'This thoughtful book manages the difficult task of talking about loving kindness in psychotherapy with clarity and compassion but without sentimentality. The breadth of disciplines it draws on means that readers will find themselves challenged to see things from a different perspective and will be both absorbed and moved'.

—**Penelope Campling**, psychiatrist and psychotherapist, author of *Intelligent Kindness and Don't Turn Away*

'*Loving Kindness in Psychotherapy* is a welcome addition to contemporary thinking about psychotherapy. Expanding on a century-old debate—originating in the contrasting views of Freud and Ferenczi—about the healing role of love in the psychotherapeutic relationship, it gets to the heart of the therapeutic enterprise'.

—**Rabbi Howard Cooper**, psychoanalytic psychotherapist

'Following contemporary neuroscience, Heather Reeves suggests that loving kindness has the potential to protect and heal us and is essential in psychotherapy. Theory, research, philosophical ideas and examples from literature and clinical practice are skilfully woven together, offering a refreshing and engaging new perspective'.

—**Gill Westland**, body psychotherapist, author of *Verbal and Non-Verbal Communication in Psychotherapy*

Loving Kindness in Psychotherapy

This book explores the way in which loving kindness, contained within professional boundaries of practice, is essential to the building of trust necessary to the psychotherapy relationship.

Arguing that loving kindness has both biological and ethical relevance in assisting recovery from the trauma of emotional injury, Heather Reeves brings forth a renewed philosophical and cultural discourse about its importance in professional work with vulnerable people. The philosophical premise of the book is the concept of alterity, or awareness of the subjective reality of others, developed by Emmanuel Levinas and expressed in psychotherapy theories since the mid-twentieth century. Understandings drawn from attachment theory, affective neuroscience and psychodynamic psychotherapy are applied to case studies (one of them written by a client) from the author's practice and themes from literature and biography, including the long-term impact of the Covid pandemic.

Loving Kindness in Psychotherapy will appeal to psychotherapists, counsellors and other mental health professionals as well as a range of other readers, including medical and palliative care professionals, educators, clergy, theologians and philosophers.

Heather Reeves works in private psychotherapy practice in Norwich, UK. Her interest in loving kindness arose from her work with people from diverse backgrounds, facing difficulties in physical, psychological, emotional and spiritual domains.

Loving Kindness in Psychotherapy

Heather Reeves

Routledge
Taylor & Francis Group

LONDON AND NEW YORK

Designed cover image: © Getty Images

First published 2023
by Routledge
4 Park Square, Milton Park, Abingdon, Oxon OX14 4RN

and by Routledge
605 Third Avenue, New York, NY 10158

Routledge is an imprint of the Taylor & Francis Group, an informa business

© 2023 Heather Reeves

British Library Cataloguing-in-Publication Data
A catalogue record for this book is available from the British Library

ISBN: 978-1-032-20074-3 (hbk)
ISBN: 978-1-032-20070-5 (pbk)
ISBN: 978-1-003-26211-4 (ebk)

DOI: 10.4324/9781003262114

Typeset in Times New Roman
by Apex CoVantage, LLC

This book is dedicated to all those who have shown me loving kindness, sometimes in unexpected circumstances.

Do not resemble a big door which lets in the wind; or a small door which makes the worthy bend down; but resemble the threshold on which all may tread, or a low peg on which all can hang their things.

Derech Eretz Zuta, Babylonian Talmud

Contents

Acknowledgements

Of all who have participated in the making of this book, I would especially like to thank my psychotherapy clients from whom I have learnt so much. I would like to express my gratitude to those who have kindly allowed me to write about their experience of psychotherapy and those who have written about it themselves.

I would like to thank Ned Henderson, George Mak-Pearce and Gill Westland for their advice about the case studies and their helpful comments on draft chapters. I would like to gratefully acknowledge the following for their feedback about various aspects of this book: Lisa Baraitser on maternal subjectivity, Penny Campling on intelligent kindness in health care, Howard Cooper and Peter Coxon, for their advice on the concept of *chesed* as a definition of loving kindness, and Paul Gilbert on compassion focused therapy.

I would like to acknowledge the writing of Sue Gerhardt, Jeremy Holmes, Arietta Slade and Peter Fonagy, all of whom have been influential in the writing of this book. My thanks go to Tania Unsworth and Rachel Clarke for permitting me to quote at length from their experiences, both personal and professional.

I would also like to acknowledge the work of the late William Notcutt, for the example of kindness he demonstrated in his medical practice and for his outstanding expertise in palliative care and pain management, both of which have influenced my work.

My thanks go also to the Guild of Pastoral Psychology and to the George Eliot Fellowship, the Dickens Fellowship and the Thomas Hardy Society, for their deep fund of knowledge about those authors, each of whom recognised loving kindness as the most important of human instincts.

I am very grateful to Joanne Forshaw at Routledge for her interest in my proposal for this book and to Grace McDonnell for guiding it through to publication.

Permissions acknowledgements

An excerpt from *Dear Life* © 2020 and an excerpt from *Breathtaking* © 2021 by Rachel Clarke. Reproduced with permission of Aitken Alexander Associates and Little, Brown & Company through PLSclear.

Excerpts from *My father said I had done something unforgivable*, by Tania Unsworth. Copyright © 2020 Guardian News & Media Ltd. Reproduced by permission of Guardian News & Media Ltd.

An excerpt from Hardy's 'Loving-Kindness' by Peter Coxon, 2018. Courtesy of *The Hardy Society Journal*.

An excerpt from *Metta: The Practice of Loving Kindness* by Ratnapani et al., 2003. Courtesy of Windhorse Publications.

Excerpts from *The Mystery of Charles Dickens* © 2020 by A.N. Wilson. Reproduced with permission of Atlantic Books Limited through PLSclear.

An excerpt from *The Sovereignty of Good* © 2001 by Iris Murdoch. Reproduced by permission of Taylor and Francis Group, LLC, a division of Informa plc.

Excerpts from *Eros Unveiled: Plato and the God of Love* © 1994, by Catherine Osborne. Reproduced with permission of Oxford Publishing Limited (Academic) through PLSclear.

An excerpt from *Borderland: Volume 111 of the Wormingford Trilogy* © 2005 by Ronald Blythe, by permission of Canterbury Press.

Excerpts from *Etty Hillesum: A Life Transformed* © 2009 by Patrick Woodhouse, by permission of Continuum Publishing, an imprint of Bloomsbury Publishing Plc.

An excerpt from *The Secret Life of Cows* © 2017 by Rosamund Young. Courtesy of Faber & Faber Ltd.

Case studies

Introduction

Much has been written about the psychotherapy relationship and the experiences of clients within that arena. It is interesting to also explore whether there are characteristics demonstrated by psychotherapists, as well as techniques, which actively benefit the psychotherapy process. In this book, I shall propose that warm-blooded, mammalian behaviours, consistently contained within professional boundaries of practice, are essential for building the sound relationship of trust so necessary for psychotherapeutic progress to be made. This is because feelings and instincts allow the development of empathy between people, a deeper understanding of the experience of others and, consequently, the building of trust in the psychotherapy relationship. Positive human feelings and instincts are discussed within the history, literature and philosophy of human behaviour, and some of these have been described as loving kindness, perhaps most often within a lay person's approach or in religious observance. But I shall suggest that loving kindness also has a place within professional practice, because it provides a foundation for good, ethical work with vulnerable people.

Use of the term loving kindness

It is first of all necessary to clarify that I have chosen to use the term *loving kindness* generically, whilst being aware that it can be interpreted in a number of more specific ways. Gilbert et al. (2019: 2259) helpfully discuss the potential semantic pitfalls which arise when using various terms which may be associated with loving kindness. Considering the use of prosocial words—those which 'relate to behaviour which is positive, helpful, and intended to promote social acceptance and friendship'—they observe that whilst terms such as compassion, kindness, caring, cooperation, empathy, sympathy, love, altruism and morality can overlap, and are sometimes used interchangeably, 'they also have distinctive features that require careful elucidation'. They draw particular attention to the difference between 'two related prosocial concepts: compassion and kindness'. So it is important to point out that, for the purposes of this book, I will rely on the term loving kindness being interpreted in a familiar sense, found within the universality of belief, in faith traditions and in common cultural language. The origins of this term within

DOI: 10.4324/9781003262114-1

these contexts, and the reasons why it appears to have meaning within the setting of psychotherapy, are discussed in Chapter 1 and throughout the book.

Loving kindness in psychotherapy and the caring professions

This book presents a discourse about psychotherapy which may be of interest not only to psychotherapists and counsellors but also to others in the caring professions, and any reader interested in the way in which human distress can be transformed by the psychotherapy encounter. I have borrowed the term loving kindness from other contexts, some of them ancient, where it can be found in the major world religions, in Buddhism and as a prominent theme in the literature of the nineteenth century, for example in the work of Dickens, Eliot, Hardy and Tolstoy. Often, these writers were grappling with the emotional and psychological challenges presented to a society experiencing rapid technological and social change. And their contemporaries in the fields of neurology and psychology—Charcot, Breuer, Freud and Janet—were beginning to explore and to develop the possibilities of what would become psychoanalysis and psychotherapy, through a deeper understanding of the human mind.

Psychotherapy can be described as a sympathetic dialogue, enacted in words and gestures and through the communication of feelings, within which a person decides, often with difficulty, to enter the psychotherapy arena, looking for something important. Frequently, this will be solace for recent or ancient wounds. Often, the search in which the psychotherapist is invited to participate is accompanied by puzzlement: about how these wounds occurred, and who was responsible, and curiosity about the part played by the client in these dilemmas, which tend to be repeated until their ownership is recognised. Psychotherapists hear about and respond to many of the facts of the lives of their clients which may not have been shared with anyone else. But for healing to take place in the psychotherapy encounter, something is needed which is wider and deeper than a response to the facts, or the use of a therapeutic technique, important though these are. This is the presence of loving kindness.

For loving kindness to have taken its place in the language of human belief systems, something older and possibly wiser than even those systems may have been at work. Therefore, I will suggest that loving kindness is not only desirable but essential to the successful development of the mammalian state which human beings share with all warm-blooded life. This is not only because survival depends upon it, but beyond that, loving kindness gives meaning and structure to our lives and relationships, without which the everyday challenges of living are much more difficult to negotiate. Loving kindness can be understood as a powerful potential in all human beings and, in psychotherapy, one which needs to be nurtured and developed in order for practice to be effective. This is because human emotional life thrives and struggles in relationship with others. Relational experience is at the core of psychotherapy, where neglect, or wounds sustained in earlier life can be revisited and healed. The nature of human attachment is such that it will always seek to be completed successfully, even in later life, and for this reason there is no age limit to the possibilities of psychotherapy. The practice of loving kindness demonstrates a willingness and a capacity to listen freely and carefully to another, whatever their story. This can include listening to dark and difficult things, without judgement. Where a spirit of loving kindness is present in any psychotherapy encounter, respect for the human state will be tangible in that exchange. It forms the basis of a relationship of trust, experienced through feeling.

Psychotherapists can develop loving kindness instinctively in their practice, through their prior experience of life and relationships, some of this successful, some not necessarily so. The wider and deeper the range of life experience, the greater the opportunity there will have been to develop the practice of loving kindness. But for experience to count, there also needs to be the capacity for self-reflection and the deeper understanding and ownership of feelings which it can give, supported in practice by the ability to fully utilise personal psychotherapy, training, supervisory support and feedback. All of these experiences contribute to a fund of stored emotional memory, which can be retrieved for potentially sensitive, attuned communication. And for the often fragile exchanges within psychotherapy to take place, and to progress, the boundaries of professional practice, especially those of confidentiality, reliability and consistency, need to be clearly established and explicit. This enables the necessary trust to develop between psychotherapist and client.

The psychotherapy relationship provides an opportunity for people to express their concerns and deepest worries and for the psychotherapist to witness these and offer a response. It is contained within a confidential arena, a safe place for disclosures which may not be able to be expressed in the outer contexts of a client's personal and working life. Everything shared within this arena is of interest to the psychotherapist, even small and apparently trivial details, such as a slight change in facial expression, breathing or tone of voice. Even the unique way in which each new client requests their first appointment will have already communicated a great deal about the person seeking psychotherapy. From that point onwards, everything should make an impact upon the psychotherapist, offering opportunities for interest, reflection and possible response. But the use of the term loving kindness does not necessarily imply ease within the psychotherapy encounter, because the nature of psychotherapy means that people may bring darkness and trauma to the relationship. This can manifest as fear, rage or resistance, when the impact of deeper therapeutic relating begins to be felt. Conversely, others find comfort and enjoyment in the process, given the varied nature of individual personalities and their unique responses to psychotherapy. Over time, the psychotherapy process can bring about a deep knowledge and understanding of the experiences a person has encountered, wherein they feel that they have truly been seen and heard. This kind of reciprocation makes change and healing possible.

The biological nature of loving kindness

During the mid-twentieth century, an understanding of the essential role of emotional warmth in human development and relationships became more explicit within psychotherapeutic practice and research. Since then, advances in the study of infant attachment have progressed towards a greater awareness of its essential role in child development and the emotional maturation of adults (Winnicott, 1957, 1960, 1961, 1965, 1969, 1971; Bowlby, 1969, 1973; Fonagy et al., 1991, 1995; Holmes, 1993, 1998, 2014; Fonagy, 2001; Fonagy & Target, 1996, 2003; Gerhardt, 2004, 2015; Fonagy & Campbell, 2015; Fonagy et al., 2004, Bateman & Fonagy, 2016 and Holmes & Slade, 2018). These studies have demonstrated consistently that the presence of warm contact between parent and infant, especially during the early years, has a direct impact upon the development of what can be called the emotional brain. The repetition of attentive and reciprocal acts by the carer begins to be stored in the emotional memory of the infant for future reference and comfort. Thus, meaning and association begin to attach to the carer and these experiences become 'biologically embedded', providing a developing capacity for feelings to be regulated (Hertzman, 1997).

In this way, the developing infant acquires sensory reference points, through feelings, which provide the foundations of interactive, relational experience. Consequently, it becomes possible for the infant to trust these internal states, to use them as a guide and to be able to discriminate between those human events which feel trustworthy and safe, and those which do not. On developing into adulthood, this becomes a growing capacity to be open and trusting of human warmth and also to protect oneself from harm. It is a common experience for people to seek psychotherapy when life has become difficult and stressful, because they have not been able to develop this level of sensory, experiential discrimination during their developmental years and, consequently, have been unable to rely on their feelings to guide them towards nurture and away from harm. This can explain why a new psychotherapy client, whose emotional life appears to be chaotic, may seem to have a continuing attraction towards harm and away from nurture, and an apparent reluctance to reverse the habit.

An understanding of the importance of emotional warmth in child development is not a counsel of perfect parenting. Indeed, Winnicott (1965, 1971) devised his idea of the 'good enough' parent partly to challenge the idealised focus upon the 'good mother'. Instead, he emphasised the central importance of the facilitating environment, which can be provided by parents and by any significant carer able to offer a reciprocal relationship of warm attachment to their infant. The facilitating environment can be replicated in the psychotherapy relationship, as described by Gerhardt (2015: 234–246), who observes that: 'The qualities of good parenting (and of close relationships in general) are essentially regulatory qualities: the capacity to listen, to notice, to shape behaviour and to be able to restore good feelings through some kind of physical, emotional or mental contact, through a touch, a smile, a way of putting feelings and thoughts into words'. She describes how the independent psychotherapy tradition offers the opportunity for people to establish 'a personal relationship for therapeutic purposes only', within which they can learn how to regulate feelings in relation to others, find out how to modify emotional habits and learn new ones. This provides the mental space for feelings to be reflected on, owned and developed, rather than being experienced as strange, or as a threat. It is as though the attachment process, when interrupted by difficult circumstances in childhood, is able later to be progressed, and even completed in an emotionally satisfying way, once a facilitating relationship is consistently available.

Holmes and Slade (2018: 135) have identified two fundamentals of effective psychotherapy which enable this relational opportunity to be provided. These are trust and a capacity to help people who are exploring pain and unhappiness. This implies that the ability to offer these fundamentals is not merely technical, because it proposes a framework of emotional and ethical motivation. Thus, if emotional warmth has a central function in the formation of secure and meaningful attachments, it follows that psychotherapeutic motivation can be expressed through the language of feelings. But emotional warmth and reciprocity are not just innate mammalian qualities; they require action through expression, matched with reflective thinking, to support the emotional and psychological development without which human beings cannot fully thrive. I therefore suggest that their philosophical framework can be described as loving kindness, which occupies the domains of both thinking and feeling and demonstrates the necessity of emotional warmth in positive human interaction. The psychotherapy relationship is complex, in that it also requires the therapist to be able to listen, without 'memory or desire' as Wilfred Bion (1967a) saw it. This suggests that the therapist tries not to seek, through a motivation of well-intentioned kindness, any avoidance of the psychological and emotional discomfort, or even pain, so often integral to sound psychotherapy practice, through which people attempt to become more aware of their feelings, thoughts and motivations.

The contents of this book

This book presents a discussion of both the nature and the necessity of loving kindness in human development and its application to effective psychotherapy. It includes psychotherapy theory, research and clinical themes, five anonymised case studies from my practice, illustrations from literature and biography, and ideas from philosophy. The central premise of the book relies upon the concept of alterity, or awareness of the subjective reality and vulnerability of others, as developed by Emmanuel Levinas (1981, 1989).

I also discuss the way in which some presentations of apparently warm feelings, such as symbiotic, merged relating and sentimentality, can be misleading versions of loving kindness; how the shadow aspects of loving kindness may be understood; and the ways in which loving kindness can assist clinical work with clients who have experienced trauma and moral injury, or who find that psychotherapy does not seem to work for them. I conclude with a discussion of the view that mind and body are dual entities, and the way in which this meets a challenge, when considering feelings as a reliable basis for understanding how relationships work. Finally, I note that this book was written during the Covid-19 pandemic of 2020/2021, which prompted the inclusion of a chapter concerning loving kindness applied more widely to the caring professions, with particular reference to the specialism of palliative care. I have used the terms *psychotherapy* and *psychoanalysis* synonymously in the text, to indicate therapeutic work which engages with both conscious and unconscious components of the experience of individuals. The terms *client* and *patient* are also used synonymously.

Chapter 1

The nature of loving kindness

A poignant illustration of loving kindness is given in Thomas Hardy's novel *The Mayor of Casterbridge* as it arrives at its apparently hopeless ending. Throughout his life the Mayor, Michael Henchard, has made just about every possible human error, including a series of wrong decisions, causing harm to those who love him and, finally, alienating the townspeople of Casterbridge. Defeated, he walks away to die on his own, and yet one person follows him. This is Abel Whittle, who occupies about the lowest position in the pecking order of the town. He is not very good at anything and cannot wake up in time for work, for which Henchard has rebuked and humiliated him publicly. But, nonetheless, it is Abel Whittle who knows instinctively where Henchard is going, who follows him and stays with him to the end. When afterwards asked why, he replies that it was because Henchard was kind to his mother, providing her with food and coal in the winter months. Abel Whittle recognises these acts of human kindness, some of the few Michael Henchard ever offered to anyone, and he simply responds in kind and without question. This action demonstrates a loving kindness which does not depend upon status, affluence or power. It is a human quality which can be seen to flourish within reciprocal human relationships, sometimes in the most unusual circumstances, and this is its function in psychotherapy.

Origins of the term *loving kindness*

The term loving kindness seems to be warmly and culturally familiar and its origins can be found, with varied interpretations, in many cultures. Coxon (2018) observes that it resonated for Thomas Hardy because of its origin in the *Book of Common Prayer*, for which it was used by Miles Coverdale, the Bible translator. Hardy attended church services throughout his early life and as Coxon notes: 'the constant repetition of the psalms in those services would have left an indelible impression on his mind' (Coxon, 2018: 56). He suggests that Coverdale was attempting to convey the meaning of the original Hebrew, by using the phrase loving kindness to translate the term *chesed*. This term has a number of English renderings, which creates a difficulty in pinning down a precise meaning, but also signals a complex depth which may include kindness, loyalty and

DOI: 10.4324/9781003262114-2

a capacity for mercy. Coxon notices how the term loving kindness appears in Hardy's novels, quoting a famous scene in Chapter 20 of *Far from the Madding Crowd*, when Gabriel Oak learns that Bathsheba has sent a thoughtless Valentine card to Squire Boldwood. Gabriel confronts her by saying: 'Leading on a man you don't care for is not a praiseworthy action. And even Miss Everdene if you seriously inclined towards him you might have let him discover it in some way of true loving-kindness'.

The universality of loving kindness

Various examples of Hardy's writing convey the humane essence of loving kindness, sometimes found in unlikely people and not confined to a particular belief system. This raises the possibility of loving kindness being a human quality recognised universally, both within and independent of formal belief systems, having some structural and developmental function, not necessarily as a virtue but as an expression of purposeful, human warmth in relationship.

The idea of loving kindness can be found in many faith systems. In Islam, the concept of *ihsan* derives from an Arabic term, meaning a state of excellence arising from an inner faith, demonstrated by actions, deeds and a sense of social responsibility. This includes *sadaqah, or* charitable acts, which can be motivated by generosity, love, compassion or faith. In this belief, precedence is given to kindness, selflessness, altruism and righteousness, which are associated with human nature, their roots being found in honesty, sincerity and truthfulness. These qualities are emphasised particularly in Sufism. Similarly, in Sanskrit, the primary sacred language of Hinduism, the term *maitri* describes benevolence, loving kindness, friendliness, goodwill and active interest in others. And in Buddhism, loving kindness is represented by the term *metta*. Here again, there is: 'a wish for the welfare of other beings, human and non-human, without any self-reference—that is, without wanting or expecting anything in return. In simple language, *metta* is 'universal loving kindness—with no strings attached' (Ratnapani et al., 2003: 3–9). It includes compassion (*karuna*), sympathetic joy (*mudita*) and equanimity (*upekkha)*, and is a quality which can be cultivated through the meditation practice of *metta bhavana.* '*Bhavana* is a Pali word meaning development or cultivation, and it is important to note that in these practices . . . we are talking about the *development* of metta'. The premise of the metta bhavana practice suggests that the ideal of *metta* is distinct from the word *love*, as used generally, which can suggest a state involved primarily with ourselves:

> These 'loves' are often self-referential; we love them for the pleasant sensations they bring us, we like the experience of being close to them, so we move towards them and become attached to them. If these loves of ours are people, we are happy when they behave as we want them to behave, but when they don't we become unhappy and may withdraw our affection. When frustrated

in this way, when we no longer get the desired effect from the object of our affection, our emotion can too easily turn to ill will, to anger or hurt or annoyance. So love, as a definition of metta, is a word that needs to be treated with caution.

(ibid.)

Ratnapani et al. propose that metta is closer to the ideal of parental love which is never withdrawn but remains constant, whether correcting or encouraging. Our responses do not depend upon the recipient behaving in a certain way that pleases or displeases us. Moreover, with metta this well-wishing extends to all beings, whether we know them or not and its cultivation has effects which are reliable and cumulative.

The distinction drawn by Ratnapani between love and loving kindness seems somewhat similar to that which is found in Greco-Christian concepts of *eros* and *agape*. *Agape* can be defined as charity, as distinct from *eros*, which represents the human desire for love and sex. We might say that *agape* is unconditional love whereas *eros* is often conditional upon the desirability or acceptability of another. For example, Plato's *Symposium* seems to illustrate a view of love as 'primarily a desire for something that you lack and need and hope to gain' (Osborne, 1994: 54). But Osborne observes that there is not an easy dichotomy to be drawn between the self-seeking *eros* and the generous love of *agape*, because the motives for giving to the other, or for cherishing the rewards received from another, may be various:

> Within the Greek tradition of *eros* it is necessary to account for the other-regarding devotion to a beloved whose benefit is sought for her own sake; and within the Christian account of love and charity it is plain that the generosity shown to the beloved can, or should, also be a joy to the giver. In both cases the loving relationship can be more than a one-sided transaction. But even if one assumes a simple dichotomy between, on the one hand, love that is directed towards the other, and, on the other hand, a self-seeking love, both *eros* and *agape* can be found to incorporate both kinds of love in parallel ways.

(ibid., 69)

Therefore, Osborne suggests that 'it is a confusion to explain love by seeking motives for love, or by identifying possible aims and rewards that are sought or desired' (ibid., 71). This opens up the possibility of loving kindness being an innate and unconditional human quality, capable of endurance and not dependent upon any particular belief system. Interestingly, Saslow et al. (2013) found that less religious individuals were motivated to a greater extent by levels of compassion than were more religious individuals. Nonetheless, it seems possible to state that loving kindness can be seen to be a universal human capability.

Eros, agape and loving kindness

It could be argued that loving kindness has a unifying quality, capable of holding human instinct in concert with generosity, care and responsibility for another, and that a synthesis of this kind is the aim and purpose of the psychotherapy encounter. Codes of conduct and common sense determine that the psychotherapist is not free to engage merely in a 'desire for something that you lack or need or hope to gain'. With only such an egocentric perspective in mind, the psychotherapy relationship will be likely to fail and cause harm, because it will not be free to fully consider and prioritise the needs of the client, who is generally the more vulnerable party to the encounter. On the other hand, a mere sense of duty will not be sufficient to engender the necessary warmth, energy and interest needed for the psychotherapy relationship to be authentic and for it to thrive. It is, after all, a human relationship.

It could also be argued that the concepts of *eros* and *agape*, and an understanding of the differences between them, mainly arise within adult cognitive experience where choice, discrimination and responsibility are more able to be employed than would be possible in infancy. And yet loving kindness appears to be recognisable and necessary within the earliest experiences of infants. It has become possible to observe and to understand this through observational studies of young children with their carers, and when separated from them (Bowlby, 1969, Gerhardt, 2015). Rees (2018: 103) when discussing, in a very different field, the future possibilities of human-level artificial intelligence, observes that learning about human behaviour involves the observation of people in their homes and workplaces. Thus, our understanding of the necessity of loving kindness in child development has been enhanced by direct observation of the experiences of infancy and parenthood, such as that initiated by John Bowlby when developing attachment theory in the 1950s. This continues to be a 'major paradigm for theory and experimentation in developmental psychology' (Holmes, 1993: 430). Bowlby demonstrated how emotional warmth supports the developing relationship of attachment between infant and parent, thereby illustrating that infants are innately capable of recognising, and reciprocating, loving kindness.

The development of attachment theory invites a debate containing similar themes to those of *eros* and *agape*. Gerhardt (2015: 30–31) mentions a comment of the neuroscientist Doug Watt that, in the earliest stages of life, we experience that which is 'unrememberable and unforgettable'. We do not consciously recall this but neither do we forget it, because it has become part of us, influencing our perceptions and behaviour. We could go on to say that *eros* is 'built into our organism and informs our expectations and behaviour', and that the unrememberable and unforgettable things are bodily instincts experienced by the human animal, but which require social interaction to support awareness, consideration and inclusion of others; not because we ought to learn these responses, but because we need to. Thus, Gerhardt observes that: 'Our minds emerge and our emotions become organised through engagement with other minds. . . . The unseen forces which shape our emotional responses through life, are not primarily our biological urges, but the patterns of emotional experience with other people, most powerfully set up in infancy'.

Here, we might say that this 'engagement with other minds' corresponds with aspects of *agape*, in that to engage with other minds, there needs to be a sense of the other person as important, allowing the self-seeking *eros* to be modified by the generous love of *agape*. Bowlby and others have illustrated how this kind of accommodation occurs through the bond of attachment formed between infant and parent. Their studies demonstrate that qualities of both *eros* and *agape* are present in the capacity of the parent who is able to offer a pleasurable sense of both physical and emotional safety, and containment of the infant, leading to the development of a secure attachment. This combines an instinctive responsiveness with a sense of responsibility, expressed through care for another. Within the bond of a secure attachment, an infant can reciprocate both the instinctive response and an early form of altruism, which can be seen, for example, in first efforts to generously offer a piece of half-chewed rusk back to the giver.

Gerhardt (2015) proceeds to describe the difficulties which can arise in child development when loving kindness is not experienced during the early stages of life, and a bond of attachment is not able to be formed on a secure basis. It is usually the outcome of these difficulties which presents unresolved in later life within the arena of psychotherapy. However, it is noticeable that her discussion is free of judgement of parents when things have not worked out well for the child. Instead, she emphasises the emotional, physical and psychological needs of children as the starting point for understanding human development and, therefore, the importance of prioritising and making secure the primary experiences of human beings, and of supporting parents in raising their young.

It is sometimes said of Gerhardt's work that it only seems applicable to babies and to early child development and is therefore not of particular relevance to the experiences of adults. However, if the essential foundations of successful emotional and psychological development are found in infancy within a sense of safety, warmth and predictability, it stands to reason that these same features, when provided by the psychotherapy encounter, will be able to establish an environment within which the necessary tasks of emotional development and repair can be completed in adulthood. So loving kindness may be represented as much in the actions and attitudes of the psychotherapist as in theories and techniques, important though these are, because there needs to be a sense that the practitioner has good intention and warmth of feeling towards his or her client. In the early stages of a psychotherapy encounter, a client may not be able to reciprocate through feelings but may sense sufficient goodwill in the practitioner to enable the experiment to continue. But if feelings of warmth and goodwill are to be more than transient and pleasurable sensations for psychotherapist and client, they need to be contained within a quality of reliable substance, able to weather initial hesitancy and, later, the occasional storms and possible ruptures which can be an important part of the developing psychotherapy relationship.

Loving kindness as steadfastness in psychotherapy practice

The capacity to acknowledge, accept and understand the client's experience relies upon the psychotherapist being able to provide a consistent presence and attention to that individual. Without this, the therapeutic relationship cannot develop and thrive. For the purposes of this discussion, I have therefore chosen to use the concept of steadfastness, because this quality seems to me to provide the basis for warm, consistent relating, from which to proceed in building the psychotherapeutic alliance. This appears to be the foundation of the idea of *chesed*, which I introduced earlier in this chapter. Snaith (1997: 102–130) suggests that this term does not mean kindness in general to all and sundry and is not used 'indiscriminately where any kind of favour is desired, but only where there is some recognised tie'. He states that it 'presupposes a covenant, and has from first to last a strong suggestion of fixedness, steadfastness, determined loyalty'. Strassfeld (2006: 221) places acts of loving kindness in the same context of 'a steadiness resting on the support of others . . . an assurance based upon support . . . an ability to rely on one another'. This suggests that loving kindness is accessible, because it can be developed and practised in a conscious way in adulthood. It is deeply recognisable to the person receiving it and not merely as a romantic or transient notion. The concept of *chesed* includes characteristics of kindness, loyalty and a capacity for mercy but requires this foundation of steadfastness. In psychotherapy this quality would signal to people that the practitioner takes them seriously and cares enough to offer them consistent attention. For this to be developed, the psychotherapy practitioner would have experienced a demanding and challenging training, including his or her own journey through personal psychotherapy. These experiences enable the aspiring practitioner to evaluate whether they wish to proceed in practice with client work which is potentially lengthy, sometimes difficult and occasionally dangerous, although deeply satisfying and rewarding. The practitioner needs to be clear that they wish to offer a reliable level of commitment to people, sometimes over extended periods of time and, in this sense, the psychotherapy relationship is parallel in quality with all other relationships of lasting value.

Loving kindness as steadfastness in literature

Good examples of this definition of loving kindness are found in the literature of the nineteenth century, often in novels of personal development, where it appears as a subtle but consistent presence. It can be seen in the characters of Clara Peggotty and Betsy Trotwood in Charles Dickens's novel, *David Copperfield;* in Joe Gargery, the faithful friend to Pip in *Great Expectations;* and in Bob Jakin, a minor character in George Eliot's novel *The Mill on the Floss*, ill-treated by Tom Tulliver, but who finds books for Maggie when the family estate is sold and who, in the end, tries to rescue them both from the flood. These examples show how loving kindness can mitigate and lend later understanding and compassion to even the most harsh childhood circumstances.

Loving kindness portrayed in *David Copperfield*

In her biography of Charles Dickens, Tomalin (2011) observes that *David Copper-field* is his first book to be narrated in the first person and she recognises how it gives a voice to a child who is taken seriously as a narrator. This is confirmed in Michael Slater's introduction to the novel, which he places in its autobiographical context, reflecting how closely Dickens associated David Copperfield's emotional experiences with his own. He liked this novel most of all and David Copperfield was his favourite imagined child (Slater, 1991: xiii). Tomalin shows how Dickens's parallel experiences of attachment and loss in childhood formed his description of the frame of mind and consequent behaviour of David Copperfield as an adult. In particular, she notices the delicate intensity with which he wrote about the pain experienced by a child when separated from his mother, treated cruelly by his stepfather and sent away to a school where he was again treated harshly. Such experiences were so common that readers readily responded to Dickens's writing about them. And, emphasised, by contrast, his illustration of the loving kindness shown to David by Peggotty, the Copperfield family servant, generated the same ready response because it was recognisable in such human terms. As David Copperfield's childhood passed interminably slowly, because he was unhappy, Dickens describes how the love shown to him by Peggotty came to occupy an essential, comforting place in his feelings, after his mother died. 'She did not replace my mother; no one could do that; but she came into a vacancy in my heart, which closed upon her, and I felt for her something I have never felt for any other human being' (1850, in 1991: 61).

Dickens's working notes identify David's difficult childhood experiences as his own, because he knew them so well. He too had experience of a rapid reversal of family fortune and knew how quickly ties of loyalty can unravel as a consequence. Following his father's imprisonment for debt in 1824, Dickens was sent to work in a boot-blacking factory, in absolute contrast to his comfortable childhood at home and at school. He was a sensitive and imaginative child who quickly saw that any dreams and aspirations he might previously have had were now beyond his reach. He felt acutely the shame and unhappiness of his new situation and, even worse, the realisation of his parents' sudden neglect of his needs (Slater, 1991: xiii–xiv).

Dickens has been accused of mawkish sentimentality in his writing, and this is sometimes certainly true, as in the example of the life and death of Little Nell in *The Old Curiosity Shop*. And yet, equally, he had a deep understanding of authentic emotion, probably derived from his earlier experience of childhood, before the changes in his parents' financial circumstances intervened and altered that childhood forever. The infant brain is supremely able to recognise and remember genuinely warm feeling. Doubtless, there were contradictions and conflicts in his character, so obvious in his writing and most evident in his eventually cruel treatment of his wife, which could undermine any perception that he truly understood feelings of loving kindness. But I will suggest that it was precisely the harsh experiences of his early life which made him so able to recognise loving kindness when he saw it and to write about it so accurately. A.N. Wilson (2020: 172) comments in his biography that Dickens is 'often described as sentimental, and that is because he is. In this, however, the belief that doing the decent and kindly thing is not merely our duty, but the way to a sane and happy life, is something he holds to be a simple truth'.

In *David Copperfield* Dickens portrays, especially, the sensory memories of a child and the emotional safety conveyed by a warm and loving human presence, as in this description of David's early formative impressions of Peggotty:

> The first objects that assume a distinct presence before me, as I look far back, into the blank of my infancy, are my mother with her pretty hair and youthful shape, and Peggotty, with no shape at all, and eyes so dark that they seemed to darken their whole neighbourhood in her face, and cheeks and arms so hard and red I wondered the birds didn't peck her in preference to apples.
>
> (1850, in 1991: 13)

And David describes the familiar objects he comes to associate, throughout his life, with that loving presence, as he sits with Peggotty by the parlour fire and tries to stay awake:

> I had reached that stage of sleepiness when Peggotty seemed to swell and grow immensely large. I propped my eyelids open with my two forefingers, and looked perseveringly at her as she sat at work; at the little bit of wax-candle she kept for her thread—how old it looked, being so wrinkled in all directions!—at the little house with a thatched roof, where the yard-measure lived; at her work-box with a sliding lid, with a view of St. Paul's Cathedral (with a pink dome) painted on the top; at the brass thimble on her finger; at herself, whom I thought lovely.
>
> (ibid., 16)

Later, when trying to survive the cruel actions of his stepfather, David is again made acutely aware of Peggotty's steadfast presence, even when she has been removed to a distance by his mother's second marriage. When, as a punishment, he is confined to his room, he is woken up by the sound of Peggotty whispering his name through the keyhole. He can hear that she is crying, and so is he, but she is able to convey her love for him by breaking the rules of the household to come and talk to him. She tells him that he is to be sent away to school:

> 'When, Peggotty?'
>   'Tomorrow' . . .
>   Then Peggotty fitted her mouth close to the keyhole and delivered these words through it with as much feeling and earnestness as a keyhole had ever been the medium of communicating, I will venture to assert: shooting in each broken little sentence, in a convulsive burst of its own . . .
>   'My own!' said Peggotty, with infinite compassion. 'What I want to say, is. That you must never forget me. For I'll never forget you'.
>
> (ibid., 60–61)

She does not forget him, and remains, though often in the background of the novel, an enduring and loving presence. It is noticeable in Dickens's account that Peggotty is very ordinary. She does not need high status, money or power in providing the essential components of a warm relationship; most importantly, a relationship which feels genuinely secure. Contemporary evidence from behavioural and neuroscientific research (Gerhardt, 2015; Holmes & Slade, 2018) supports the essential function described by Dickens, that the process of child development thrives when infants *feel* loved. To be able to feel love requires it to be expressed in the first place and to be felt by the infant as authentic. In the example of Peggotty's love for David, it is experienced by him as a totality of thoughts, feelings and physical sensations of comfort. Her steadfast and unambiguous presence is the foundation of his knowledge of her love. He knows, from his prior experience of her actions towards him, that he can rely on her to be consistent and caring, even at times when he does not know if he will see her again. The foundation built between them has been established sufficiently for him to be able to later soothe and comfort himself, having learnt this from being soothed and comforted by her. She is the familiar, reliable and delightful object of his trust and affection. At the same time she is not an idealised or perfect person. She and her family live in close proximity to poverty and have to make the most of their lot. But Peggotty knows who she is and has no inflated ideas of becoming someone more grand. She gives David what she has, which is a kind heart. As discussed later in this book, emotional security provides the basis for resilience. Dickens illustrates this when portraying not only the harshness David endures but the way in which his secure foundation with Peggotty helps him to endure it.

Dickens skilfully presents the dark and the light of David's childhood experience. Peggotty is unable to protect David from the cruelty of his stepfather, Mr Murdstone, and sadistic treatment by Mr Murdstone's sister. In portraying the exquisite pain caused to David by their 'educational' methods, and their attempts to shape him into an image of their own, he provides pointed examples of the way in which a child's feelings and capabilities can be profoundly injured but also how David is able to keep going because he knows that he is loved. In this scene he describes how David tries his best to prepare himself for an ordeal in which the Murdstones are going to test his memory of what he has read. David's mother has been reduced to a state of compliance by her fear of them and has to sit quietly, unable to help him:

I trip over a word. Mr Murdstone looks up. I trip over another word. Miss Murdstone looks up. I redden, tumble over half-a-dozen words, and stop. I think my mother would show me the book if she dared, but she does not dare . . .

'Now, Clara,' says Mr Murdstone, 'be firm with the boy . . .' 'He knows his lesson, or he does not know it.'

'He does *not* know it,' Miss Murdstone interposes awfully . . .

There is a pile of these arrears very soon, and it swells like a rolling snow-ball. The bigger it gets, the more stupid *I* get. The case is so hopeless, and I feel that I am wallowing in such a bog of nonsense, that I give up all idea of getting out, and abandon myself to my fate.

(1850, in 1991: 53–54)

And yet, the factor which protects David in the midst of all of this is his earlier memory of the loving kindness of Peggotty, which prevails. This has given him a sufficient foundation of early emotional experience to sustain him, to give him hope to survive and eventually to thrive.

Loving kindness portrayed in *Great Expectations*

The characterisation of an early, secure attachment, providing the foundation for a lasting and supportive relationship, is repeated in another of Dickens's novels of personal development, *Great Expectations*. The central character, Pip, has a protector and champion in the form of Joe Gargery, the husband of Pip's much older and punishing sister. Joe has solid qualities and, as the village blacksmith, he knows who he is. He has no aspirations beyond the seemingly narrow confines of his local community and the limitations of his marriage. He is able to survive the onslaughts of his wife and to help Pip do the same. When Pip leaves the forge to pursue his fortunes in London and later comes to a final collapse, it is Joe who knows where he is, who finds him and restores him to health, even though Pip has treated him with disdain when at the height of his fortune seeking. Here, Pip describes his sustained and renewed awareness of Joe:

But, above all, I knew that there was a constant tendency in all these people— who, when I was very ill, would present all kinds of extraordinary transfor-mations of the human face, and would be much dilated in size—above all, I say, I knew that there was an extraordinary tendency in all these people sooner or later to settle down into the likeness of Joe.

After I had turned the worst point of my illness, I began to notice that while all its other features changed, this one consistent feature did not change. Whoever came about me, settled into Joe. I opened my eyes in the night, and I saw in the great chair at the bedside, Joe. I opened my eyes in the day, and, sitting on the window seat, smoking his pipe in the shaded open window, still I saw Joe.

(Dickens, 1861, in 1996: 462–463)

Here again, Dickens illustrates the steadfast quality of a secure attachment. But how do we understand these lyrically described characteristics in the setting of psychotherapy? Returning to my opening discussion, it seems to me that both Peggotty and Joe demonstrate the qualities of *chesed*, which provides: 'a steadi-ness resting on the support of others . . . an assurance based upon support . . . an ability to rely on one another'. And the essential component of loving kindness as a form of steadfast attention also offers the opportunity of a secure attachment in psychotherapy, for as long as it is needed. Loving kindness can be held safely within the bounds of a professional relationship.

The essential nature of emotional memory

Historically, much emphasis has been placed upon the cognitive development of children as the channel through which educational and career progress flow and consequently, on this view, personal progress must follow. But, more recently, attention has been drawn to the fact that cognitive progress, vital though it is, cannot on its own provide the foundation for secure experience and self-esteem, unless there is corresponding progress in emotional development and memory. As a consequence, therapeutic questions arise as to why it is that people who may have succeeded in their cognitive development, and perhaps risen to the heights of a successful career, may not necessarily at the same time have been able to achieve satisfying personal and professional lives. This kind of dilemma is often encountered in the psychotherapy consulting room because, eventually, the internal strain of keeping going without the support of a sound emotional structure has proved overwhelming. This conflict will have been compounded by the unrealistic expectations of a society in which cognitive and material achievement are highly prized, often at the expense of securely attached relationships and emotional bonds. An adult facing this dilemma eventually may feel that he or she has failed, precisely because they could not keep going through the agency of thinking alone. The missing ingredient in childhood will have been the consistent, embodied, sense that their parents loved them. However many words of love may have been offered, they have not *felt* loved, because they have not been able to gradually develop a reliable awareness of the physical presence, interest and attention of their carers. Further, Duffell and Basset (2016: 26) have commented on the increasing body of evidence that the physical development of children's brains is facilitated by close bonds with loving parents and the relational stimulation thus provided. Within these conditions children grow more healthy brain tissue, whilst learning how to regulate their feelings and consequently their nervous systems. When lacking these conditions, they fail to grow in this way.

According to the work of Feldman, these optimum conditions depend upon a process of 'entrainment' of baby and mother brains, beginning *in utero* as the mutual regulation of physiology, behaviour, and affect. He states that this is based upon *biobehavioural synchrony*, which is a: 'co-wiring of parents' and infants' brains and behaviour into a synchronous unit that supports the infant's brain growth and buttresses social competencies' (Feldman, 2015b: 387). Discussing this process, Holmes and Slade (2018: 55) observe that: 'Heightened sensitivity to danger and the need for protection . . . *works synergistically alongside pleasure and reward* in bonding'. And they note Feldman's observation that this is not confined to mother–infant relationships but has also been demonstrated in both primary and secondary caregiving fathers as well as non-biological parents: 'Seeing infants appears to elicit the motivation to care in all adult members of the species, which may have functioned to enhance survival throughout human history when many mothers died at childbirth, thus leaving infants to non-parental care' (ibid., 390).

The impact of attachment difficulties

The work of Gerhardt (2004, 2015) illustrates in detail the various impacts upon the developing infant, where circumstances do not allow for the development of biobehavioural synchrony between infant and caregiver. She describes the variety of emotional strategies the infant brain has to employ for purposes of psychological and emotional survival. Insecure patterns mean that children can become hostile to feelings which have not had opportunity to become embodied and familiar; thus, they cannot understand and reflect upon them. Consequently, they have less capacity to contain and express what they are truly feeling, and their emotional reactions can be experienced as rapid and unsafe, even catastrophic at times. Another strategy is that of avoiding feelings, which have to be shut down as soon as they arise, in order to prevent experiences which would not be emotionally manageable. Children with resistant attachment, paradoxically, are immersed in strong states of feeling but are not able to reflect upon them, nor upon the impact their full expression has upon others. This prevents any flexibility or modulated flow between different states of feeling and stands in the way of reciprocal interaction with others. This sets up an extremely distressing cycle wherein the child feels unable to understand his or her own feelings, or the reactions of others which unintentionally they may provoke. Children with these difficulties may become labelled 'difficult' and consequently are easily scapegoated, which of course adds greatly to their distress and confusion. Gerhardt (2015: 44–45) describes how these adaptive processes in fact deprive children of access to emotional information which could help them navigate their relationships with others. Thus, their emotional and social repertoire is restricted, which means that the necessary coordination they need between their personal and their social experience is hampered. This gives rise to continuing limitations and inhibitions in adult life, which are the factors people often identify when seeking psychotherapy.

The beginnings of therapeutic conversation

Psychotherapy offers the opportunity for dialogue, within which difficult experiences can be put into words. The language used may not necessarily be verbal. Non-verbal communication often provides signals to express the experiences encountered by a person (Westland, 2015). The case study of Amanda which follows in this chapter demonstrates how her silence implied a great deal of what she wanted to say. And by working within that silence, we gradually developed a rapport which enabled her to begin to achieve a resolution to her difficulties. Then she became more articulate with words to express herself more openly. Amanda came to rely on a steadfast therapeutic presence through which she gained a sympathetic and attuned hearing. With this support she learnt how to use feelings as prompts and as a guide to actions that might be helpful. This required a lot of persistence because she had learnt in childhood to fear her emotions, having experienced ridicule and further punishment if she cried when upset. In suppressing natural feelings of distress, she had not acquired the emotional skilfulness of discrimination between positive and negative experiences. One central function of emotional arousal is that of signalling approaching danger, which provides opportunities to avoid it. Arousal of anxiety is useful when it can motivate constructive action. On the other hand, trying not to have that uncomfortable feeling means we cannot choose from available and appropriate options in responding. As seen in the case study, a lack of discrimination between different states of feeling led Amanda into relationships which did further harm to her self-esteem. She made a significant therapeutic advance when she withdrew permanently from a relationship of this sort, painful though this was, having identified and allowed herself to admit how unhappy it made her feel.

So relationships seem to succeed when each of the parties feels that the other person is genuinely available, present and attentive and, if ruptures to the relationship happen, there is the possibility of repairing them. Thus, Gerhardt identifies the psychotherapy relationship as an opportunity to learn how to regulate feelings in reciprocation with another. Unhelpful emotional expectations arising from difficult experiences in the early years can be transformed into new and positive ones with the assistance of a reciprocal and attuned relationship for 'therapeutic purposes only' (ibid., 234). This therapeutic process may take time, as the emotional habits learnt previously can have a powerful capacity to hold on and resist change. This is because the early adaptation helped the child to survive the difficulties he or she faced. Arousal of new kinds of feeling can raise anxiety and a sense of threat to the previous *status quo*, however uncomfortable it may have been. The psychotherapy relationship provides a place of experimentation with the experience of new feelings, and it offers encounters with those which previously were not allowed expression at all.

The combined knowledge base of psychotherapy and affective neuroscience

Nowadays we have the benefit of knowing how behavioural change of this kind is at the same time both personal and neurological. The brain makes new adaptations as the client progresses in psychotherapy. This is discussed further in Chapter 8 with reference to the discoveries made by affective neuroscience in the late twentieth century (Damasio, 1994, 2000, Panksepp, 1998; 2010, Panksepp & Biven, 2012). Gerhardt describes the process whereby old neural networks become activated automatically through neurotransmitters when feelings are aroused. This is how the emotional *status quo* is maintained by an old neurological habit, adapted to controlling unpleasant states of arousal. She observes that psychotherapy offers a new opportunity to regulate feelings, this time with sympathetic support and understanding. Consequently, the need to suppress or deny feelings and to activate the old system of neural defence slowly becomes redundant when a better alternative is available. A space opens up for reflection and more effective decision making. New states of arousal become able to be tolerated. This activates the positive functions of stress hormones, which stimulate the development of fresh cortical synapses and networks of sensory and cognitive interaction (Gerhardt, 2015: 234–237).

The healing function of psychotherapy

As with the acquisition of any skill, such life-changing processes take time, consistent application and repetition until consolidated. A central aspect of the work involved is that of supporting clients to apply their newfound capability to their personal lives and relationships. These sequential developments establish mental and emotional wellbeing and healing, as each new step is recognised and affirmed. As clients begin to acquire a level of personal agency, this signals that in due course the treatment will come to an end and psychotherapeutic assistance will no longer be needed. Both psychotherapist and client will witness this development as it grows, and together they can assess for how much longer the psychotherapy will be required. People often ask at the outset of psychotherapy how long it will take. This is usually unanswerable because each individual is unique in their need, and in their prior experience of relationship. But where it is possible to develop a sound therapeutic alliance, people begin to trust the deepening process and the question of how long it will take becomes less urgent. Through becoming more soundly acquainted with their own feelings, people become able to trust themselves and to know what to do, even in quite challenging emotional circumstances, and to transfer the skills they have acquired to their lives outside the psychotherapy arena. The capability to negotiate differences of view and ruptures in the therapeutic relationship is an important way in which people come to rely on their own experiences and feelings to navigate their way through the challenges of relating to another person. However, people vary widely as to how long it takes them to arrive at this point. And, paradoxically for some, the prospect of achieving greater personal agency can become such a threat to their emotional *status quo* that it feels like the better option to keep things the same. This can bring about an apparently sudden decision to finish, because the possibility of acquiring such a level of personal freedom seems too overwhelming. This dilemma is discussed further in Chapter 6.

But, as Gerhardt has observed, the psychotherapy relationship can offer an opportunity for real healing to take place. A secure sense of personal agency can come about through 'a mental process by which an individual implicitly and explicitly interprets the actions of himself and others as meaningful on the basis of intentional mental states such as personal desires, needs, feelings, beliefs and reasons' (Bateman & Fonagy, 2004: xxi). In other words, just as infants learn *how* to know, instinctively, when they are genuinely being seen and heard and are able, concurrently, to see and hear the intentions and feelings of others, the psychotherapy client learns this too. It is the most important of all psychotherapeutic encounters, most especially when it has been absent previously from a person's experience. Fonagy et al. (1991) have furthered our contemporary understanding of this process of mentalisation by studying the intergenerational transmission of attachment security. For example, they found that mothers whose personal experiences were those of secure attachment were more able to reflect on their own and others' internal experience, and their children were more likely to have a secure experience of attachment. They could interpret the thoughts and actions of others by noticing what they were thinking about, and then reflecting on it. When a parent is reflecting responsively on the experience of his or her infant, this signals by definition that the infant is 'in the mind' of the parent and is the focus and the priority of the parent in that moment. Equally, attunement between psychotherapist and client can come about, over time, when 'being in the mind of another' becomes deeply felt and securely known to the client, both cognitively and somatically. Consequently, the world feels more secure and predictable. This is illustrated in the following case study.

Case study of Amanda

Amanda came to see me at the suggestion of her boyfriend Sean, because he was worried about her low mood and her tendency to withdraw into silence, sometimes for days, when she was distressed. Amanda was 24 years old and the only child of her parents who had separated many years previously, because of domestic violence by her father. She was four years old when they separated and she had three sisters, each with a different father. Her mother had wished to protect her from any further risk and therefore prevented her from having contact with her father. He contested this and a court order reinstated unsupervised contact with him, during which he was aggressive and violent towards Amanda. He would silence her with threats and blows if she made any protest. Her mother appealed to the court and Amanda's contact with her father was stopped when she was 12. She resumed contact with him voluntarily when she was 18. Throughout her childhood and onwards, Amanda experienced great emotional distress which she could not articulate.

Amanda received some counselling when she was 12 and since her teenage years had been prescribed antidepressant medication. She was unhappy at school and experienced a series of unsatisfactory and wounding relationships, all of which seemed to confirm her fixed belief that she was unworthy of love and care. Of the sibling group of four, she seemed to be the one most affected by her father's behaviour. She lived with her sisters, her mother and her mother's partner who for a time, after her mother's previous traumatic experiences of relationship, became a relatively stable part of the family group. He encouraged Amanda and helped her to find employment as a postal worker on a rural post round. At one point in our conversations, she disclosed that if it had not been for finding this job and sticking to it, she would have killed herself. I noticed, as the psychotherapy progressed, that this capacity for healthy stubbornness and determination, which had protected her from self-harm in the past, illustrated some of the enduring qualities of her character.

Amanda was worried about the psychotherapy sessions at first, because she thought she would not be able to find any words to express what she was feeling and thinking. Often, we would sit in silence for most of the hour together. This felt like the right thing to do, but I sometimes wondered if I was doing anything by sitting quietly and I had to resist the temptation to speak. Gradually, as Amanda discovered that it was alright to not be able to find words, she became able to find them. I came to realise it was possible that no one had spent time like this with Amanda, without doing anything, thereby signalling quite simply that she was worth the time. Her mother had been busy working and providing for her four children as a single mother; she had been preoccupied, and was herself unsupported by unsatisfactory and sometimes abusive relationships. Amanda had, emotionally speaking, got lost in the busyness of the family. This was made especially difficult because her mother loved her but, at the time of Amanda's birth, did not have the resources to offer the consistent, caring presence Amanda needed. Later in the psychotherapy, Amanda remembered that her mother told her she had considered terminating the pregnancy. Her father also had perceived the pregnancy as an unwanted disaster, and he told Amanda that this was how he felt at the time. However, it seemed to me, that the fact her mother did not go ahead with the termination must have signalled that she wanted Amanda, despite the difficulties. Amanda and her sisters were all named after precious stones. And eventually, her mother was able to provide a more stable and supportive foundation for her children.

So often, people engaged in the psychotherapy encounter find that it is the past and often early experience of developmental trauma which emerges more fully, just as the psychotherapy process begins to feel safe and secure. It is as though their internal emotional system, by growing more confident and robust, gradually becomes able to accommodate the unbearable, original pain of being 'lost in the family'; to feel this, to articulate what happened, to be witnessed and properly heard in doing so. This was particularly important for Amanda, because one of the difficulties experienced by her mother had been that of not always being able to protect her from harm. During Amanda's psychotherapy, her mother disclosed that she felt bad about not leaving Amanda's father sooner, to protect her. Amanda's father had been violent when misusing drugs and alcohol. This meant that he was unpredictable, which held particular fear for her because she could not know what to expect from him, or what he would do next. She developed an *internal working model*, which told her she must have caused his rage and the attacks upon her, because she was 'bad'. As Bowlby (1969) understood, the relationship of attachment is a mental representation of a child's bond with her primary caregiver.

Consequently, it becomes a template or internal working model for future relationships, helping individuals to predict and manage their social and emotional environment. Ideally, this can become the child's secure base and so it follows that if it is disrupted or damaged, there will be consequences for the development of self-esteem and future relationships. Crittenden suggests that:

> Internal representational models are postulated to assist individuals in two ways. First, such models can help an individual to interpret the meaning of others' behaviour and to make predictions regarding others' future behaviour. 'Open' models are open to new interpretations and predictions. 'Closed' models interpret all behaviour in terms of the existing model. Second, such models can facilitate the organization of a response. 'Working' models allow cognitive manipulation of possible responses. 'Nonworking' models do not allow cognitive exploration of behavioural alternatives. The responsiveness of the model to new information and the ability of individuals to use the model to organize their responses are relevant to the adaptiveness of the model.
>
> (Crittenden, 1990: 265)

For Amanda, the impact of threat when in contact with her father, augmented by the sense that at times her mother was unable, despite loving her, to protect her from harm, had caused her to live in fear, which she could not express. This generated a traumatic reaction and difficulties in the 'cognitive exploration of behavioural alternatives'. Amanda's feelings became internalised, frozen and unutterable, and her closed, internal working model was one of self-blame. As Tanzer et al. (2021) have observed: 'the child may be left with little option other than to adopt self-blame as there is no 'other' to take the blame or to be blamed for these experiences'. They go on to comment that experiences of neglect reduce feelings of trust and create higher levels of guilt and shame. These negative resolutions of psychosocial crises are thought to reawaken with particular acuteness during adolescence, leading to lower levels of personal autonomy and more isolation, which may be expressed by internalising symptoms. The impact upon adolescent development, where attuned emotional responses have been lacking in childhood, causes difficulty with the regulation of feelings. This means that stressful experiences are much more difficult to negotiate and, further, the adolescent may learn to blame herself for the lack of social support she received when she most needed it. This was the case with Amanda, which led to her adopting a strategy of self-blame which limited her capacity to integrate and appraise new and more positive information about herself. Consequently, she withdrew from social situations, or felt unsafe within them, which further exacerbated her low mood and feelings of anxiety and worthlessness. She came to see herself as a needy person with whom no one would want to spend time. As Tanzer et al. point out: 'The increased impact and value of social relations in adolescence heighten the intensity of the affect associated with self-blame, generating greater distress and potentially leading to increased social impairment'.

I met with Amanda at individual sessions and for a brief period I saw her and Sean together. It quickly became apparent that the internal working model, which told Amanda she was worthless and to blame, had transferred itself into her feelings about Sean. Initially, they had been drawn to each other through feelings of irresistible attraction, which belied the fact that they both felt unworthy of love and unsafe in an intimate relationship. Amanda was convinced that Sean was attracted to other women and that he would leave her. She felt that her depression and low mood proved she was bad and made her unlovable. The irony being that from Sean's point of view, he didn't seem at all interested in other women. Instead, he was constantly distracted by a group of his peers who had an established social life, from which Amanda seemed to be excluded. He would go clubbing with his friends, the main impetus for this seeming to be access to drugs, after which he would be moody, withdrawn and out of contact with Amanda. It seemed as though, when he felt like it, he would then get back in contact with her and the same cycle of events would repeat itself, with Sean alternating between intense loving feelings, absence and resentment of what he felt were her demands, when she was simply wondering where she stood with him. Amanda found him charming, attractive and seductive, at the same time as feeling hurt and tormented by his casual treatment of her. Often she would ask 'Why doesn't he want me?', and this seemed to me to be a direct echo of her emotional experience of her father.

During the couple sessions, Sean disclosed that his father had left when he was quite small, having been violent to his mother. His mother was a recovered drinker, but he said he felt sceptical about her remaining abstinent. He described occasions when, as a teenager, he had witnessed his mother becoming intoxicated in public and how humiliating this had been, leaving him feeling he had no control or capacity to influence these bad experiences. He had been left with mixed feelings of humiliation and a desire to look after his mother. He said that he didn't invite Amanda to join in with his social life with his friends, because he feared that she would 'get smashed'. He said this with real anger, as if this outcome would be entirely inevitable, even though Amanda pointed out to him that she didn't enjoy drinking very much and anyway she could look after herself when out socialising. But Sean was able to discuss the possibility that he had developed an internal working model from his early experiences, which told him that he must try to protect someone close to him who might, at the same time, let him down and humiliate him. His experiences had led him to believe that he must have an escape route open at all times, to allow him to get away from what he imagined would be a demanding emotional trap, against which he must always remain in control.

Sean seemed to find it much more difficult to discuss the possibility that he used drugs to try to cope with his conflicting feelings and that he might have become dependent on them for this purpose. And it was difficult for him to see that whilst Amanda was clearly deriving benefit from the psychotherapy sessions, she was not 'the problem to be solved'. Rather, she was a person who had sustained considerable emotional wounds, for which she was engaging in beneficial treatment. Sometimes he would contact me by email to express his difficulties with Amanda and I suggested he might wish to engage in individual psychotherapy himself, with a different therapist. Although he expressed some interest in this possibility, he did not seem to follow up on it. This distressed Amanda further, because she felt that this was another example of her 'not being worth the bother' as far as he was concerned. However, it was finally his avoidance which assisted her in finding a way out. The couple would get together and all would seem well for a time, then the same cycle of events would repeat itself, with Sean withdrawing into silence and absence and Amanda reacting with extreme anxiety, distress and the belief that, if only she did not have these strong feelings, then Sean would want her. But, together, Amanda and I would also consider the fact of her father's rejection and anger against her and how this had coloured her view of relationships, making her believe that no one could love her and show her the care she wanted. Slowly we began to consider the fact that Sean had difficulties of his own, which meant that he also feared relationship but in a different way to Amanda. Her greatest fear was of abandonment, his was that of being controlled.

Gradually, Amanda became able to differentiate between her early experiences and those which were occurring in the present. She came to see that her fear of her father had been a legitimate response to an actual threat and that, as a child, she had not been in a position to avoid the danger or protect herself. Now, as an adult, she was able to exercise choice and could remove herself from situations causing her fear and distress. Instead of being caught up in a continuing cycle of harm and self-blame, she began to develop a healthy sense of resentment towards Sean's inconsistent treatment of her. She suggested to him that, unless he also sought help for his difficulties, she could not see a way forward for them as a couple. When he continued to behave towards her in the same way she broke contact with him. This was an extremely painful experience, but she stuck with it. Sean continued to contact her and said he would seek help. They got back together for a while, but when it appeared that nothing had changed Amanda withdrew a second time. On this occasion she seemed quietly stronger and more determined to make a life for herself, in which she would feel respected and supported. She began to make plans to undergo training for a new aspect of her work and to save up to buy a home of her own. Her mood, her appetite and her sleep pattern improved, and she became more confident to put her point of view forward in discussions, especially with her mother. Although hurt by the ending of her relationship with Sean, she became less overwhelmed by her feelings about this and more able to cope with them.

It used to be commonly believed that harm done during the formative years of early development might not be able to be put right and therefore that certain kinds of mental ill health were not susceptible to successful treatment. But as Gerhardt has explained, processes of emotional rehabilitation and recovery are possible when underpinned by a rearrangement of neurological function, facilitated by the agency of dialogue with a supportive and sympathetic listener. She refers to the work of Pennebaker (1993), who found that recovery from childhood trauma depends on talking about it. This activates the appropriate parts of the left brain to put the traumatic experience into context within organised memory. Thus, 'Putting stress into words has been found to be an effective way of coping with it, in many circumstances' (in Gerhardt, 2015: 167). However, because children in their early years have not yet fully developed these verbal parts of the left brain, they are more likely to store traumatic experiences in the amygdala and subcortical areas, which are associated with emotional events, and with fear conditioning (ibid., 168). A child who has been traumatised during the early years is therefore less able to self-soothe, lacking a stored memory of secure and reassuring experiences which needed, first of all, to be provided by a carer. During later development, and with support, dialogue makes possible a coordination between the conscious verbal processes of the left brain and the powerful store of memories in the amygdala. This means that information can be updated and adapted to the present moment, rather than being continually overridden by traumatic memory. Consequently, self-soothing can become an established part of the individual's emotional repertoire, assisting the process of regulating feelings.

Thus, Amanda found that with consistent weekly support, free from any pressure to do or to say anything, she became able to speak about the traumatic experiences of her childhood and to express her legitimate feelings associated with those memories. Consequently, she discovered that she was not the primary cause of her low mood and poor sense of self. She became less afraid to express her point of view and began to project a more positive sense of herself into the future. Her experience became less defined by the trauma of the past. During the early stages of psychotherapy, she was able to signal that she needed a lot of extra support and reassurance. She could express destructive thoughts and be honest about her emotions, even though her words were limited. During one of the couple sessions with Sean, she became so distressed that she left the session in panic and in tears. However, she made contact soon afterwards by phone and was able to continue the psychotherapy process with me from then onwards. I was also able to respond by offering the extra support of email dialogue in between meetings, for several weeks. By various ways of communicating to her that she mattered and could be a cause of caring concern, she began to value herself more highly and to know that she was visible and noticeable to others, not for being 'bad' but simply for being herself.

Negative capability in psychotherapy

In considering loving kindness as a form of steadfastness, it can be argued that this approach allows for a quality in psychotherapy which Wilfred Bion (1970) described as *negative capability*. This was a phrase discovered in the correspondence of the poet John Keats, by which he meant a capacity to be 'in uncertainties, mysteries, doubts, without any irritable reaching after fact and reason'. Keats compared human life to 'a large Mansion of Many Apartments, two of which I can only describe, the doors of the rest being as yet shut upon me. . . . Now if we live, and go on thinking, we too shall explore them' (Keats, 1899: 277–326).

Bion came to use this term in the context of psychotherapy and psychoanalysis, in which he sought to promote new ways of understanding the growth of the whole personality. Bion had himself faced extreme situations as a tank commander in the First World War, in which he demonstrated great bravery. Later, in his psycho-analytic work, he proposed that we may often be unaware of that which is new and distinctive in each moment, when we are caught up in 'reaching after fact and reason'. By being open to uncertainty and mystery, we may become more capable of allowing a process of transformation to emerge in the psychotherapeutic encounter.

When I began seeing Amanda as a client, I could not know what lay behind her silences. I did not know if I was doing anything helpful and frequently had doubts about this. But by waiting in uncertainty, her need to be accompanied in silence became clearer, as something which seemed new and reassuring to her. She had not known that her early experiences were the cause of her present difficulties in relationship. Concurrently, she had no awareness that she was a worthwhile and competent human being, with whom people liked to spend time. By waiting together we discovered these things, which gradually affirmed themselves and became a routine part of her awareness. An important part of the waiting included some long periods of sitting with her belief that nothing could get better and that, having lost Sean, she had lost all hope of happiness. This was a form of griev-ing, which she needed to experience in full, with a supportive presence. As the sessions slowly progressed, I noticed that each time she entered that despairing place, it had less hold over her and the accompanying feelings she experienced gradually became less urgent and overwhelming. Eventually, when taking part in a training course at work, she found herself sitting next to a man who looked, to her anyway, identical to Sean. However, on this occasion she experienced an unexpected shift in her memory of Sean, when she found that she was seeing this man as ordinary, and merely a human being like herself. She discovered a new perception of Sean, in which he was no longer unique and sublime, and in which she was capable and competent. This shift in perception began to confirm her recovery from the additional emotional wounds which had been inflicted by that unsatisfactory relationship.

Loving kindness as a form of good

In this chapter I have suggested that loving kindness, as steadfast presence, repre-sents the capacity to offer the following within the psychotherapy relationship: an ability to stay present and still; to remain available and responsive during times of uncertainty; to accept and work with strong feelings and negative thinking, even despair, sometimes for long periods of time, when more positive outcomes are not yet visible; to challenge destructive patterns and always to acknowledge and affirm the emergence of positive feeling and increased self-confidence. Con-sistent and steadfast attention encourages and supports the mobilisation of the psychotherapeutic imagination. It is not possible for the psychotherapist to relate to all the myriad experiences shared within the consulting room. But through deep listening it becomes possible, using imagination, to develop empathy and compassion; or at the very least some sympathetic comprehension of the client's dilemma. Through this process, Amanda gradually came to believe that she had a worthwhile future and could be loved for herself, as she was, rather than for the person she thought she should become.

Conclusion

The philosophical writing of the novelist Iris Murdoch includes reflections on the nature of love which, when engaged, becomes the focus of our attention. She states that:

> Love is the general name of the quality of attachment and it is capable of infinite degradation and is the source of our greatest errors; but when it is even partially refined it is the energy and passion of the soul in its search for Good, the force that joins us to Good and joins us to the world through Good.
>
> (Murdoch, 2001: 100)

So it is possible to define loving kindness in psychotherapy as a form of good, in that its central function in the forming of attachments positively promotes security in the development of human life, both biologically, in the form of survival, and emotionally, in the making of secure relationships upon which human beings rely in order to thrive.

Chapter 2

Expressions of loving kindness in psychotherapy

My definition of loving kindness in psychotherapy as a form of good, in its central function of forming attachments through steadfastness, implies the making of a secure relationship of trust with a psychotherapist. That relationship necessarily develops within the human context. And it is within the complexity of its uniquely human setting that loving kindness can make such an essential contribution to the task of psychotherapy. This is demonstrated in a variety of psychotherapy theories, some of which are the subject of this chapter, where I discuss the progress made in psychotherapeutic thinking and neuroscience during the twentieth century. These theories have allowed the disposition of loving kindness to be understood more clearly in professional practice, through forms of therapeutic conversation.

In first of all describing something of the wider human context within which psychotherapy takes place, it can be helpful to use lyrical descriptions from literature which capture its essence. A metaphorical example is given by Ronald Blythe, the rural essayist, in a vivid account of Thomas Hardy's origins in the isolated hamlet where he was raised (Blythe, 1978: 462–463). This microcosm of Hardy's early experience was represented in his novel, *Far from the Madding Crowd*. Blythe describes a small community viewing life through a protective barrier, constructed by generations of inherited habit, and designed to move with the seasons. The annual round is the thing that moves and turns, taking the villagers with it. It holds no assurance of happiness and is entirely subject to chance, as harvests and fortunes change for better or worse, without consideration for the finer feelings of the inhabitants. Nonetheless, this natural order of things continues unquestioned, as long as endurance is possible.

A parallel experience in psychotherapy emerges when, within the familiar microcosm of lifetime habit, endurance itself becomes no longer possible and a process of change is demanded by circumstances. Thus, the description of Hardy's experience introduces the very human conflict between habit and the possibility of a life lived beyond it. Hardy was never able to resolve this, once his writing succeeded and he acquired fame and fortune. He remained forever divided between his rural background and the life he made as a writer. But, as a writer, he was supremely able to depict his background authentically, whilst at the same time standing outside it looking in, a capability not available to those who had

DOI: 10.4324/9781003262114-3

never left or had never been raised within it. Thus, he did not depict a romantic view of the countryside, and his portrayals of character comprised the whole of human experience, including disappointment, pain and loss, as well as joy and deep good humour. Of Hardy's world as a writer, Blythe describes an 'intricate coppice' wherein sharp facts combined with his imaginings.

Equally, the psychotherapy process could be described as an intricate coppice of inner and outer experience, and of habit, in competition with the challenges presented by life events which may demand a change of view. The task of the psychotherapist, in responding, is to represent faithfully the background story of the client whilst at the same time offering an honest and independent commentary about it. In order to take these steps, it is necessary to offer loving kindness as a disposition, allowing a relationship of implicit trust to form, so that any differences of view can be weathered collaboratively. I will now discuss the progress made in psychotherapeutic thinking during the twentieth century, which has encouraged this disposition to be expressed in professional practice.

The therapeutic conversation

Phillips and Taylor (2010) have observed that kindness is not a matter of moral superiority, charitable power or a need to feel good. Put straightforwardly, they state that people need other people, not just for companionship or support in hard times but to fulfil their humanity. They propose that kindness arises from something already known and felt but not always acted upon. Indeed, we may even feel a need to resist this impulse, but they believe that it unites us with experiences held in common with others who share the same variety of human needs and vulnerabilities. Thus, acts of kindness can directly include us in different kinds of conversations.

Psychotherapy is itself an involvement in different kinds of conversations. Indeed, Hobson (1985) and Meares (2001) developed a conversational model of psychotherapy, to assist the growth of the client's self, through the encouragement of a kind of conversational relating called 'aloneness-togetherness'. Developed from within a psychodynamic framework, this model relies upon empathic listening and a common 'feeling language—a language of the heart', rather than psychoanalytical interpretation (Hobson, 1985: 15). Hobson asserted that:

> Understanding is achieved, here and now, by an imaginative exploration in different but related languages between persons who are at once alone and together. Learning how to correct misunderstandings is one (and, perhaps, *the*) most important therapeutic factor.
>
> As a climate of trust develops, fear and avoidance activities diminish. Problems, usually involving conflicts in intimate relationships, are enacted and explored. Solutions are applied to situations outside therapy. It is a matter of learning how to be with *persons*, as distinct from relating to and manipulating *things*.

A conversation involves providing conditions for on-going growth as a person. Moments of insight are steps in a progressive realisation of potentialities. A relatively unknown 'myself' extends beyond 'I'.

(ibid., 16)

Thus, he believed that the psychotherapy process was not 'talking about' the problems but 'an enactment of them with a testing out of solutions within a conversation of mutual trust'. He proposed that learning how to engage in a personal conversation 'is the heart of psychotherapy' (ibid., 7). Further, he suggested that: 'A personal feeling-language means a progressive increase in mutual understanding and its form must be such as to promote that creative process within a relationship. It is not a mere matter of discharging affect' (ibid., 89). This assertion is borne out in the case studies in this book, wherein loving kindness as a steadfast focus upon the subjective experience of the client assisted a progressive increase in mutual understanding, enabling the creative process to develop within those relationships.

In the following passages, the term *therapeutic conversation* will be understood to include both verbal and non-verbal forms of communication. As Westland (2015: 105–106) explains: 'We observe how clients speak and what their bodies are telling us non-verbally. We keep the conversation going and notice our internal experiences. Being able to keep two levels of interacting going on simultaneously comes from the skills developed by awareness practices. . . . The different experiences, those observed and those experienced, build a picture of the therapeutic relationship'. She notices that:

Clients have different ways of talking, and we can learn more about the non-verbal communications expressed or missing in their speech by listening in a low-key way to the content of their words. This frees us up to listen more intently to the way that clients are speaking. It is a question of getting used to listening not so much to content as to form. Listening to the form of the client's words will tell us about the non-verbal level of our relating in the present. It also hints at what communication the client may have initiated (non-verbally) that was not fully expressed in babyhood because of lack of attunement, or frightening or abusive interactions.

(ibid., 108)

Historical perceptions of loving kindness

Phillips and Taylor (2010: 69–70) observe that fellow feeling is a universal tendency and an essential resource in times of trouble. They speak of a 'kindness instinct', the perception of which evolved during the Enlightenment period of the seventeenth and eighteenth centuries, from being a possible solution to a human problem, into a version of kindness which viewed self and other as interdependent (ibid., 28). Hobson's 'personal feeling-language' in the therapeutic conversation implies this interdependence in relationship, which assists the development of a fuller sense of personal being and self-knowledge. Some of the origins of this Enlightenment thinking are found in the essays of the Renaissance humanist, Michel de Montaigne (1533–1592), who asserted, with a colourful foresight applicable to modern psychotherapy, that:

> It is an absolute perfection and virtually divine to know how to enjoy our being rightfully. We seek other conditions because we do not understand the use of our own, and go outside of ourselves because we do not know what it is like inside. . .
>
> The most beautiful lives, to my mind, are those that conform to the common human pattern, with order, but without miracle and without eccentricity.
> (Montaigne, 1588. In Frame, 1965: 857)

Hobson's 'personal feeling-language' demonstrates an evolved sense of kindness through interdependence, where steadfastness is required in achieving his 'progressive increase in mutual understanding'. These are characteristics of the psychotherapy relationship, which allow the possibility of Montaigne's ideal of 'enjoying our being rightfully' through our common humanity.

Montaigne and Freud

Montaigne believed that an understanding of human life and experience could not be established through rational theory, because human beings are so diverse; therefore, it was not possible for one person to determine how another should live. He was more interested in the anecdotal experience of people and the capacity to reflect on one's actions and thoughts within a common language of ideas. Thus, his distinctive legacy was an emphasis upon self-knowledge, liberty of speech and thought (Boutcher, 2005: 2, 49). His viewpoint opened up an understanding of human behaviour later evident in the thought of Freud (Bloom, 1987). Montaigne posed questions about humanity which remain relevant now: on the nature of human civilisation and the part played in it by individuals. Freud's development of psychoanalysis applied similar questions to the realm of personal experience.

Expressions of loving kindness in practice

Phillips and Taylor (2010: 58) point out how Enlightenment ideas about kindness, and their inherently social emphasis, present a challenge to Western thought on questions of human nature and morality, because the capacity to form bonds between people implies an ability to construct relationships of all kinds. Within this framework they describe ordinary kindness as a simple exchange which can enable people to encounter negative experiences and emotions with greater equilibrium. This is a central task of the therapeutic conversation. By now examining of some of the models of therapeutic conversation which emerged during the twentieth century, it becomes possible to discuss their positive impact upon psychotherapy practice.

Carl Rogers and the person-centred approach

Pereira (2012: 161–162) observes that Carl Rogers's basic perception of the nature of human beings has sometimes been contrasted with that of Sigmund Freud on the one hand and with that of personality theorists on the other. He asserts that Freud's view of human nature was essentially negative, seeing the human person as 'fundamentally hostile, antisocial and carnal'. Personality theorists, on the other hand, took a neutral view of human nature. Pereira compares Rogers to the French thinker Jean-Jacques Rousseau, who believed that 'every human being comes from her/his Maker an essentially perfect being, and that, unfortunately, this pristine splendour is corrupted by an imperfect society'. However, he states that Rogers, in speaking for himself, would not have compared himself to anyone. Rogers formed his distinctive views of human behaviour through his direct experience as a therapist, remarking that:

> When an individual is studied in the context of a relationship that is characterised by safety, absence of threat and complete freedom to be and to choose, he may initially express all kinds of bitter and murderous feelings, abnormal impulses, bizarre and antisocial desires. But as the individual continues to live in such a relationship, expressing and being more of himself, a certain innate nature emerges. He shows up to be a basically trustworthy individual, whose most deep-seated tendency is towards development, differentiation, co-operative relationships; whose life tends fundamentally to move from dependence to independence; whose impulses tend to harmonise into a complex pattern of self-regulation; whose innate tendency is to preserve himself and his species and move it towards its further evolution. In short, the human being is the most widely sensitive, responsive, creative and adaptive creature on earth.
>
> (ibid., 162)

This view of the nature of the human person, which Rogers called the person-centred approach, represents his perspective concerning the potential of every helping profession (ibid., 163). He proposes that each individual has extensive inner resources for self-understanding and a capacity to change his or her own self-image, attitudes and behaviour. But he also sees that the right climate for change is required, in order for persons to engage with their own unique resources. He identifies three conditions which contribute to such a climate and which promote personal growth (Rogers, 1967: 61–62). These are congruence, unconditional positive regard and empathic understanding, which find expression in attitudes and behaviours demonstrated by the facilitator and are 'the most delicate and useful ways we have of using ourselves' (Rogers, 1980: 137). They can be expressed through the facility of listening very attentively to clients and reflecting feelings back to them.

Rogers views empathy as a way of being, where the therapist can enter the private perceptual world of another person and feel at home in it. This requires a sensitive response from moment to moment 'to the changing felt meanings which flow in this other person, to the fear or rage or tenderness or confusion or whatever'. He compares it to temporarily living in the life of the client, without making judgements, whilst perceiving meanings of which the client is scarcely aware, and not trying to uncover feelings of which they are unaware, since this could feel threatening. To be with another person in this way means that for the time being you lay aside the views and values which you hold for yourself, so as to enter the world of another without prejudice: 'In some sense it means that you lay aside yourself, and this can only be done by a person who is secure enough in himself that he knows he will not get lost in what may turn out to be the strange or bizarre world of the other, and can comfortably return to his own world when he wishes' (ibid., 142–143).

Empathic understanding focuses attention upon the client in a relational approach which places emphasis upon mutuality, intersubjectivity and active intervention. In these aspects Rogers was influenced by Ferenczi (1873–1933), who criticised Freud's method of neutral interpretation. Ferenczi collaborated with Otto Rank in devising a 'here and now' perspective, which can be seen in Rogers's development of the person-centred concept (Kramer, 1995). The person-centred approach is most evident at the outset of psychotherapy engagement, when the aim is that of setting a reliable tone of sympathetic attunement and acceptance. This is illustrated in the case study of Olivia in Chapter 5. In that chapter I also discuss the necessary transition in the developing psychotherapy process from those prior stages, where non-impingement upon the client's subjective experience is paramount, to later developments capable of accommodating more robust emotional exchanges, which nonetheless continue to be empathic as well as congruent and authentic.

Hans Loewald and the therapeutic action of psychoanalysis

Loewald (1960: 16–20) was a psychoanalyst influenced by the thought of Freud, which he adapted in practice to a focus upon 'the significant interactions between patient and analyst which ultimately lead to structural changes in the patient's personality'. This he called 'psychoanalytic process'. He proposed that psychoanalysis resumed the process of ego-development and that modern psychoanalytic ego-psychology represented far more than an addition to the psychoanalytic theory of instinctual drives. He suggested that it was the elaboration of a more comprehensive theory of the organisation of the psychic apparatus. He observed that an analysis could be characterised as 'a period or periods of induced ego-disorganization and reorganization'. This is illustrated in the case study of Gemma, in Chapter 3 of this book, confirming his opinion that 'new spurts of self-development may be intimately connected with such "regressive" rediscoveries of oneself as may occur through the establishment of new object-relationships'. These opportunities permit the rediscovery of earlier paths of the development, 'leading to a new way of relating to objects as well as of being and relating to oneself'. The psychoanalytic process described by Loewald represents a fuller discovery of oneself and of objects, and is made possible by the encounter with a 'new object', the analyst, who makes him or herself available to the client throughout the analysis. This is one meaning of the term *positive transference*.

This fuller discovery of self reveals characteristics of the core of a person. It helps the analyst to interpret the transferences and defences of the patient, rather than 'some abstract concept of reality or normality'. In doing so the analyst avoids moulding the patient in his or her own image and imposing upon the patient his or her own concept of what the patient should become. Loewald observes that it requires an 'objectivity and neutrality the essence of which is love and respect for the individual and for individual development. This love and respect represent that counterpart in 'reality', in interaction with which the organisation and reorganisation of ego and psychic apparatus take place' (ibid.). This is what is meant by loving kindness in psychotherapy, as our steadfast focus of attention upon the patient, in a true representation of him or herself.

Orange (2016: 21–23) identifies Loewald as an 'ethical thinker', placing his approach to psychoanalysis at a midpoint in the history of psychoanalysis, between Freud and the present time. She comments that in his paper, *On the Therapeutic Action of Psychoanalysis* (1960), he brought together object relations, transference, the relations between instinctual drives and ego, and the function of the analyst in the analytic situation 'into a *tour de force* of just sufficiently deferential subversion, opening the subsequent history of our field for nearly everything that has followed in American psychoanalysis and in psychotherapies related to it'. Orange states that he 'relationalised' Freud, when he asserted that 'the therapeutic power of psychoanalysis resulted from the relational—that is, transferential—transformation of old miseries' and that without transference, 'human life becomes sterile and an empty shell. On the other hand, the unconscious needs present-day external reality (objects) and present-day psychic reality (the preconscious) for its own continuity, lest it be condemned to live the shadow-life of ghosts or to destroy life'. Thus, Loewald (2000: 248–250) concluded that: 'In the daylight of analysis the ghosts of the unconscious are laid and led to rest as ancestors whose power is taken over and transformed into the new intensity of present life, of the secondary process and contemporary objects'.

Alterity and the 'ethical turn' in therapeutic conversations

Orange (2016) and others (Baraitser, Katz & Corpt) have discussed the philosophy of Emmanuel Levinas (1906–1995), in developing the concept of the 'ethical turn' in contemporary psychoanalysis. Katz (2013: 72–73) explains that the 'ethical turn' means the guiding condition of our lives needs to become that of putting the Other first, so that 'the self is turned toward the Other'. Thus, Orange asserts that the practising clinician or humanitarian is also a practising philosopher who can internalise 'the crucial resources needed to nourish and sustain the kind of practice that clinical work in the best of the psychoanalytic tradition, including the ethical turn, requires. The required capacities and attitudes involve not only wisdom and compassion but also vulnerability and fallibilism, courage and humility' (Orange, 2016: x). Her use of the term *fallibilism* includes:

> a disciplined recognition that one might always be mistaken, that one is fallible, and, moreover, that one is likely to be mistaken insofar as one takes one's own opinion to be the whole, final, and absolute truth. It does not mean a flippant, 'Oh, I could always be wrong', but rather describes the attitude of someone who always and genuinely wants to learn more.
>
> (ibid., 174)

Levinas was a French philosopher, of Jewish and Lithuanian heritage. He introduced a particular focus upon the nature of being through his belief in alterity, meaning 'otherness, or an awareness of our being the "other of two"'. On this view he proposed that ethical encounters are philosophy in practice, the 'wisdom of love' rather than the 'love of wisdom'. He believed that the primary impulse towards philosophy, or that which makes us seek reasons and justifications, is our ethical responsibility to others, or love (Levinas, 1981: 162). Orange observes that he transforms the concept of subjectivity through his attention to the suffering of the other: 'Only in the suffering of the other, and in my response, do I . . . come into being . . . called into being by the other's naked and vulnerable face. The sovereign self, with its 'place in the sun,' always trying to have more, would be indifferent to the plight of the other'. And she goes on to enquire:

> What can the working clinician make of all this? Where is *our* discourse of hospitality and welcome? Though only recently have words like 'compassion' (Orange, 2006), 'kindness' and 'generosity' (Corpt, 2009) found their way into psychoanalytic literature, if we look carefully, we can find their forebears. Sandor Ferenczi wrote to Freud about tact: 'I merely think that one must from the outset place oneself in—feel oneself into—the patient's situation' (Ferenczi, 1949, p. 248) . . . Ian Suttie (1935) wrote of tenderness, Winnicott & The Institute of Psycho-Analysis (Great Britain) (1975) . . . of maternal care. Hospitable spirits have also existed in the other humanistic psychotherapies . . .

Oddly, however, psychoanalytic reticence has combined with the worship of efficiency and cost- effectiveness to render invisible, and even disparaged, clinical warmth and unhurried welcome, but it remains an indispensable need. Such emotional availability . . . involves being prepared for whatever openhearted empathic stretching the other may need of me.

(Orange, 2016: 36)

Orange provides an illustration from her own practice, of this 'open hearted empathic stretching', when she describes how a patient of hers, 'brilliant but always hovering on the edges of madness, protested to me that everything about psychotherapy and psychoanalysis was arranged for the protection and convenience of the clinician, and had nothing to do with the needs of patients'. It was only when she invited him to help her design something that might better meet his needs, and to try this out for a while, that they settled into a treatment arrangement for many years. She points out that as a human being herself, with her own limitations, she must set contracts with her patients 'in advance for time, place, and payment, and work out the rest as best and hospitably as possible in a spirit of welcome, a tent-open spirit. Otherwise they too may notice the closed-off spirit, and turn away in despair once more' (ibid., 37–38). And she reflects upon how she began to think about the place of compassionate discourse in psychoanalytic literature, when she observes that:

Psychoanalytic compassion is not reducible to moral masochism on the part of the analyst, nor is it to be contrasted with properly psychoanalytic work, usually seen as explicitly interpretive. It is, instead, an implicitly interpretive process of giving lived meaning and dignity to a shattered person's life by enabling integration of the pain and loss as opposed to dissociation or fragmentation. A compassionate attitude says to every patient: your suffering is human suffering, and when the bell tolls for you, it also tolls for me.

(Orange, 2006: 16)

Baraitser (2008) discusses alterity in the context of motherhood, when considering the needs of mothers in the encounter with the enigmatic 'otherness' of their infants. She reflects on how the mother is presented with the task of separating her subjectivity from that of her child and how, in this process, the mother may be isolated and seen as 'otherwise' to a discourse of care which understandably prioritises the infant. This ethical consideration is highlighted in the case study of Gemma in Chapter 3, where Gemma's mother was unable to allow a healthy emotional separation from her daughter, because of her own unmet needs. These are important reflections when considering the discussion in Chapter 1 of this book, concerning the central importance of attachment between infant and parent. The case study of Gemma illustrates the need for her mother to be viewed as 'an ethical subject'; even when she was situated 'otherwise' to my discourse of care with her daughter. Whilst it had to be faced, therapeutically speaking, that Gemma's mother had been unable, for reasons of her own vulnerability, to disentangle her own subjectivity from that of Gemma in childhood, resulting in harmful outcomes; respect for her humanity, though stretched to the limit at times, was included and not diminished. As the psychotherapy progressed and deepened, Gemma was able to move away from the symbiotic intersubjectivity she had shared with her mother. And at the end of her mother's life, their final farewells were able to be said in a spirit of alterity. Parallel dilemmas can occur in the developing therapeutic relationship when a symbiotic, intersubjective merger is unconsciously sought by the client. The psychotherapist needs to remain disentangled from it, in order for the client's development to proceed without inhibition.

Empathic conversations in psychotherapy

Akhtar (2018a: xiv–xv) states that psychoanalysis is both a listening and a talking cure, in which he places silence 'on an equal footing with speaking by emphasising that both have the ability to serve similar aims'. He observes that the aims and consequences of the patient's silence and the analyst's silence might differ, and he describes the phenomenon of 'mutual silence' in the therapeutic hour, which I have illustrated in the case study of Amber in Chapter 1. And, in referring to the work of Jacobs (1991: 104), he draws attention to the sort of information the psychotherapist can draw from listening to herself, her inner emotional state, passing associations, reverie or distractions. Even the way she is dressed and postural changes can signal events that are taking place between psychotherapist and client: 'but are just so slightly out of the conscious awareness of both' (Akhtar, 2018a: 6). Thus, empathic attunement can be brought about through consistent attention to the seemingly small details of therapeutic engagement.

Jacobs describes how the manner in which the analyst begins and ends the session, including posture, facial expression and vocal tone, 'convey kinesic messages of which he may or may not himself be cognizant'. He emphasises the fact that listening itself gives rise to bodily movements and non-verbal gestures of which the therapist may be unaware. A sigh, a barely suppressed yawn, or slight movements will generate low-level sounds, which may be conveyed as conscious or unconscious communications to the client. These could express an otherwise unexpressed attitude or feeling on the part of the therapist. The development of an attuned, embodied, self-awareness on the part of the psychotherapist therefore supports congruent therapeutic communication and the possibility of verbal dialogue about all of its aspects. Jacobs calls this 'body empathy', through which the psychotherapist can become attuned to the unconscious communication of the client and offer more accurate mirroring of their experience.

Empathic attunement and projective identification

Empathic conversations are not always easy and the more difficult the early developmental experience of the client, the more challenging will be the feelings which arise within the therapeutic relationship. But equally the empathic process will provide a source of accurate information about how the client feels. As Akhtar (2018a: 8–9) has pointed out: 'the use of projective identification on the patient's part leads the analyst to experience what the patient cannot bear to feel or think'. Klein (1946) described the concept of projective identification as a process which begins in early infancy when parts of the rudimentary self become 'split off and projected into an external object. The latter then becomes identified with the repudiated part as well as internally controlled by it'. Listening empathically engages the psychotherapist with the hidden shaming, which is so often the experience of persons who have been deeply wounded during their infant development. Thus, one possible impact for the psychotherapist may be that of feelings of inferiority or inadequacy, which in fact represent 'an identification with the projected shame-laden parts of the patient'. These are the parts of the client's experience which are the most hidden. But it is essential to know about them and to allow them gradually to be brought into view, if their hold on the client is ever to be loosened. Issues such as these therefore require long-term, painstaking and tenacious work, because their origins have arisen in early infancy, creating a set of assumptions which feel completely real for the client. These are examples of Bowlby's *internal working model*, wherein the relationship of attachment, as a mental representation of a child's bond with the primary caregiver, becomes a template for future relationships. Projective identification serves defensive purposes, as a response to the neglect or abuse of childhood needs, and these purposes can include:

> attempted fusion with external objects to avoid the existential burden of separateness, extrusion of bad internal objects that cause persecutory anxieties, and preservation of endangered good aspects of the self by depositing them into others. Bion (1967) extended the notion of projective identification to include the depositing of unthinkable thoughts ('beta elements', in his terminology) into a receptive other who can metabolise them and return them to the subject in a piecemeal manner.
>
> (Akhtar, 2018a: 8)

It is therefore essential that the 'beta elements' are metabolised by the psychotherapist and returned to the client kindly, in a piecemeal and digestible manner, yet one which is robust enough to be able to name and discuss the client's previously unthinkable thoughts. This is especially important in situations of self-harm and suicidal thoughts. The responsiveness of the internal working model to new information and the ability of individuals to use it to organise their responses are factors which influence its adaptiveness (Crittenden, 1990: 265). Psychotherapy seeks to build a relationship with all aspects of a person's experience and most especially those which have been rejected. This is not always possible, as discussed in Chapter 6. Nonetheless, until those aspects are addressed, they will continue to influence negatively the client's view of self, of relationships, and of the world in general.

Akhtar observes that the opposite of projective identification is empathy. 'The former involves the patient's actively putting something into the analyst's mind.

The latter involves the analyst's actively seeking to resonate with the patient's experience' (Akhtar, 2018a: 9). He discusses the work of Fliess (1942: 212–215), who explained the process by which one comes to understand what someone else is actually saying. In order to empathise with someone, 'one "*introjects this object transiently, and projects the introject again onto the object*" '. This alone enables a perception to be viewed both from without and from within. This is an important definition of empathy when considering loving kindness as steadfast attention towards another person. The quality of this attention enables the introjection of the other, which can then be projected back to the 'object of attention', through a process of accurate mirroring. Only when a client is properly seen in this way is it possible for him or her to begin to let go of the projective identification, as the rejected and split-off parts are reunified and a true self is acknowledged. This is beautifully illustrated in a verse by George Herbert (1593–1633), from his poem *The Elixir*:

> A man that looks on glass,
> On it may stay his eye;
> Or if he pleaseth, through it pass,
> And then the heav'n espy.

Thus, Schwaber (1981: 378) proposes a mode of attunement, which emphasises a focus upon the subjective reality of the client. This approach aims to avoid imposing the therapist's point of view. Instead, the role and the point of view of the therapist, and the context of the consulting room, are recognised as intrinsic parts of the client's own experience and reality, where 'the observer is part of the field observed. As a scientific modality, empathy employs our cognitive, perceptual, as well as affective capacities . . . empathy draws upon modalities which are significant components of the essentials of parental empathy—attunement to and recognition of the perceptive and experiential states of another'. Experiences of empathic listening are provided in the case studies in this book, with particular reference to Mark in Chapter 4 and Coral in Chapter 5, who concludes with her own reflections.

The humanistic therapies and the experience of the client

The humanistic therapies are distinctive in their attention to the experience of the client, as illustrated earlier in the example of Carl Rogers's person-centred approach. Applying a different emphasis, the client as focus of attention in Gestalt therapy is perceived as a figure in the ground of a particular therapeutic context or event where: 'If both attention and excitement are present and working together, the object of attention becomes more and more a unified, bright, sharp figure against a more and more empty, unnoticed, uninteresting ground. This form of unified figure against an empty ground has been called a 'good gestalt' (Perls et al., 1989: 56–75).

A human gestalt experience, as an organised whole which is more than the sum of its parts, sees the individual as paramount within that authentic experience. By contrast, the alternative experience of tolerating without question the external assumptions which may be made about that individual will 'tend to perpetuate its present undesirable aspects'. The contribution of Gestalt therapy therefore lies in its emphasis upon the reliability and validity of subjective experience.

The relevance of client subjectivity

In the psychotherapeutic setting it is therefore important for the therapist to be aware that the experience of the client is paramount, and empathic listening by the psychotherapist has to allow an accurate sense of attunement with that experience to develop. Akhtar (2018a: 94–95) provides an example of this from his own practice, when a distressed client, Olga, who was going through a difficult divorce, broke down in tears and he felt a strong urge to cross the room and hold her in his arms. Olga had no other family living close by and felt trapped within her legal and financial predicament. In that moment, Akhtar felt that to physically hold her would be right thing to do, because it would calm her and she would feel better. He noticed that his impulse was strong, but seemed humane. He was also aware that the sensual experience of holding her would give him sexual pleasure. He resisted the impulse to hold her and gradually it passed. Olga became more composed. The importance of Akhtar's decision became evident the following day. He writes that:

> A far more relaxed, if not beaming, Olga appeared in my office. She announced that upon leaving my office the previous day, she somehow felt better, stronger, and empowered. As if someone was truly on her side. As if she were not alone. Buoyed by such feelings, she fired her inept divorce lawyer and called a highly recommended attorney of great repute in the area. 'Had you not been with me the way you were yesterday, I don't think I could have done this,' she said.
>
> (ibid.)

Akhtar later reflected that his wish to hold and comfort his client had somehow conveyed itself to her. Referring to Winnicott (1960b), he suggests that abstaining from his impulse was in fact a 'firm holding' which more accurately represented the need of his client. He goes on to comment that he did not enquire further about his client's experience because that would have been 'analytically greedy and, by making the "holding" function a topic for intellectual discussion, would, paradoxically, rob the experience of its value. This was the kind of stuff that, in each session, we leave uninterpreted, while focusing upon other material'. Referring to Loewenstein (1951) and Poland (1975) Akhtar defines this kind of attuned abstention as a form of discretion or tact and he points out that we can make such choices about where to place our therapeutic focus: 'what to focus and what to leave alone are integral to our daily work. More often than not, we are able to contain our impulses and learn about the patient (and ourselves) from this'.

Compassion-focused therapy

Compassion-focused therapy (CFT) is a development of the twenty-first century, devised by the clinical psychologist Paul Gilbert, which incorporates theories, principles and techniques from a range of psychological modalities and spiritual practices. These include cognitive behavioural therapy, developmental psychology, evolutionary psychology, social psychology, neuroscience and Buddhist philosophy. In 2006 Gilbert established the Compassionate Mind Foundation, a charity with an international network of practitioners and researchers promoting CFT and Compassionate Mind Training (CMT). As a comprehensive approach to psychological therapy, CFT has responded to the considerable emotional and psychological needs of people living in modern, complex societies; where pressures of work, or a lack of income and meaningful employment, rapid technological development, the impact of climate change, conflict, and the necessity of migration together present a bewildering array of external circumstances which can diminish human equilibrium, health and wellbeing. Within these contemporary realities, the overriding impulse of CFT arises from Gilbert's belief that a lack of self-kindness and warmth is central to many states of mental suffering (Gilbert, 2013: ix). Gilbert defines human warmth within its evolutionary context when he observes that:

> It is very easy to think of our 'old brain/mind' as containing only the difficult emotions of anger, anxiety, tribalism and so forth. However, the evolution of mammals brought new emotions and motives into the world—this was a brain that could care about others. Now, of course, the way early mammals cared for their offspring was automatic, their brains responding to specific cues or stimuli such as the cries of the chick in the nest. . . . But it was the first glimmer of a brain that would build a nest to protect an infant, that would detect, recognise and respond to distress calls and behave in ways that would benefit an infant . . . its behaviour was aimed at supporting, protecting and helping another living being, not just itself. . . . Some would say that this behaviour was aimed at supporting, protecting and helping its own genes. However, over millions of years, such caring was so successful as an evolved strategy to maintain genetic lineages that, in the flow of life, it has flourished into complex potentials within the human brain, including building the competencies that gave rise to our abilities for compassion.
>
> (ibid., 48–49)

Gilbert states that the human brain has evolved both to be caring and to need care in its development. Referring to the work of Cozolino (2007), he observes that the patterned interconnections of the brain are directly influenced by the amount of love and affection received. So the care shown by parents to their infants not only soothes distress but also helps children gain a sense of how their minds and emotions work. This enables children to talk about their feelings and the things that happen to them and to generate warm responses. Knowing that they exist in the mind of another, as a loved person, stimulates their capacity to self-soothe. This makes the world feel safe, so that children and adults 'who receive kindness, gentleness, warmth and compassion are, compared with those who don't, more confident and secure, happier and less vulnerable to mental and physical health problems; they are also more caring and respectful of others' (ibid., 49–50). Thus, Gilbert asserts that kindness is fundamental to the human state: '*we are a species that has evolved to thrive on kindness and compassion*. The challenge here is to recognise the importance of kindness and affection and place them at the *centre* of our relationship with ourselves, with others and with the world' (ibid., 51).

Here, Gilbert has clearly described the conditions necessary to engender emotional warmth in human beings. And we can illustrate what this emotional warmth feels like. Some examples have been provided in Chapter 1 of this book, with reference to Charles Dickens's descriptions of the sensory experiences of children in the care of people who loved them unconditionally. The children—David Copperfield with Peggotty, and Pip with Joe Gargery—knew, and more importantly *felt*, that they were loved. Dickens's writing communicates the deep mental and physical response to being soothed and comforted, in which children feel safe and content because, in that state of body and mind, all feels well. Both Peggotty and Joe are steadfast in their focus upon the children for whom they care, young children who develop and thrive on kindness and compassion.

The significance of having feelings

Within the arena of affective neuroscience Damasio (2000: 42) has helpfully drawn a distinction between emotions and feelings. He suggests that: 'Emotions and feelings of emotions, respectively, are the beginning and the end of a progression, but the relative publicness of emotions and the complete privacy of the ensuing feelings indicate that the mechanisms along the continuum are quite different'. He proposes that the term *feeling* should be reserved for the private, mental experience of an emotion, while the term *emotion* should be used to designate the collection of responses, many of which are publicly observable. This is a useful observation because it clearly identifies the finely tuned subjective and distinctive experience of another person as different from one's own subjective response. 'In practical terms this means that you cannot observe a feeling in someone else although you can observe a feeling in yourself when, as a conscious being, you perceive your own emotional states. Likewise no one can observe your own feelings, but some aspects of the emotions that give rise to your feelings will be patently observable to others'. Damasio's view not only supports the subjectivity of personal experience but opens a discussion about how emotions and feelings are experienced and communicated between human beings. Within this context, Westland comments that:

> Emotions are accompanied by physiological and energetic changes, movement patterns, and thoughts. Emotional expression is part of self and interactive regulation. If we are to connect non-verbally with our clients, we have to tune into and tolerate the basic emotional energies coursing through our bodies. This is the starting point for helping clients to link their feeling, thinking, and action. . . . With some practice, we can observe these physical changes in our clients and we can keep track of our own autonomic nervous system and emotional responses. This is part of a collaborative, intersubjective approach.
>
> (Westland, 2015: 170)

And here, she describes the variety of emotional experiences encountered within the psychotherapy arena:

> Broadly speaking, clients may be flooded with feelings, lurching from one feeling to another, one moment angry, then crying and afraid, that is, overwhelmed with their feelings. On the other hand, some clients have a limited emotional repertoire. They may have difficulty recognising their feelings, and if they do experience their feelings, recognition of the changing contours and rhythms of their feelings may be stilted. They may find it difficult to withstand the intensity of their emotional experience. Emotionally overwhelmed clients are left without really knowing what they want as the torrent of their feelings leaves them unable to think and reflect . . .
>
> At the other end of the spectrum, clients may not know what they are feeling, let alone be able to put feelings into words. Clients who are overwhelmed with feelings benefit from discovering ways of dampening the intensity of their emotions, being able to contain them so that they can be experienced more slowly, reflected on, and thought about. This enables discrimination between different feelings, gaining some perspective on them, and being able to make choices about tactful ways of expressing them in words in different relationships, or keeping them (relatively) private. Psychotherapy may end when emotionally overwhelmed clients have taken charge of their emotions rather than being at their mercy. For some clients in this emotionally overwhelmed grouping, once they are more in command of their feelings, they are equipped to continue and deepen into the therapeutic relationship.
>
> (ibid., 161–162)

As Westland has observed, emotional life for some clients is limited and feelings may not be able to be recognised at all. Or, if they are recognised at some level, there may be little capacity to differentiate between states of feeling; the only reference point being a generalised sensation of anxiety. And for some there may be either overt or hidden hostility to feelings. Where this is the case, it is noticeable that emotional memory is often lacking and clients may not be able to remember previous therapy sessions, or cannot hold on to a therapeutic 'thread' in the same session. A slow and progressive opportunity to become acquainted with feelings and to recognise each one distinctly is a therapeutic priority here. Westland suggests the use of an approach which helps clients to join thinking, feeling, and action together and to learn how to express feelings to others. It can be done by underscoring and gradually amplifying denied and inaccessible feelings. This helps clients widen their capacity to recognise and name feelings and to experience an increasing repertoire and range of intensity. She goes on to describe the necessity of talking both in words and non-verbally to 'different levels of consciousness in clients from the matter-of-fact to the deep emotional level' (ibid., 163). And she comments that body psychotherapies, creative arts and humanistic psychotherapies have emphasised the non-verbal and have found ways to communicate this through movement, sound, music and drawing.

Loving kindness as the core of psychotherapeutic conversations

The development of psychotherapies where loving kindness is integral to practice has opened up and deepened the reparative work of therapeutic conversation. It has become possible to demonstrate—through theory, research and practice— how people experiencing emotional distress can gain a full and lasting sense of the healing function of loving kindness, through the therapeutic relationship. This reparative work is illustrated in the case studies provided in Chapters 1, 3, 4 and 5 of this book.

Chapter 3

False friends of loving kindness

The symbiotic merger and sentimentality

The term loving kindness could imply that the psychotherapeutic work involved will always be pleasant or even 'nice'; the paradox being that, as consistent therapeutic presence gives room for deep and difficult experiences to be explored, progress can sometimes be very challenging for both client and psychotherapist. It is therefore necessary for the psychotherapist to be able to avoid misleading representations of loving kindness, in order to be of most assistance to the unfolding process of each individual client. In this chapter I will describe two common yet understandable pitfalls: the symbiotic merger and sentimentality.

The symbiotic merger

Generally speaking, a symbiotic relationship can be described as one where people co-exist beneficially and each party experiences advantage from it. However, to acquire a distinct level of adult functioning, it is necessary to develop a level of separation from the symbiotically merged representation of self which characterises early infant development. Therefore, an understanding of the importance of symbiosis between infant and parent is helpful when considering the necessity of independence at a later stage. A symbiotic merger is characterised by the need for both parties to feel that their responses to experience are identical and that they think and feel as one. This is natural in early infancy and in the early stages of intimate adult relationships, and is a key point in the life of teenagers, when becoming part of a peer group is so important. However, as Lowen (1974) observed, the child also requires opportunities for exploration outside the symbiosis, to later achieve adult independence and to form collaborative relationships with others in a social group. In this chapter, I will illustrate how obstacles to emergence from the symbiotic stage of infanthood can present later as difficulties in adulthood, and why it is important for the psychotherapist to be consciously aware of them, in order to avoid entering into a repetition of the same relational pattern.

DOI: 10.4324/9781003262114-4

Symbiosis in infant development

In making these observations, it is useful to apply the object relations perspective developed by Mahler, Spitz and Bowlby, concerning the early expressions and challenges encountered in childhood development (Johnson, 1985: 13). Direct observation of young children, including infants in hospital, found that when they were removed from their carer/object of attachment for significant periods of more than five months, they were seen to deteriorate emotionally and psychologically. The object relations perspective enhanced understanding of the impact of such deprivation. It also provided a significant bridge between psychoanalytic, cognitive and behavioural approaches to the support and repair of adaptive functions. It shed light upon the ways in which infants master developmental tasks towards adulthood or, on the other hand, become inhibited in their efforts.

Mahler et al. (1975) viewed the symbiotic phase of child development as a transition, from the stage at which the infant is self-absorbed and merged as one with his or her parent, towards the possibility of individuation, where a sense of other persons as separate beings begins to develop. They emphasised the necessary establishment of a 'sound symbiosis', influenced by the non-verbal cues of the infant to signal his or her needs and feelings. They proposed that this phase lasts until around five months of age, when the infant becomes more aware of his or her parent but as yet has not acquired a sense of individuality. The separation phase signals the end of the symbiotic phase of infancy. At this stage, limits to the unconditional experience of a merged symbiosis begin to develop, alongside the growing sense of differentiation between infant and parent. This allows for the development of individuation, leading ultimately to a sense of self and an individual identity which enhances emotional and cognitive capability. This essential stage in child development is what Mahler (1968) described as an 'expansion beyond the symbiotic orbit'.

Johnson states that the first stage of separation and individuation begins at approximately six months. This represents the first attempts of the infant to push away from the mother and to begin to perceive her more distinctly. The processes involved in developing an entirely separate identity continue from this point until about two and a half years or more. It is during this process of differentiation that the child begins to focus his or her attention outward. The shift occurs more smoothly if a 'safe anchorage' has already been established, making the experience of symbiosis secure. Thus, the secure symbiotic merger is the foundation from which a safe separation begins to become possible.

> During this differentiation period, the self-representation is still merged with the object-representation but the infant begins to discriminate the specific identity of the other part of the symbiotic unit. During this period, a *specific* smile of recognition will develop for the mothering figure, indicating

that a specific bonding has taken place. This discrimination is the essential 'seed' of the separation from symbiosis. Another marker event of this period involves responses which indicate that the child discriminates strangers from the mothering person.

(Johnson, 1985: 16–17)

As development proceeds, greater mastery of the child's environment begins to become possible. And it begins to dawn on the emerging toddler 'that the world is *not* his oyster; that he must cope with it more or less "on his own", very often as a relatively helpless, small, and separate individual, unable to command relief or assistance merely by feeling the need for them, or giving voice to that need' (Mahler, 1972: 9). Masterson (1976) therefore discussed the inevitable and sometimes intense challenges, for both parent and infant, in negotiating this essential stage of development. Infants will naturally feel a longing to remain in the comfort zone of a symbiotic fusion which provides warm feelings of safety and consistency. And if a parent is emotionally vulnerable it is easy to see how, if the infant withdraws from developing a new autonomy, the parent may mirror that reluctance by encouraging the continuation of the symbiotic merger and the comfort zone they share. In these circumstances, the individuation process can be impeded or prevented altogether. Johnson (1985: 33–34) observes that the consequence of this will be the maintenance of the symbiotic attachment, possibly throughout life, which may in future be transferred to another primary attachment figure. He notices that the 'symbiotic character' in adulthood tends to have a history of difficulty with separation and may, for example, have faced considerable challenges in going to school, or moving from primary school to high school, or from high school to college or work. 'Continued separation anxiety is the most common and obvious complaint in this structure and the individual may be prone to develop symbiotic attachments to other objects or persons, experiencing a good deal of anxiety when any separation is threatened'.

The difficulties of the symbiotic merger in adulthood

A person with symbiotic difficulties will tend to seek relationships where they can continue to believe that others think and feel exactly as they do. Consequently any divergence of thought, feeling or action may be perceived as deeply threatening to the symbiotic merger and, on that view, must be prevented. This can lead to coercive behaviour, or withdrawal from the relationship following failed attempts to maintain the symbiotic *status quo*. Relationships which continue to be symbiotically merged in adulthood are not uncommon. And it is often the struggle with the unresolved pressures of such a symbiotic relationship with a parent, or other significant figure, which brings the client to psychotherapy, because they have not been able to form a confident, individual identity and cannot seem to make steady progress towards maturity in their emotional lives and relationships.

The challenges presented in adulthood, by separation from a symbiotic relationship with a parent, are described by Tania Unsworth (2020), remembering how she began to develop as a children's writer when the symbiosis with her father broke down. Unsworth has kindly permitted me to quote at length from the newspaper article which illustrates her experience. During her childhood, the symbiosis had seemed productive, supporting her in growing confidence to write. She tells how she and her sisters were attached to their father as precocious readers and writers, since demonstrating an interest in the written word never failed to win his approval:

> Every year, at Christmas, we wrote "books" for him, toiling for weeks over implausible plots and volumes of melodramatic poetry, our handwriting getting bigger and bigger in an effort to fill up our exercise books. I still have an entire Norse saga that I presented to him when I was 10.
>
> My father never laughed at these offerings, ludicrous though they must have seemed. On Christmas afternoon, I would watch in breathless anticipation as he read what I had written, slowly turning the pages, his face full of thoughtful appreciation. He was just as interested in the journals we kept when we went on holiday. We were trying to copy his habit of filling notebooks with writerly observations, although, when I sneaked a glimpse at what he had written, I sometimes wondered whether we were actually on the same trip. Where I might write: "This morning we went on a walk and it was v hot and Maddy was showing off all the time," my father's entry would make no mention of these events. Instead, he would have spent a whole paragraph describing the colour of the sea and another one on how one church reminded him of another.
>
> That was what *real* writers wrote about, I thought.
>
> In my family, stories—the ones we made up and the ones we read—featured large. Discussed over supper, told at bedtime, used to pass the time whenever we were bored. Stories were our bread and butter. Stories were gold. I knew I had got my father's full attention when, as I chattered about something or other, I saw a particular look come over his face. Intent, focused, strangely inward.
>
> There's a story in there," he would say. And suddenly I would see it, too, understanding that stories are never truly invented, but merely discovered, dug up like fossils, with language the tool of their extraction.
>
> (Unsworth, 2020: 4)

But Unsworth goes on to describe how, as the events of their respective lives unfolded and her father moved abroad, their communication became more argumentative. He didn't come to her graduation ceremony or her wedding. But she persisted:

convinced that the next letter—or the one after that—would sort everything out. That writing had the power to resurrect our relationship.

I was wrong. As it turned out, it was writing that put the final nail in its coffin. I published my first novel, The Seahorse, when I was 35 and sent him an advance copy. "Look!" I wanted to say. "Not a Norse saga this time! A real book!" But I restrained myself, settling for a coy: "I hope you like it," instead.

His reply was swift and devastating. While he thought the book was good and showed promise, none of that mattered because I had done something unforgivable. One of my characters (a villainous one) bore an unmistakable resemblance to a person he loved, although, according to him, "resemblance" was too weak a word. It was more that I had based the *entire* character (who was not only villainous, but also completely insane) on this person.

He was perfectly right. I had. And what made it even worse was the fact that this person was the source of the long-running tension between us. Writing the character had been—shameful though it is to admit—an act of private revenge on my part. But I was horrified that he had made the connection. I thought I had disguised it too cleverly for that. After all it was only how *I* saw this person. My father—who saw them quite another way—could surely find nothing he recognised. Now I was exposed in all my clumsy pettiness.

I rushed to explain and apologise. I wouldn't have done it if I had known how hurtful and obvious it was. It was *fiction*, I begged. He of all people knew how that worked. How, the minute it is written down, a story slips the ropes of its origins and becomes its own recklessly separate thing.

It was no use. My father refused to speak to me. I had one child and then another. I published a second book, Before We Began, although, like the first, it felt unsatisfactory, oddly tentative somehow. I had the sense that I was trying too hard—to be clever, literary, important—while all the time being on the wrong path. I carried on writing to my father, a letter every few years. In writing, there was hope. I still believed that, with the right combination of words, I might discover a different, better story for us.

Just after he turned 80, my father asked me to stop communicating with him. Future letters would be returned, unread. "You were always a difficult child," he wrote. I wept at that. But there was a miserable kind of relief in the finality.

Not long after, my work changed direction. It wasn't clear then, but I see now that the two things were connected. It wasn't just that I gave up writing to my father. I gave up writing *for* him, too. Having realised it was pointless, I lost interest in winning his approval, of using writing as a way to reach him. (What had that villainous character been, in all honesty, but a bid for his attention by being naughty?)

. . . For the first time, I began writing for myself—or rather for that difficult child I had once been. When the borders between worlds were still vague, and disbelief could be abandoned with the turning of a page, and the more improbable anything seemed, the more likely it was to happen.

(ibid., 5)

The symbiotic merger of her childhood, represented by the love of writing she shared with her father, had in the end not been able to offer Unsworth a true experience of being seen by him. Her father's attention had seemed to be drawn more to the colour of the sea, or the shape of a building, than to the day-to-day experiences she was writing about in her journal and in which he could have shared. Their symbiotic relationship dissolved through the passing of time and the sometimes painful process of change brought about by events in their lives, leaving her free to develop as a person and a writer.

The symbiotic merger and psychotherapy

Within the context of psychotherapy, it is necessary to avoid the symbiotic merger, otherwise it will become part of a process which blocks the client's progress, or stops it altogether, instead of psychotherapy being a vehicle for real and lasting change in the life of a person. So it is important for psychotherapists to be able to recognise the difference between symbiosis and empathy, which can deceptively, and usually unhelpfully, appear to be identical. Rogers (1959: 210) defined empathy as perception of 'the internal frame of reference of another with accuracy and with the emotional components and meanings which pertain thereto, as if one were the person, but without ever losing the 'as if' condition'. An easy mistake to make in psychotherapeutic work is the loss of the 'as if' condition. It is of course flattering and sometimes quite seductive when a client says 'you are the only person who has ever heard and understood me'. This may well be true, where a person has not previously experienced attunement in relationship. And experiences of attunement as a shared and occasionally even as a merged reality are essential to the healing processes of psychotherapeutic work. However, the psychotherapist is not the same person as his or her client and these experiences of attunement need to be accompanied always by the psychotherapist's own sense of self as distinct and separate from the selfhood of his or her client. Thus, by progressively beginning to explore the possibilities presented by differing points of view and varieties of experience, the way can be opened up for the beginnings of individuation. The resolution of the symbiotic merger can be achieved through the active presence of—and dialogue with—the distinct and individual personality of the psychotherapist; if he or she is able to resist the emotional merger and continue as a supportive, separate and consistent therapeutic presence.

This process can be fraught with difficulty because, for the client, it may signal the prospect of separation from a merged, long-term relationship in her personal life, as illustrated in the following case study. Resolution of the symbiosis will mean that she is faced with the inevitable grief of loss, before a renewed sense of self can emerge. She may feel that the psychotherapist is trying to take her away from a loved one, or even replace that person. Thus, if the psychotherapist were to be emotionally merged with the client, then the individuation process could once again be blocked by a shared reluctance to disturb the relational *status quo*. The case study of Gemma illustrates the tenacity of a symbiotic merger

between an adult client and her mother, the difficulty of challenging that symbiosis, and the need for sometimes lengthy psychotherapeutic work to support
the individuation process.

Case study of Gemma

Gemma came to see me at a critical stage in her life. She was 51 years old and
apparently devoted to her mother whom she visited or phoned daily. Gemma
worked as a lecturer at a university school of education. The crisis which prompted
her to seek psychotherapeutic help happened at a staff development event. The
participants had been invited to disclose something more personal than they usually might do and in this moment Gemma felt immobilised with distress. She
was able to maintain her composure but afterwards spoke with a sympathetic
colleague about what had happened and later decided to seek professional help.

As the early stages of our work developed, Gemma spoke of feeling under
pressure, tired and frustrated. She worked extremely hard both in her job and
in her support of her mother but seemed to gain little joy or real satisfaction in
either. She could not see a way out of this *impasse* and felt that her life was slip-
ping away, with no future prospect of real fulfilment. Nor did she believe that the
kind of satisfying life she witnessed in other people could ever apply to her. As
our sessions progressed, Gemma told me that when she was about four years old
her father had suddenly left the family home. He never returned. Her mother did
not seem to have been able to explain this very important event to her, and he was
not spoken of again. Consequently, Gemma did not feel able to ask about him.
She was further disrupted by the fact that she and her mother then moved away
from their close, networked urban community, to a village in Norfolk where they
seemed to know no one. This separated Gemma from family members and childhood friends to whom she was attached and who had been warmly affectionate to
her. Since moving to Norfolk, she had never been able to gain any understanding
of why her father left so suddenly and why these separations had taken place.
She and her mother lived in isolation from the local community, and her mother
seemed reluctant to make friends locally.

Gemma came to believe that, somehow, she was the cause of this unhappy
state of affairs. She also became aware that there must be a better life somewhere
and eventually she asked if she could go to a residential high school. Her mother
agreed to this and as a result Gemma made her first steps towards self-assertion
and independence. But, crucially, she had to do so whilst lacking the foundation
of knowing she had a right to exist in the world as an individual person and to
be loved as such. She did not have the emotional basis of a secure attachment,
and she missed the previous bonds with her father, her extended family and her
childhood friends, which had been broken so abruptly. At boarding school she
made good lifelong friends. But she also learnt, perhaps inevitably, to appear quite
tough and independent and not to show that she had needs and vulnerabilities. She
came to believe, as her mother had done, that to show need was to be weak and

foolish and might open one up to exploitation. During her psychotherapy, Gemma wrote a poem expressing the solitary bewilderment she had felt at that time and which she had not been able to articulate.

CALCULUS (math) Particular method of calculation—OED.

Life

Is just like mathematics.
If you miss out in Foundation Stage,
It will never make sense.
In Maths -
Without a secure understanding
Of object/number correspondence,
You won't ever really get it.
Never spend sufficient time,
Experimenting with concrete materials
And you don't really understand the concepts,
You just learn to follow the rules.
You never think to question why
The hypotenuse is found by squaring the sides,
Or that to find the circle's circumference
You need to multiply with pi.

CALCULUS (med) stone, concretion in some part of the body—OED

Love

Like mathematics, relies on
A number of practical experiments.
And if things don't add up.
You're fucked! -
If first loves change or vanish without trace,
You don't ever really get it.
If you never have enough evidence
that you are more than acceptable,
Just as you are—loved with all your faults,
You can't ever really understand
The nature of love.
You will spend your life following the rules,
But often wondering how come -
Whatever the equation,
The solution always equals one.

Despite achieving a successful career, having married and separated, travelled widely and made a strong liaison with a man whom she later left, the alienation and loneliness expressed in Gemma's poem remained. And in psychotherapy, she began to question the symbiotic relationship with her mother, which she could see had blocked her ability to live freely in the knowledge that she had a right to exist as herself and to be loved without conditions and obligations.

Gemma often spoke of the frustration she felt when she would devotedly attend to her mother's needs, including numerous and time-consuming visits to the G.P. and the hospital, and yet would seem to receive only criticism in return. It felt as if, however hard she tried, she could not win and could never get it right. She blamed herself for this and would go to any length to complete domestic chores to her mother's satisfaction, only to be further ignored or criticised and sometimes ridiculed. I remarked upon the sheer amount of effort Gemma put into this, including the 25-mile return journey and the responsibility she took for walking her mother's dog. I marvelled at her efficiency in managing both an extremely demanding schedule at work and the domestic support of her mother, without being late or forgetting things. The cost of this was that Gemma rarely had a satisfying break and only saw her close friends as an occasional and brief luxury. The prospect of going away on holiday provoked anxiety about how her mother would cope. Her mother continued to live, by choice, in isolation from her neighbours and local community and insisted that only Gemma could assist her. From time to time she would address Gemma as 'my little slave'. Gemma felt she had no right of reply to such comments and consequently was left full of rage and distress which she could not express openly. She told me that she hoped her mother would die, and she believed that she would soon follow her. I heard how she felt that her mother stood between her and the achievement of a satisfying intimate relationship of her own. On one occasion her mother commented, 'we two don't attract men do we?'.

As we got to know one another better, I began more often to challenge Gemma's belief that she could never have a life of her own. I asked practical questions about whether it might be possible for her and her mother to consider employing someone other than Gemma to complete at least a few of the domestic chores. At first Gemma said 'no', as she thought her mother would never accept this idea, or even discuss it. She even believed it was necessary for her to be personally present when her mother's coal delivery arrived and she would make a special journey for this purpose. At the same time she would complain bitterly, and justifiably, about the weariness she felt concerning her mother's lack of gratitude for her efforts. I could see that my questions provoked anger. This erupted when Gemma arrived very late for one of our appointments and did not seem to feel that this mattered. I was annoyed, and it showed. Gemma had arranged for someone to walk her mother's dog, and it transpired she could have left her mother in time for her appointment with me. She was very angry to be challenged about this and yet in her anger she was able to say that she hadn't wanted to leave her mother because she felt jealous of the dog walker.

At our next appointment, Gemma was still angry and upset. She said she felt betrayed, that I had exposed her feelings and taken advantage of her vulnerability. She was affronted. She had previously talked about her psychotherapy with a good friend, who was pleased that she was taking this step, but on this occasion she told him she was thinking of finishing. He had himself experienced the benefit of psychotherapy and responded by saying he would be disappointed for her if she stopped. Gemma became very tearful and said that she told him she just wanted me to tell her what to do. I replied that I thought it would be a brave person who might try this and she laughed in recognition and with goodwill. She then told me she felt angry with everyone and with the fact that many of her friends' elderly parents were dying. I said this must be a very lonely feeling and that I wondered if she was, in fact, beginning to form an attachment to me and that this also might feel frightening. I wondered if the strong expressions of feeling I witnessed at these sessions, so new as an experience for Gemma, and the fact that she had allowed herself to suggest her mother might ask someone else to walk the dog, indicated that she was beginning to review her own established pattern of dependency on her mother. Maybe, in beginning to form an attachment to me, she felt the possible threat of being drawn away from her. Later, I mentioned that I was soon going to take a holiday, and we would have a break from our appointments. I offered her a small photograph of myself, so that she would not feel that I had 'disappeared' whilst I was away. I noticed that she took it from me very quickly and stashed it in her bag as though she had stolen it. And during a later session, she told me of a dream in which she was at the back of my house, on one side of a bridge, looking across it. As time went by, we would refer to this dream as a reference point in her progress through psychotherapy, indicating how far she was moving across that metaphorical bridge towards independence from her mother and a life of her own.

Gemma told me that she had a previous experience of psychotherapy some years before, which arrived at a similar challenging place. On that occasion she left the psychotherapy and contemplated making a spurious complaint about misconduct by the psychotherapist. But now she brought insight to that past experience, by beginning to develop an understanding and a reluctant acceptance of how terrifying, and yet how desirable, it was to even imagine making an emotional separation from her mother. A great deal of steadfastness and resolve is needed in supporting a client who is extricating herself from a symbiotic relationship with a parent. After all, one is encountering a strongly bonded pair, however brittle and ultimately fragile that bond may actually be. Gemma, wisely, never disclosed to her mother that she was having psychotherapy, and this allowed her to feel free to express whatever she needed to, without fear. However, we shared our amusement when, after some of our sessions, her mother would seem to know what we had been talking about. Gemma would then ask me in fun if I had phoned her mother and told her everything. This communicated the real fears Gemma experienced: of disloyalty to her mother, of betrayal and the possible loss of her 'only' relationship, of personal abandonment, of criticism, and of guilt about moving away from the merged relationship with her mother, whilst at the same time wishing she was dead.

The deep distress incorporated in this relationship was clearly expressed in a drawing she made to illustrate it. Gemma is a talented artist and able to express complex emotional themes in her drawings. In this one she had drawn what looked like two foetuses, without mouths, both standing facing each other and umbilically attached, whilst trying to tear at each other. No more graphic account could have shown how she really felt. Also, the drawing illustrated that the symbiosis had grown out of a mother's immaturity and vulnerability as a parent. Gemma's parents had been married for a number of years before she was born and, after her birth, it seems their relationship broke down. Gemma carried this understanding with her as a terrible kind of legacy, having been led to believe that it was she who had caused her father to leave. When we explored this further, it emerged that she could remember waiting as a small child at the garden gate, every day, when it was time for him to come home from work. After he left the family, she would still wait there. We talked about how this must have meant that there was an attachment between them. During the psychotherapy, she got in touch with a cousin who remembered her father. Her cousin told her how he had attended her father's funeral, at which Gemma was named as her father's daughter. To hear this was a very healing moment for her.

Progress in psychotherapy rarely follows a straight and uninterrupted line. Sometimes it feels as though progress is being made, sometimes there is a plateau, or an impasse, and sometimes it feels as if the process has gone into reverse. In these ways the psychotherapy process mirrors not only the wide variety of all human development but also the individual history of each client. But the gains in awareness which are made tend to be kept. Often, it is through the repetition of unhelpful yet familiar patterns of behaviour, with a psychotherapist to witness them, that self-awareness has the opportunity to grow. Gemma told me at one point that she had been looking online for a house she thought she might buy on the Norfolk coast, where she could live with her mother. However, she quickly came round to seeing for herself that this was the last thing she really wanted. We talked through what this actually would have meant, living in a fairly remote place, with only her mother for company. This theme repeated itself when her mother needed to go into hospital for a short period. Gemma moved into her mother's house, even though this was not necessary. She began to speak about how nice it would be to live there and, should her mother die, how she might move in. Once again, after a while, Gemma realised that this wish arose from something she had never had since her father left, and still would not have in her mother's house, which was a properly loving and secure home.

These imaginings took place during the most challenging phase of the psychotherapy, when I was increasingly encouraging Gemma to consider and prioritise her own needs. She began to talk more about the things she would like to have, and which she felt were disallowed, like the time and space to engage in painting and printmaking. At around this time, there was an occasion when she was returning from work and decided for no particular reason to pay a visit to her mother. Minutes after making this decision, she made an error of judgement driving into a bend and crashed the car which had recently belonged to her mother. The accident took place in a quiet village, but there were people around who came to help, including some friends of hers who lived opposite the accident site, although she had not previously known that they lived there. She was relatively unhurt and her friends invited her into their house. During their conversation she discovered that they owned a printmakers' press of the kind that she wanted to own. This coincidence came to represent a turning point in Gemma's escape from the merger with her mother. It woke her up to the fact that visiting her that day had been aimless and had nothing to offer her, that there were things she longed to do, and in fact could do, in preference to being her mother's 'little slave'. She began to explore the idea of finally giving up her lecturer post, which no longer gave the satisfaction she had once gained from it, as a 'respectable' career of which her mother approved. And together we began to develop a series of ideas about how her mother might be persuaded to accept help from sources other than Gemma. This was a long and rather tortuous path, but it culminated in her mother's eventual acceptance of a carer visiting her most days to take up the role of the 'little slave'. But in this case the carer was being paid and was a good-humoured and wise presence who could deal with the demands made upon her, whilst also being a support to Gemma.

But it was difficult for Gemma to let go, and more than this, to see her mother transferring her loyalties to the new carer. It was very painful and shocking for Gemma to gradually become aware that her only value to her mother seemed to have been in her role as 'little slave'. She continued valiantly to show her artwork to her mother and to try and share the pride she felt when her pieces were sold. And yet, finally, she came to accept that her mother appeared to take no real joy from her daughter's talent. In fact, it seemed to make little difference to her whether Gemma visited her or not. This was a very difficult stage of the psychotherapy where Gemma was faced with the fact that she had never really been seen or felt loved by her mother, as an individual person, and probably never would be. Her mother did not seem to need her now that she had a carer with whom she did not have to have a close relationship. But Gemma began to find it easier when she gave up trying so hard to please and started to take increasing time for herself and her artistic work. She resigned her post at the university and organised a process of renovating her home, creating a studio to accommodate her own printmaking press. And, gradually, she came to accept her mother's limitations as a vulnerable woman who had not been able to accept the bounty that life could have given her, due to the harsh conditions of her own childhood.

As the psychotherapy progressed and Gemma began to rearrange her life to meet her own needs, her friends began to comment on a noticeable change in her appearance and her enthusiasm for life. She found that she was able to be more open with them about her feelings and about how much her friends meant to her. Consequently, her friendships deepened. Gemma had more time and energy to give, and she was able to take holidays without believing that she must be 'on call' for her mother. Interestingly, as she progressed in this way, her mother became calmer and more accepting of the new arrangements. Her visits to the hospital and the doctor lessened. She would still make hurtful comments from time to time, but Gemma was less affected by them. It was as though the disturbing fusion between them, illustrated in Gemma's drawing, had been loosened at last. Gemma continued not only to make art but to sell her work at exhibitions. And she showed me a piece of writing by the poet Mary Oliver (2016), describing the space she had always needed in order to allow this creativity to emerge. It spoke of the privacy, solitude and absence of interruption needed for the deep concentration Gemma could not create whilst continuing to be distracted by the merger with her mother.

Gemma's progress arrived at a point where she began a new intimate relationship. She had not expected this. We were in the process of completing the psychotherapy, and she still seemed to believe that the possibility of a relationship of her own was beyond reasonable expectation. When I challenged this belief, she would say 'I just can't see it myself', and she seemed to feel that her creative work and her friendships were sufficient. And yet she would also speak from time to time about how she saw her friends in their couple relationships and how she longed to have the same easy intimacy they seemed to enjoy. Her new relationship began quickly, and it lasted. She negotiated some early misunderstandings with her partner in the confident belief that she was worth loving. And she found that she could make demands on him and have demands made upon her, which deepened their bond. He was supportive and understanding about her relationship with her mother and was able gently to question and challenge some of her remaining anxious concerns. They began making plans for a life lived together, in which each of them could include their long-established individual interests and activities. By letting go of the symbiotic merger with her mother, Gemma was able to find closeness, trust and satisfaction, and a life which she had thought was closed to her. And thus we moved towards the ending of the psychotherapy.

An unexpected postscript arrived at our final session, when Gemma told me that her mother, at 90 years of age, had died the week before. Gemma had spent Christmas Day with her and, before she died, her mother was able to tell her how she regretted the way she had treated her, that she was very proud of her and grateful for all the support Gemma had given to her. She said that now Gemma had a partner and was happy with him, she felt she could leave. They were able to say their farewells in peace. Gemma told me that the ending of their symbiotic attachment had freed them both.

This case study illustrates how necessary it is for the symbiotic merger with a parent to be dissolved if a person is to be able to form satisfying and emotionally intimate relationships in adulthood. Even if the dissolution does not come about through psychotherapy, symbiotically merged relationships are inevitably so brittle that they tend to break down anyway, or at least become the source of ongoing tension, conflict and unhappiness. A vital life cannot thrive if it is permanently merged with the unmet needs of another person. Two people cannot share one personality without the sacrifice of the individual. Gemma's mother's description of her as 'my little slave' was psychologically accurate. When Gemma resigned from this role, which had been assigned to her when she was too young to choose any other, her own life came alive and she began to develop in ways which brought her true satisfaction. Loving kindness, as an activity of steadfast attention in psychotherapy, was not always perceived by Gemma as kind, because I needed to exercise strong, determined, support of my client's emerging process of individuation, in conflict with her desire to maintain the *status quo* with her mother. But by witnessing and remaining faithful to what I had witnessed of Gemma's longing to have a vital experience of life, we formed an alliance, which helped her cross the bridge to life itself and to say farewell to her mother, in peace.

How an understanding of early attachment assists the resolution of symbiosis

Holmes and Slade emphasise the key therapeutic skill of securing the therapist–patient relationship by forming an attachment:

> Attachment provides the scientific basis for the exploratory curiosity, emotional empathy and responsiveness, validation, appropriate verbal interplay and developmental narrative constructions that are the hallmarks of good clinical practice. The responsibility for the formation and maintenance of the therapeutic relationship rests squarely on the shoulders of the therapist, whose patients' insecurity will inevitably mean that they struggle to form a solid alliance and working relationship. Therapists who are able to provide a secure and safe base for their patients, to remain emotionally present and compassionate, while managing complex and potentially intense affects, are likely to be those best able to facilitate their patients' development.
>
> (Holmes & Slade, 2018: 36)

It can be seen in the case study of Gemma that the journey travelled by the patient and the therapist, whilst constructing a secure base, is potentially hazardous and at times even vulnerable to breakdown. Therefore, if loving kindness is representative of a focus upon the client as our object of attention, it follows that the psychotherapist needs to have resources of steady determination in order to sustain it, sometimes during long periods of engagement in the work. Quite often, this will include a seemingly mundane process of just keeping going, whilst continuing to put one therapeutic foot in front of the other. And where a process of change is engaged with symbiotic difficulties, it is almost inevitable that intense feelings will arise, which at times may test the therapeutic alliance potentially to destruction. We have seen how Gemma, in her prior experience of psychotherapy, felt unable at that time to prevent herself from turning her back on the therapeutic relationship which was beginning to develop. Early efforts of this kind are not necessarily wasted. She had made a start, and the fact that she later gave psychotherapy another chance probably signalled that she knew, somewhere in her consciousness, that it was of benefit to her. So in her second attempt at psychotherapy, Gemma was able to weather the storm between us when faced with the real, if terrifying, prospect that our work together was urging her towards something which deep down she really wanted; a separation from the symbiotic merger with her mother.

When reflecting on the anger which emerged between us, when Gemma was late for her appointment and gave no convincing explanation, it seemed to me that a transference had developed wherein I was possibly being cast in the role of *her* 'little slave', who could be kept waiting whilst her emotional priority in that moment was her envy towards her mother's new dog walker. If this trend had continued, we would both have been at risk of enslavement to her mother's symbiotic need. And if Gemma's own needs were to gain priority through the progress she was making in psychotherapy, then less attention would be able to be devoted to her mother. She arrived at an impasse where it became obvious she could not have both. Thus, the features of emotional empathy and responsiveness in the therapeutic attachment have to include confrontation of such elemental experiences and the visceral emotions they bring with them. This means that the psychotherapist has to be drawn right in, but without losing herself and being swept away. If she were to be already symbiotically merged with her client, she would be carried along and unable to resist the stronger currents of the merger. When Gemma reacted to my confrontation, I of course had to ask myself whether I was overreacting and just being petty. But as is so often the case, this challenge, which was motivated by care for Gemma's progress away from a stultifying and frustrated life, sparked an insight which allowed her to begin to feel a growing attachment to me, including the fears and desires which were inviting her to experience a taste of the life she really wanted to have. She began to feel that she mattered.

The therapeutic structure which allowed this confrontation to be experienced and understood by both of us was based upon the dynamic aspect of mirroring as a feature of our growing relationship of attachment. Holmes and Slade state that in the parent-infant dynamic, 'the mother *contingently* waits for the child to initiate an expressive communication' (ibid., 44). This kind of dynamic applies equally to the therapeutic relationship. Gemma and I had already experienced a substantial period of therapeutic interaction, with sessions taking place once, then twice, each week. There had been opportunity for a wide range of communication, both verbal and non-verbal, with silences and mutual reflections included, as well as pleasurable sharing in discussions about art, books and Gemma's own creative work. These opportunities had given plenty of scope for Gemma to initiate expressive communication and to receive my mirrored experience of her. I noticed how her view of herself, initially based upon the negative mirroring she had received from her mother, began to soften as our work progressed, although she often found this positive development difficult to accept and believe. But as Westland (2015: 260) has pointed out, by working from an embodied stance and staying with the process we can keep track of presence and make continual adjustments to the experience of the client. Holmes and Slade confirm this when observing that mir-roring between psychotherapist and client is sometimes 'confined to the eyes and the vocal tone, but can also be seen in the verbal and gestural give-and-take of therapeutic exchange' (2018: 45). They quote Winnicott, who noticed that: 'Psy-chotherapy is not making clever and apt interpretation; by and large it is a long-term giving back to the patient what the patient brings. It is a complex derivative of the face that reflects what is there to be seen' (1971: 158).

Thus, I had many opportunities to give back to Gemma my interest in what she had to say, in how she felt during any particular session, and my pleasure in being invited to see her drawings and to hear her poems being read. I was able, in Holmes and Slade's phrase, to wait contingently for Gemma to initiate an inter-est, which then gave me the chance to mirror my experience of her, back to her. Gradually, and together, we found that Gemma's adult adherence to the role of 'little slave' had arisen long ago in her early years when she had come to believe, through negative mirroring, that the only role she could be allowed in life was that of being in permanent service to her mother's emotional demands. This gave rise to the false yet potent belief that if she at any stage resigned from this role, she would not be able to survive. Hence, the view she expressed early in the psycho-therapy process, that when her mother died, she also would die.

I think that we can assume that Gemma's mother, who was raised within an austere, rather masculine, respectable and hard-working community, had from childhood onwards experienced extensive, unmet emotional needs, and responses of negative mirroring, due to the lack of material and emotional resources avail-able. Her way of parenting Gemma was what we can describe as a re-enactment of those unmet needs through her woundedness and vulnerability, masked by an external toughness and determination to survive against all the odds. Gemma, prior to psychotherapy, was susceptible to a similar re-enactment. In other words, she had developed the habit of repeating her mother's belief that relationships are fundamentally power-based and exploitative, that her mother was 'top dog' in their relationship, and by definition Gemma was the 'underdog', unable to control her impulse to visit her mother, even though there was no prospect of a satisfying reward for the visit. Attachment behaviour increases in the face of external threat, and Gemma's childhood anxieties had caused her to continue clinging on to her mother, despite the harm being caused by their symbiotic merger.

A key turning point for Gemma in her withdrawal from the pattern of re-enactment arrived when she crashed her mother's car. It was as if her uncon-scious mind, in seeking a path to health, took over and steered her somewhat risk-ily in the right direction. Re-enactments are crisis points in psychotherapy, often repeating only their negative features, until the adoption of greater self-awareness allows real change to take place. But this re-enactment included a number of positive, life-changing aspects. As if from nowhere, it transpired that the accident occurred outside the house of her friends, who were at home and came to help her. She had not known they lived there and, up to that point, had somewhat lost touch with them. When they invited her in, she discovered that they owned a printmaking press of the kind she herself had wanted to own for some time. Later, this prompted her to think about not only buying her own press but also allowing herself to follow her desire to work as a creative artist and leave a career which had been chosen to please her mother, and in which she was now losing interest.

Gemma and I had previously talked about a dream she had, in which a rather shady kind of trickster figure from the street came into her home and invited her to discover many hidden rooms of which she had not been aware, and we remembered the words of the New Testament: 'In my Father's house are many mansions' (John 14: 2). We wondered if Gemma's recent rediscovery of her own father, the memory she experienced of her attachment to him, and the new knowledge that she was remembered at his funeral, had been part of a positive re-enactment of some sense of security, of belonging and vitality which she had once known in her childhood. The accident wrecked her mother's car, which meant that Gemma bought a car of her own without any close associations to her mother. She came out of the accident without injury. And the accident awakened her to the aimlessness of her journey that day when she had no real interest, nor satisfying purpose, in randomly deciding to visit her mother. It was the beginning of a break with the symbiotic merger and an opening up of her 'many mansions'.

Jung proposed that events such as this occur when attention and concentration are eased, allowing inhibitions to be loosened. This permits the unconscious contents to emerge unimpeded. His earlier mentor, Pierre Janet, had introduced this concept of *l'abaissement du niveaux mental*, which Jung saw as the prior condition for what he described as *synchronicity*, or the *acausal connecting principle*. Jung asserted that synchronicity was quite distinct from simultaneity and he defined it as 'a coincidence in time of two or more causally unrelated events which have the same or a similar meaning' (in Jacobi, 1973: 49). For Gemma, the apparently unrelated events were: her rather random decision to visit her mother, and the accident which followed outside the house of her friend who owned the much-desired printmaking press. Jung identified synchronicity as the simultaneous occurrence of a certain psychic state with one or more external events, which appear as meaningful parallels to the momentary subjective state (Jung, CW8). The unconscious contents released by the synchronicity, and later recognised by Gemma in our discussions, were her desire to have a printmaking press and thereby follow a creative path towards a life of her own, and acknowledgement that visiting her mother had nothing rewarding in it. But the accident could only take Gemma's process so far. What was required, in order for Gemma to have this experience relatively safely and with understanding, was our therapeutic attachment, which provided the basis for 'exploratory curiosity, emotional empathy and responsiveness, validation, appropriate verbal interplay and developmental narrative constructions' (Holmes & Slade, 2018: 36). This provided the safe holding needed for Gemma to come through the accident uninjured and more attuned to her own process, through conscious recognition of the meaning of these apparently random events.

Sentimentality

One of the characteristics of the symbiotic merger between Gemma and her mother was that of an active and undermining kind of sentimentality. This was particularly evident in the way in which her mother appeared to ask for attention and pity by becoming ill. Fear concerning her mother's health was a key factor in Gemma remaining 'enslaved', and feeling sorry for her mother meant that she could not go away on holiday. Her mother had physical health difficulties, and these would regularly come to crisis point whenever Gemma began to take up enjoyable activities of her own. It became noticeable that once Gemma began to assert more of her own needs, and allowed another carer to attend to her mother, the medical emergencies and visits to the hospital diminished, only then occurring infrequently. In parallel, at one particularly challenging point in the psychotherapy when Gemma said she was thinking of finishing, she told me that she was tempted to do so by her fears that psychotherapy was jeopardising her own mental health. When I gently asked some basic questions about what led her to believe she was at risk in this way, we were able to establish that her mental health seemed to be quite robust, but her fear of being separated from the merged relationship with her mother was causing her acute distress and anxiety. She described a visceral sensation of having an iron cage around her heart which made her feel that it would burst. This provided a graphic image of her desperate feelings of emotional confinement, her longing to escape the prison of the merged relationship and her terror at the prospect of doing so. The sentimentality of self-pity concealed what was in fact an intensity of rage in both mother and daughter, so dramatically represented in Gemma's drawing of the two foetuses attacking each other.

Aggression masked by sentimentality

The writer James Baldwin recognised and wrote about the intensity of repressed feelings belied by sentimentality. He had witnessed this as a person of colour experiencing racism, which prompted him finally to leave the USA. He described how an ostentatious parading of excessive, spurious emotion was actually a sign of dishonesty, a hidden but violent inhumanity and a mark of cruelty (Baldwin, 1955). This understanding corresponds with the view of Jung (CW15), who asserted that: 'Sentimentality is the superstructure erected upon brutality. Unfeelingness is the counter-position and inevitably suffers from the same defects'. In the experience of Gemma, her mother had developed a hostility to warm feelings which, she had come to believe, were a sign of weakness and something to be suppressed. Due to the emotional austerity of her childhood, she had acquired a fear of life and a cold-heartedness which allowed her to be cruel to Gemma, whilst feeling sorry for herself and demanding pity from others. Consequently, Gemma tried to suppress her own heartfelt emotions within an iron cage, but as the psychotherapy progressed and she began to accept kind attention from another, she felt as though her heart was bursting out of its prison which, of course, it was. As

Winnicott (1965: 148) observed: 'The True Self comes from the aliveness of the body tissues and the working of body-functions, including the heart's action and breathing'.

There followed a progression of therapeutic work during which I offered continuing, steadfast attention and support to Gemma, as her wounded feelings were gradually released from their caged prison. Therapeutically, we had the prior advantage of having formed a good working alliance, within which I was able to mirror my experience of Gemma and give her authentic and congruent feedback, even when this seemed to clash with her negative impression of herself and her belief that nothing could get better. It could be said that we were, for some time, engaged in a 'transfer of power', from Gemma's allegiance to the sentimentalised, symbiotic merger with her mother, to an authentic and life-giving relationship with herself. My role was that of providing support to this bridge-building work.

Sentimentality illustrated in literature

A vivid illustration of the connection between sentimentality and the misuse of personal power is given in Charles Dickens's novel *Little Dorrit*. Jung (CW15) stated that: 'Where love reigns, there is no will to power; and where the will to power is paramount, love is lacking'. This view is demonstrated by the example of William Dorrit and his misuse of parental power through the manipulation of sentimental feelings.

It is interesting to see how the personality of William Dorrit, in many ways, reflects the character of Charles Dickens's own father, John Dickens. Throughout his life, Dickens was haunted by the emotionally traumatic events which occurred during his childhood and for which he held his parents responsible. As a result of these events, and their impact upon him, he developed the habit of making 'experience into fiction, to the point where he was no longer able to distinguish what he had undergone and what he had invented' (Wilson, 2020: 70). Whilst his father came to be seen by him as an irresponsible figure, Dickens also retained his early childhood experience of him as a 'zealous, useful and cheerful spirit' and did not blame him for the later trauma. It was his mother who 'bore all the weight of that cruel story' (ibid., 26). Nonetheless, his shrewd portrayal of William Dorrit's deceptive fantasy life probably betrays much of what Dickens really felt about his father.

Tomalin (2011: 4–22) observes that John Dickens was a somewhat mysterious figure in the family history. His parents' origins were humble, and they were employed in domestic service. He did not follow their path and was described by his mother as lazy. Later, he was favoured when he gained employment in the Navy Pay Office, proceeding to promotion in a post which commanded a salary far in excess of anything his father had earned. It seems that he viewed himself as a man of taste and acquired a collection of books, at that time expensive items in a household budget. Tomalin describes him as expansive by nature, identifying himself as a 'gentleman' in documents. He was likeable and fun-loving. He had habits of extravagance and debt but he was a character—and lucky—later becoming the model for one of Dickens's most famous characters, Mr Micawber.

John and Elizabeth Dickens seem to have been a cheerful couple and apparently she spent the night before the birth of her son out dancing. But gradually their good fortune appears to have diminished and, when Charles was five months old, they were obliged to move to a smaller house. However, they continued to thrive when John was transferred to the naval dockyard at Chatham, at that time a prosperous and lively town. The years at Chatham, until Dickens was 12, were probably his happiest and most secure and he remembered them as idyllic. Chatham was a pleasant riverside town where he acquired what was to become a lifelong attachment to Kent and its landscape. At that time his family life felt secure, he enjoyed school and was taught well. But soon the idyll began to come to an end, when John Dickens's employment with the Navy Pay Office required the family to move back to London, into a small terraced house in Camden Town. Here, Dickens found none of the sense of community he had known in Chatham and he had no other children to play with. Shortages of money prompted his mother to take a lease on a large house in Gower Street, in order to start a school, and the family moved once again. The young Dickens was sent out with advertising circulars which raised his hopes about being sent to school himself. These did not materialise because his mother's enterprise did not succeed and the family was pursued by creditors, when his father would hide upstairs until finally arrested for debt.

It is not difficult to see how easily Dickens was able to invent the character of William Dorrit, an imprisoned debtor, from these experiences which culminated in the final humiliation of his being sent to work in a factory, in complete contrast to his rich memories of the years in Chatham. When only 12 years old, his most traumatic realisation was that his parents did not seem to make strenuous efforts to support him or attempt to repair his situation. Effectively, he was abandoned to fend for himself. Tomalin refers to the account Dickens wrote, 25 years later, of this most formative time, in which he dwelt with horror upon his parents' proposal that he should work in a factory and their apparent indifference to what it meant for him. Dickens as a writer became capable of the kind of searing wit and cynicism which is generated by profound disappointment and disillusionment. The events following his unwanted move to London, and the collapse of family security they represented, opened up a split between harsh reality and his capacity to retreat into fantasy. These experiences later enabled him to write the most engaging and persuasive fiction. But as Wilson observes:

> Inside, there was the burning anger and resentment: 'I never shall forget, I never can forget.' There was also, however, the never-so-aptly named False Self. Whereas the mother, frivolous, young, still little more than a teenager herself, and exhausted by the birth of Charles so soon after his elder sister, was simply not equipped to offer him love, the father urged him to perform, act and write. Dickens would be placed on the table, as on a stage, to entertain the

guffawing aunts and cousins. He wrote a tragedy called *Misnar, the Sultan of India*, which his father urged him to put on for the entertainment of the larger family, and he wrote and performed sketches—in one he pretended to be a deaf old man, and in another he cruelly imitated the old woman who cooked their meals in Bayham Street, Camden Town. They could not give him the inward reassurance of knowing that he was loved, but they offered a knowledge that was much more seductive: the knowledge that he was entertaining.

(Wilson, 2020: 96)

Later as an adult and, perhaps inevitably, Dickens led a double life divided between the image of the much-loved writer, father, family man, founder and active supporter of charitable organisations, the secret assignations with his mistress Nellie Ternan and finally, the cruel rejection and abandonment of his wife. He was therefore in a strong position to know about, and represent in *Little Dorrit*, the image which William Dorrit built upon a fantasy version of himself.

William Dorrit is the personification of the false self. In the novel, he is captive for many years in the Marshalsea Prison, a 'close and confined prison for debtors':

Crushed at first by his imprisonment, he soon found a dull relief in it. He was under lock and key; but the lock and key that kept him in, kept numbers of his troubles out. If he had been a man with strength of purpose to face those troubles and fight them, he might have broken the net that held him, or broken his heart; but being what he was, he languidly slipped into this smooth descent, and never more took one step upward.

(Dickens, 1857, in 1985: 103)

But, as the 'the shabby old debtor with the soft manner and the white hair', he becomes the 'Father of the Marshalsea', thus claiming the dominant position in this community of inmates. In fact, the role he develops is that of a confidence trickster and extortionist, who uses his position to manipulate and exploit the other inmates, including Amy his daughter—Little Dorrit—who goes to work outside the prison to provide him with money.

All new-comers were presented to him. He was punctilious in the exaction of this ceremony. . . . He received them in his poor room (he disliked an introduction in the mere yard, as informal—a thing that might happen to anybody), with a kind of bowed-down beneficence . . .

It became a not unusual circumstance for letters to be put under his door at night, enclosing half-a-crown, two half-crowns, now and then at long intervals even half-a-sovereign, for The Father of the Marshalsea. . . . He received the gifts as tributes, from admirers, to a public character.

(ibid., 105–106)

The hold which William Dorrit has over those he exploits is that of emotional blackmail which relies, in the case of Amy, upon her love for him because he is her father and she feels sorry for him, and for the other inmates, upon his manipulation of them through his display of exaggerated, sentimentalised feelings. On one occasion he encounters a new inmate who has settled his debt and is leaving the Marshalsea:

> The man was a mere Plasterer in his working dress; had his wife with him, and a bundle; and was in high spirits.
>
> 'God bless you, sir,' he said in passing.
>
> 'And you,' benignantly returned the Father of the Marshalsea.
>
> They were pretty far divided, going their several ways, when the Plasterer called out, 'I say!—sir!' and came back to him.
>
> 'It ain't much,' said the Plasterer, putting a little pile of half-pence in his hand, 'but it's well meant.'
>
> The Father of the Marshalsea had never been offered tribute in copper yet. His children often had, and with his perfect acquiescence it had gone into the common purse to buy meat that he had eaten and drink that he had drunk; but fustian splashed with white lime, bestowing halfpence upon him, front to front, was new.
>
> 'How dare you!' he said to the man, and feebly burst into tears.
>
> (ibid., 106–107)

The effect of this emotional outburst is that the Plasterer offers, once he is let out, to visit William Dorrit at the Marshalsea.

Enslavement is the theme of *Little Dorrit* and, more than anything, the enslavement of living as a false self through dissociation from true feeling. William Dorrit eventually leaves the prison and travels abroad in grand style. But instead of feeling free, his health declines and he becomes confused, acting as though he is still the 'Father of the Marshalsea'. When dying, he reverts emotionally to the prison where he spent years of his life in retreat from himself and where the sentimental manipulation of the feelings of others kept them tied to him. As an example of the power of sentimentality, Dickens's portrayal repeats the theme of Gemma's case study. She too was enslaved by the sentimental self-pity of her mother, until she allowed herself to challenge its damaging impact upon her. By beginning to resist the temptation of giving in to her mother's unreasonable demands, she found that she could claim a vital life for herself. Her mother came to no harm as a consequence and, within her own limitations, became calmer and more contented. And the resolution of their symbiotic relationship allowed them to say, in a spirit of goodwill, a final farewell to the life they had shared.

In the psychotherapy relationship, it is not enough to feel sorry for someone but rather to feel sorrow *with* them. When this sorrow is heartfelt, it signals authentic empathy and connection in the therapeutic alliance. By contrast it is noticeable, where sentimentality is dominant in the client's experience, that the psychotherapist may not feel anything at all, which is in fact a true reflection of what is happening for the client, who at that point has no vital connection with their own feelings. But as Akhtar (2007: 12) observes, in these circumstances 'the analyst does not actually stop listening. What he does is to stop listening to the surface material'. Beneath the surface of sentimentality lies a depth of unexpressed feeling which can emerge if the therapeutic alliance has a foundation of loving kindness, as an act of faith in the client's capacity to seek a more authentic experience.

Embodied feelings in the therapeutic resolution of symbiosis and sentimentality

It is necessary, in concluding this chapter, to ask questions about how challenging and provocative interventions can be justified in psychotherapy, where loving kindness is the focus of the work, what we mean by authentic empathy and connection in the therapeutic alliance, and how these can guide the practitioner in taking the most appropriate and helpful steps with each individual client. In addressing these questions, I propose that loving kindness is an embodied, human function which becomes available as a skilful intervention, when there is a level of self-awareness in the practitioner which combines both feelings and reasoned thinking. In this respect, Damasio (2000: 312–315) views consciousness as feeling: 'consciousness *feels* like a feeling, and if it feels like a feeling, it may well be a feeling'. And he goes on to say that: 'We only create a sense of good and evil as well as norms of conscionable behaviour once we know about our own nature and that of others like us'. He states that awareness of what we are feeling assists the process of not just self-awareness but active participation in and awareness of the experience of others. I suggest that this includes those psychotherapy encounters where the therapist picks up on something important that may not, as yet, be in the awareness of the client. Often, at these times, it is feelings which are the most reliable guide, even when the wider and deeper meanings of an encounter are not yet fully understood. The example of my angry exchange with Gemma illustrates this. Our shared cultural norms could have led both of us to avoid this kind of emotional exchange but, in fact, doing the 'wrong' thing culturally, turned out to be the 'right' thing, therapeutically.

But on what valid basis can we trust such instincts in psychotherapeutic practice? A useful guide to answering this question has been provided by the findings of affective neuroscience, enabled by the advent in the 1990s of brain scanning, using functional magnetic resonance imaging (fMRI). This technique detects changes in blood oxygenation and flow in response to neural activity, making it possible to devise a visual map of the brain as emotions are experienced. Affective neuroscientists Damasio (1994, 2000), Panksepp (1998, 2010) and Panksepp and Biven (2012) have developed new access to information about how emotions and thinking work together in human behaviour and relationship. Consequently, Damasio (1994: 128) is able to assert that: 'Nature appears to have built the apparatus of rationality not just on top of the apparatus of biological regulation, but also *from* it and *with* it'. Thus, as Gerhardt explains:

> The higher parts of the cortex cannot operate independently of the more primitive gut responses. Cognitive processes elaborate emotional processes, but could not exist without them. The brain constructs representations of internal body states, links them to other stored representations, and then signals back to the body in a process of internal feedback, which may then trigger off further bodily feelings in a cyclical process.
>
> (Gerhardt, 2015: 6)

For psychotherapists in practice, it is not only fascinating but reassuring to know that concepts previously developed within psychotherapy theory have this contemporary validation in neuroscientific research. So when we consider the impact of loving kindness in working with psychotherapy clients, it can be clearly established that emotional warmth in relationship has a central part to play in client recovery. Jung (CW9) was aware of this when he stated that: 'emotion is the chief source of consciousness. There is no change from darkness to light or from inertia to movement without emotion'. Thus we can say that loving kindness is an embodied quality, guiding not only empathy but effectiveness in its steadfast focus upon the client as our focus of attention. By expressing loving kindness, the psychotherapist can be true to instincts of warm feeling and compassion, whilst holding boundaries and promoting real change, from negative expectations to more vital living.

Chapter 4

Loving kindness and moral injury

In the autobiography of Lynne Barber the journalist, entitled *An Education*, there is a graphic description of the way in which as a teenager she took responsibility, without knowing otherwise, for considerable neglect of her emotional and psychological needs. This happened when she most required support in growing up. She describes how, when she was still at school and studying for her A-levels, she had a two-year relationship with a significantly older man, Simon, who she later discovered had deceived her and her parents. It transpired that he was married and lived nearby, without any of them knowing. When the facts of the deceit emerged, her parents continued to support the relationship, in disorientating contrast to their having previously placed her under relentless pressure to study hard for entry to Oxford University. As an adult looking back at this experience, she realised that the only values and aspirations expected of her as a child were to do with cleverness and the achievements it might bring as a reward. It was only when she arrived at Oxford that she realised cleverness wasn't everything. She began to see other values were possible, such as kindness, tact and sensitivity to the feelings of others (Barber, 2011: 63). Lynne Barber's account of her story is humane, tolerant and forgiving of her parents. At the same time, it describes the emerging bewilderment she experienced as she discovered the facts which lay behind her naïve encounter with an unscrupulous adult. She comments that her life might have turned out differently if she had been able to say no to that seduction (ibid., 33). But she was not of an age or experience to be able to say no to something she could not have been expected to know about.

This takes us into the arena of *moral injury*. The term refers to damage caused to an individual's conscience and values by a moral transgression, causing profound guilt and shame and a sense of betrayal, anger and moral disorientation. The concept of moral injury was initially developed and studied in the context of combat. An increasing understanding of the impact of military trauma brought with it a recognition that such situations also put civilians at risk of moral injury. It was found that occupations other than military, such as health care and emergency services, present experiences which render individuals vulnerable to a similar hazard. And, although much less studied, there are

DOI: 10.4324/9781003262114-5

other kinds of events which are potentially morally injurious, such as betrayal by trusted others. The core conditions for development of this kind of moral injury are a betrayal of trust concerning valued belief systems and self-blame for such events.

Barnes et al. (2019: 99–103) discovered that moral injury is an event which can have profound effects upon all the critical domains of emotional, psychological, behavioural, social and spiritual functioning. Until quite recently it might not have been thought possible that Lynn Barber's experiences qualified as morally injurious in the same way that can be applied to extreme trauma in situations of war. However, these contemporary studies have exposed the undermining effect of betrayal by a trusted figure, and this has special potency for children and teenagers who are reliant on their carers to be trustworthy. Barber survived the betrayal and went on to achieve considerable success in her career and her marriage. And yet she writes of her experiences as a teenager having been damaging to her sense of self. Trauma of this kind is not always recognisable, as such, to the subject at the time when it is happening. It is being lived through, often with considerable feelings of unease, but without a fully coherent acknowledgement that something is wrong. The impact of such trauma can remain buried for long periods of time, and it was not until many years later that Barber became fully alert to the disturbing effects of what had occurred.

As is so often the case, the events of Barber's teenage years came back to her by chance, in an unrelated conversation with a friend who was a fellow journalist. He happened to mention Peter Rachman, known famously in the 1950s as an exploitative landlord in London. Barber mentioned that she had known him, and this prompted a strong reaction from her friend. He was astonished that she knew him when she was still at school. Barber went on to explain that she became involved with a much older boyfriend, Simon, who was engaged in property-dealing. Through him she met Peter Rachman at the nightclubs he owned. Whilst telling her friend about this she became aware of how extraordinary this account must seem in the cold light of day. Her friend asked her the kind of searching questions any journalist would ask, and she found that it was difficult to explain exactly how, as a well-brought-up Twickenham schoolgirl, she had become involved with this shadowy world. So she changed the subject.

But this conversation later prompted a train of serious thought about Simon, following an interval of 40 years during which any recollections of him had been pushed away from her immediate memory. Barber had not liked to think about him, and having gone on to a successful life there seemed no point in revisiting the experience. But thoughts continued of how odd it was that she knew Peter Rachman when she was only 16, and questions arose about how her parents had let the relationship with Simon continue, even when they knew that it was transgressive. So to try and explain it all to herself, she wrote it down and hence discovered an unstoppable flow of memory. In doing so, she felt a sense of betrayal when she became more consciously aware of the way in which she had been let down by her parents when she most needed their support and guidance. She became able to see much more clearly the wide discrepancy between the excessive enthusiasm they had imposed upon her concerning an Oxford University education and the complete reversal of this belief of theirs, when they advised her to marry Simon. When they discovered that he was married they did not intervene, leaving her to make any decisions for herself. Barber writes about how this left her feeling that she could never rely on their advice again and how it undermined any belief she had in their moral authority.

Here, not only had Barber lost faith in her parents' authority but was also placed in the impossible double bind of needing them to be her parents, whilst having to hold the moral ground as though *she* were the parent. And she learned not to trust people. The title of her autobiography is ironic, pointing to an education with Simon that she would rather not have had, which was about expensive restaurants, luxury hotels and foreign travel, but also about learning to be suspicious of people's motives and to be watchful of their actions which might be at variance with their words. This made her cautious and avoidant of trust. She writes that she was damaged by her education (ibid., 56). When she married David, she felt that compared with him—a good, kind, truthful and decent person—she was morally damaged.

Moral injury and the false self

We can see here an example of a person taking blame onto herself, for what she saw as her own moral failing, without being able to know that, as a teenager, she could not have been responsible for the neglect of her need for protection from her parents. They possibly believed that, by emphasising academic achievement, they *were* meeting her needs by encouraging her to gain that kind of success. But what seems to have been missing for her was the sense that they knew her, were interested in her, and in the things that made her feel genuinely happy and secure. What came about, as a consequence of this subtle but potent form of neglect, was the development of a false sense of who she was. And, confirmed by Winnicott (1965: 144), an overemphasis upon the intellect can cause it to associate with a *false self*. He developed this concept as a contrast to what he saw as the *authentic self*, based upon true experience rather than defensive assumptions and behaviour: 'When a False Self becomes organized in an individual who has a high intellectual potential there is a very strong tendency for the mind to become the location of the False Self, and in this case there develops a dissociation between the intellectual activity and psychosomatic existence'. Winnicott proposed that when this dissociation occurred, the false self would protectively organise itself to hide the true self, so that the true self could survive. The individual would thus try to solve the personal problem by the use of a fine intellect, in a clinical picture 'peculiar in that it very easily deceives. The world may observe academic success of a high degree, and may find it hard to believe in the very real distress of the individual concerned, who feels "phoney" the more he or she is successful'. From within the experience of a false self,

Barber was not at a point of sufficient emotional and psychological maturity to give her considered consent to what was happening. She was drawn to Simon on the basis of emotional neglect of her needs, because of his apparently genuine interest in her.

Piaget (1954) observed that children learn to judge experience by developing through various stages of thinking and, most importantly, he concluded that adaptation to the human environment and the consequent development of behaviour occur as processes of assimilation and accommodation. These processes require sufficient modelling and support from adult carers in order to be completed and, if all goes well, psychological maturity can be said to have been achieved in what he described as the stage of *formal operations*, or the capacity to think more rationally and systematically about abstract concepts and hypothetical events, rather than just being restricted to concrete assumptions on the basis of familiar facts. On this view, the identity of the child begins to form alongside, and in partnership with, a growing understanding of the behaviour and responses of others. Thus, the child gradually acquires a coherent sense of self, as a reliable reference point in reciprocal relationship.

If the course of this sequence of developments towards a coherent sense of self is interrupted or damaged and, as occurred in Lynn Barber's teenage experience, has not yet been fully arrived at, it follows that she would be unable to imagine an alternative hypothesis about Simon; that a stranger might be something other than merely charming and friendly and could have different motives. Without parental guidance, she would be limited in knowing how to protect herself from deception and harm in the face of a plausible, but dubiously motivated adult. Lynn Barber, at 16, could not have been expected to know how to respond to this challenge and yet was left with the feeling that she should have known what was happening to her and should have said no to it. Thus, her experience of herself became fragmented and she came to view herself, in the example of her comparison with her husband, as morally damaged.

The acquisition of an authentic self-image and self-esteem requires knowledge gained from the support of parents who can model the skills needed to discriminate between trustworthy and untrustworthy behaviour. Also needed is the capacity to experience and respond to feelings and to decipher what they might be telling you. Nonetheless, although Lynne Barber's actions as a teenager were not contained within a context of sufficient parental maturity and support, they also signalled something of her later, more authentic self as a creative journalist, skilfully able to examine the experiences of others through her investigative writing, especially on the complexities of personalities in the public eye. This gained her the nickname of 'The Demon Barber of Fleet Street'. It is noteworthy that it was she, and not her parents, who exposed Simon's wrongdoing, demonstrating a potential capacity for penetrating observation of other people. Thus Winnicott (1965: 147) observed that: 'When the degree of the split in the infant's person is not too great . . . it may even be possible for the child to act a special role, that of the True Self *as it would be if it had had existence*'.

The false self portrayed in George Eliot's novel *The Mill on the Floss*

Another example of the false self generated by moral injury can be seen in George Eliot's description of Maggie Tulliver, in her novel *The Mill on the Floss*. Maggie is the child who somehow is always in the wrong, even in the colour of her hair, when compared by her mother to her cousin Lucy:

> And Maggie always looked twice as dark as usual when she was by the side of Lucy.
> She did to-day, when she and Tom came in from the garden. . . . Maggie had thrown her bonnet off very carelessly, and, coming in with her hair rough as well as out of curl, rushed at once to Lucy, who was standing by her mother's knee. Certainly the contrast between the cousins was conspicuous, and to superficial eyes, was very much to the disadvantage of Maggie, though a connoisseur might have seen "points" in her which had a higher promise for maturity than Lucy's natty completeness. It was like the contrast between a rough, dark, overgrown puppy and a white kitten. . . . Maggie always looked at Lucy with delight. She was fond of fancying a world where the people never got any larger than children of their own age, and she made the queen of it just like Lucy, with a little crown on her head and a little sceptre in her hand . . . only the queen was Maggie herself in Lucy's form.
>
> (Eliot, 1860, in 1964: 54)

Here we can see how, in the absence of authentic mirroring by a mother who understood and affirmed her nature, Maggie tried to develop a false self, modelled upon what she thought would gain approval. This she could never achieve, which defines the tragedy of the novel. Of the false self, Winnicott (1965: 142–148) observed that its defensive function is that of hiding and protecting the true self, by setting itself up to seem real: 'And it is this that observers tend to think is the real person. In living relationships, work relationships, and friendships, however, the False Self begins to fail. In situations in which what is expected is a whole person the False Self has some essential lacking'. In contrast with this, Winnicott stated that: 'The spontaneous gesture is the True Self in action. Only the True Self can be creative and only the True Self can feel real. Whereas a True Self feels real, the existence of a False Self results in a feeling unreal or a sense of futility'. For Maggie, her false self developed within a setting where her mother was not able to adapt well enough to her needs as a distinctly individual child. So, as Winnicott observed, when faced with a dilemma of this kind the infant 'gets seduced into a compliance, and a compliant False Self reacts to environmental demands and the infant seems to accept them'. Thus, the point of origin of the false self can be seen as a defence 'against that which is unthinkable, the exploitation of the True Self, which would result in its annihilation'.

The theme of Maggie's story is that, despite her attempts to develop a false persona, and to comply with the expectations imposed upon her by the values of her mother and the cultural milieu of a close rural community, something about her always remains true to her authentic self. Whilst the story ends with her death, the novel portrays throughout an authentic self which could not be extinguished even though, by the values of the time, that self was deemed to have got her into all kinds of trouble. This theme is reflective of the life of the author. George Eliot was herself raised in a community which expected her to live within the confines of her father's religious assumptions and social values. As she began to develop her own ideas and could no longer subscribe to his faith, a breach opened between them. Although she remained personally supportive to him for the rest of his life, she continued to pursue and to develop her own more humane values, so evident in her writing. Her authentic self was most certainly not annihilated, even though she had to endure a painful separation from the society and culture in which she had been raised and for which she kept an enduring attachment, alongside joyful and affectionate memories of her native landscape of villages and markets, and the field hedgerows which gave a home to the wildflowers she loved (Ashton, 1996: 13).

Psychotherapy and the authentic self

It could be said that the false self is moral injury *par excellence*. Having developed a complete persona from a sense of perceived moral transgression, whose foundation is based upon fear of 'getting it wrong', a person can come to believe that they should be someone else, in order to gain affirmation from their parents, teachers or other important figures. Loving kindness as *agape* or *superego* is not adequate to the tasks of psychotherapy here, because any appeal to an already overactive conscience will be likely to encourage the sense of inadequacy and shaming. In fact, for the person who has such negative self-belief, it is necessary for the psychotherapist to encourage more *eros* and *id* through an exploration of human instincts, 'wrong' though these may seem. This work may not be easy, as the sense of perceived wrongdoing may have become for the client a distorted kind of comfort zone, however painful, at least familiar and reliable as a default setting for feelings. Resistance to authentic feelings is therefore likely, and often renewed self-blame or at least ambivalence, whilst undergoing this difficult and challenging process of transformation. Equally, the *eros and id* components need to be handled with care therapeutically, to avoid being caught up in a 'desire for something that you lack and need and hope to gain' (Osborne, 1994: 54), such as wanting the client to change for the personal and emotional gratification of the psychotherapist. Hence the need for a unifying quality of loving kindness as a consistency of purpose in the psychotherapist, willing to relate to the authentic self of the client, even where the false self insists on being the dominant version of that person, or the ego of the psychotherapist wishes to promote a particular outcome. The personal and professional challenges of holding this balance represent both the most difficult and the most rewarding aspects of the complex work of psychotherapists. They require a capability to 'reflect-in-action', which is to notice that:

> There is some puzzling, or troubling, or interesting phenomenon with which the individual is trying to deal. As he tries to make sense of it, he also reflects on the understandings which have been implicit in his action, understandings which he surfaces, criticizes, restructures, and embodies in further action.
> It is this entire process of reflection-in-action which is central to the 'art' by which practitioners sometimes deal well with situations of uncertainty, instability, uniqueness, and value conflict.
>
> (Schon, 1991: 50)

This 'art' promotes the development of reflexivity in the psychotherapist which, through deep thought and engagement with another, allows subjective self-awareness to be acknowledged and to meet and engage with that of the client. This is why the personal psychotherapy component is perhaps the most essential experience in the training and professional development of psychotherapists; through learning how to recognise, distinguish between and affirm the individual experiences of self and other. Until the psychotherapist has fully enough explored and reflected upon his or her own psychological and emotional territory, it will be difficult to discriminate clearly between his or her subjective experience and that of the client, especially where projections are in the foreground. To be able to sustain a sufficient level of clarity, and the demands this activity places upon the practitioner, it is necessary to recognise and occupy the wider and deeper context of the psyche, that totality which includes both conscious and unconscious components of awareness. Jacobi, in the context of Jungian psychotherapy, describes how:

> By 'intellect' we mean the power of conscious thought and understanding, the purely rational side of the individual. 'Spirit' is to be taken as a faculty which pertains to the realm of consciousness but also has a natural bond with the unconscious; it leads primarily to meaningful . . . insights and utterances, but it can also lend a definite coloration to thoughts and judgements as well as emotional attitudes. 'Spirit' in this sense comprises both the intellect and the soul; it forms a bond between them and is a meaningful 'sublimation' of both; it is a formative principle constituting the contrary pole to the unformed, instinctual, biological nature of man, thereby sustaining the continuous tension of opposites on which our psychic life is based.
>
> (Jacobi, 1973: 5)

Jung (CW9) thus regarded individuation and the emergence of an authentic self as a regulatory function which sustains the balance and integration of these two related opposites. He defined individuation as 'the process by which a person becomes a psychological 'in-dividual', that is, a separate, indivisible unity or 'whole'. In order to be able to function as a separate whole, a person requires a sufficient level of self-esteem and awareness to maintain a personally secure base, capable of supporting clear recognition of others. The individuation process is not finite and, once engaged, will continue. From the psychotherapist's point of view, an increasing level of experience, deeper self-awareness and flexibility will provide a foundation for greater reliance upon his or her instincts, without necessarily having to act on them immediately, or at all, because this foundation enables the psychotherapy process to unfold at a pace necessarily determined by the psyche and life experiences of the client. So we can add here that whilst loving kindness in psychotherapy is based upon an instinctive, biological capability, it also needs to be understood, assimilated and developed through the deep and searching experiences of personal psychotherapy, supported by training, supervision and continuing thought and reflection with colleagues, for the duration of a psychotherapy career. The steadfast quality which grows through meeting these demands will help the practitioner to weather the inevitable storms and ruptures which must be part of the process of change in which both client and psychotherapist are engaged.

From the point of view of the client, Gerhardt (2015: 236) notices how defences against change and individuation can have origins in an understandable attempt to manage alone, in the face of childhood adversity and to create an ideal version of self as one who *could* be loved, but only by an ideal parent. Often, this imagined parent is one who seems to have no needs. But we can see how the attempt to manage alone, even though it lacks realistic foundations, is a necessary adaptation where acceptance of feelings and the consequent ability to regulate them have not been made available as a working model in childhood. The experiential problem which arises as a consequence of this model is that authentic human feelings and the possibility of satisfying relationships pose a threat to it. Thus, engagement in a therapeutic relationship can be the first, often difficult, step away from that state of aloneness, because it offers the necessary support for the process of transition. This is illustrated in the case study of Gemma in Chapter 3, where she gradually moved towards relationships based upon her own authentic sense of self. And in doing so she became more able to accept the human fallibility of her mother, rather than the idealised version which had always made Gemma feel lacking. The therapeutic process was not always easy, because inevitably it included human misunderstandings, but these experiences also generated opportunities to repair them by recognising and accepting strong feelings. Gerhardt emphasises the importance of this aspect of psychotherapeutic work. She comments that the nature of 'rupture and repair' and the sharing of emotional states arising from such experiences mean that, although they have been missing in the past, these opportunities can now be provided by the psychotherapist and repeated as a cycle of experience until the necessary learning has been established securely.

Within this relational context, Casement poses an important question concerning the psychotherapeutic clarity needed when assisting the individuation process. He asks whether, at any given moment, it is the process of the client, or that of the psychotherapist which is in the foreground, and how the two can be distinguished from each other. He observes that, even after a personal analysis, any therapist is still vulnerable to the unconscious defences of projection and denial, especially when under pressure. Thus, one's own feelings need to be monitored, so that when defences are triggered, the therapist is able to accept what belongs to him or herself. Casement identifies two important aspects of this process:

> First, he or she needs to have access to these unconscious resonances across as wide a range of feeling as possible. Therapists do not have to remain limited to their own experiences, their own ways of being and feeling. It is possible that each person carries the potential to feel all feelings and to resonate to all experiences, however strange or alien these may be to their conscious selves . . .
>
> Second, every therapist has to learn to be open to the 'otherness' of the other—being ready to feel whatever feelings result from being in touch with another person, however different that person is from themselves. Empathic identification is not enough, as it can limit a therapist to seeing what is familiar, or is similar to his own experience. Therapists therefore have to develop an openness to, and respect for, feelings and experiences that are quite unlike their own.
>
> (Casement, 1985: 94–95)

These observations also signal the vital importance of consistent psychotherapy supervision, because it is not always possible for the psychotherapist to recognise the feelings which result from being in touch with another person. The supervisor may pick up on them, sometimes in quite subtle ways, such as a certain vocal tone when the psychotherapist/supervisee is discussing a particular client, or the fact that a client seems not to be presented very often at supervision.

Outcomes can never be predicted at the outset of a psychotherapy encounter, but it is often the idea of an outcome and a satisfactory ending which naturally preoccupy a client, especially during the opening stages of the work. At this point, the focus of the client may be upon the cost, the time taken up, or the potential impact upon family and social life. And yet, where a therapeutic alliance is able to be made over time, a psychotherapy process begins to develop which has a life and an energy of its own. Later on, timescales and outcomes often become less urgent, as layers of experience are explored and a process of individuation may be entered into. Ultimately, as Carl Rogers observed, it seems that the person increasingly discovers that his own organism is trustworthy, that it is a suitable instrument for discovering the most satisfying behaviour in each immediate situation, so that:

> Consciousness, instead of being the watchman over a dangerous and unpredictable lot of impulses, of which few can be permitted to see the light of day, becomes the comfortable inhabitant of a society of impulses and feelings and

thoughts, which are discovered to be very satisfactorily self- governing when not fearfully guarded . . .

The individual increasingly comes to feel that this locus of evaluation lies within himself. Less and less does he look to others for approval and disapproval; for standards to live by; for decisions and choices. He recognises that it rests within himself to choose; that the only question which matters is, "Am I living in a way which is deeply satisfying to me, and which truly expresses me?" This I think is perhaps *the* most important question for the creative individual.

(Rogers, 1967: 118–119)

Individuation, loving kindness and the repair of moral injury

Referring to the work of Jung, Jacobi defined individuation as:

a spontaneous, natural process within the psyche; . . . Unless it is inhibited, obstructed, or distorted by some specific disturbance, it is a process of maturation or unfolding, the psychic parallel to the physical process of growth and aging (sic). Under certain circumstances, in practical psychotherapy for example, it can in one way or another be stimulated, intensified, made conscious, consciously experienced, and elaborated; the individual can thus be helped to 'complete' or 'round out' his personality. In such cases it requires an intensive analytical effort, a conscious and absolutely honest concentration on the intrapsychic process. . . . Leading through all the hazards of a psyche thrown off balance, cutting through layer after layer, it finally penetrates to the centre that is the source and ultimate foundation of our psychic being, to the SELF.

This path . . . is not advisable for all men, nor is it open to all . . . Consequently it takes two to undertake this journey . . .

It falls into two main, independent parts, characterized by contrasting and complementary qualities. . . . The task of the first half is 'initiation into outward reality' . . . it aims at the adaptation of the individual to the demands of his environment. The task of the second half is a so-called 'initiation into the inner reality', a deeper self-knowledge and knowledge of humanity, a 'turning back' *(reflectio)* to the traits of one's nature that have hitherto remained unconscious or become so.

(Jacobi, 1973: 107–108)

The delicate emergence of the individuation process in psychotherapy takes place in what Knox (2003: 2) has described as 'the fragile co-construction of a symbolic space', which provides the symbolic holding that is a prerequisite for individuation. This holding is necessary because, as Jacobi (1973: 127–132) points out, it allows a person to know himself for what he naturally is as distinct from what he would like to be. This is a difficult task, but only when 'this midpoint is found and integrated, can one speak of a well-rounded man. For only then has he solved the problem of his relation to the two realms which make up every man's life, the outward and the inner reality'.

Where moral injury is concerned, the relationship between those two realms will be particularly vulnerable to the experience of self-blame. As Fonagy (167–187) observes, a child's tendency to 'incorporate mental state attributions into internal working models of self-other relationships depends on the opportunities that he had in early life to observe and explore the mind of his primary caregiver'. An adult with moral injury may have lacked parenting where there was tangible reflection upon and empathy towards the infant's aroused feelings of distress, wherein that infant could witness his or her existence and importance in the mind of his or her parent. The child will have lacked what Fonagy has described as 'the benefit that the experience of psychic containment brings in terms of the development of a coherent and symbolising self', which comes about through the mirroring of the infant's experience by the primary carer. For reflective function to develop, the infant needs to internalise the parent as someone with a mental image of the infant (Knox, 2003: 141).

Thus, Fairbairn (1952: 62) proposed that an infant who encounters a negative version of herself may not only develop an internalised image of self-blame but also continue to idealise the neglectful parent, thus taking the whole of the blame for feeling bad. This he described as the 'moral defence against bad objects', in which a child blames herself for her parents' emotional and empathic failures, because it feels safer to be bad, rather than having a parent on whom you depend for your safety being bad. Equally, the psychotherapy process can become very challenging when a client is faced with her idealisation of a parent figure who let her down. The prospect of letting go of this idealisation can stretch the psychotherapeutic relationship to the limits of breaking point when a client may even say, quite suddenly, that they want to leave the psychotherapy. Potentially this is the ultimate rupture and must of course be repaired if the work is to continue to a satisfactory ending, as illustrated in the case study of Gemma. The challenge lies in the fact that infant attachment, however damaged, is an intense and perfectly understandable form of biological and emotional loyalty to the parent. It is vitally important because, without some kind of bond of loyal attachment, young mammals are vulnerable and could die if their needs are sufficiently neglected. Thus, when basic needs are not met, attachment behaviour increases in one form or another and can be measured by the aroused somatic response of the infant. Rutter observed that in situations where the mother is stressed, or the child is parent-deprived, the buffering and cortisol-level lowering impact of parental presence is reduced, neuroplasticity is diminished and the child becomes more anxious, less adventurous, and more prone to anxiety disorders (Rutter, 2012, in Holmes & Slade, 2018: 59). By contrast, securely attached infants in the presence of their mothers are less frightened and have lower salivary cortisol levels when compared with insecure or mother-absent counterparts.

Where a child has taken the blame for family difficulties, has carried this moral injury into adulthood and, later, is facing her wounded state in psychotherapy, it will feel counterintuitive and disturbing for her to be disloyal to the idealised parent. Although Gemma's mother could not meet her emotional needs, she *was* her mother, and it might have seemed that without that lasting loyalty, Gemma would be cast adrift and at the same time threatened by the prospect of a replacement relationship forming with her psychotherapist. But the psychotherapy relationship was, at the same time, the bridge towards a new relationship with her authentic self and a life free from fear of blame. What also had to be faced was the reality of past mistreatment which had damaged her authentic sense of self.

The consistency of the psychotherapy relationship offers a new opportunity, through steadfastness of both psychotherapist and client, to hold this most challenging stage of the work. Sometimes, people leave psychotherapy at this point, which is their perfect right to do, but it means that the bridge leading to transformation will not have been crossed. However, the supporting structure of the therapeutic alliance usually holds firm, even though the challenges presented may have to 'go to the wire', giving pause for much mutual reflection in the weeks and months which follow. Loving kindness, as a steadfast holding of that growing process, is therefore essential in supporting the transitions and challenges which are necessary if a person is to discover, and begin to live, the life of the authentic self. Psychotherapy offers the chance to 'try out' the authentic self in relationship with another and in personal relationships outside that arena. At this point the sense of an ending to the psychotherapy begins to emerge. The goal of the individuation process achieved here is a *conscious* relation to the self (Edinger, 1972: 261). It permits a distinctive sense of individuality to be perceived by both parties to the therapeutic alliance, strong enough to be sustained by the client within relationships after the psychotherapy has ended. Consequently, Jung described individuality as:

> the peculiarity and singularity of the individual in every psychological respect . . . a process of *differentiation* having for its goal the development of the individual personality. . . . Individuation is a natural necessity inasmuch as its prevention by a levelling down to collective standards is injurious to the vital activity of the individual. . . . Any serious check to individuality, therefore, is an artificial stunting. It is obvious that a social group consisting of stunted individuals cannot be a healthy and viable

institution; only a society that can preserve its internal cohesion and collective values, while at the same time granting the individual the greatest possible freedom, has any prospect of enduring vitality. As the individual is not just a single, separate, being, but by his very existence presupposes a collective relationship, it follows that the process of individuation must lead to more intense and broader collective relationships and not to isolation.

(Jung, CW6)

The transformative function of the individuation process in the repair of moral injury is illustrated in the following case study.

Case study of Mark, written in his own words

08/09/20

In a few weeks I will complete a seven-year period of psychotherapy.

I guess it's not unusual for a client to begin therapy with an issue they believe to be isolated. Maybe a passage of crisis that seems not to be connected to their history and which only needs some short-term attention. I also imagine that for some people the therapeutic work can be relatively short-term. I began therapy in a troubled state and needing urgent help and advice. Although I don't recall having links with deeper-seated issues clearly in mind, I was aware that my misery had a lot to do with regrets over past experience and I remember being open-minded about how long the therapy would last.

I had scarcely any idea how things would unfold and knew little about the rich world I was entering. Years earlier I had spent eight months seeing a counsellor. While I recall that this experience didn't seem to involve much intervention by the counsellor, I remember feeling gratefulness for the positive feelings that arose from talking over things that I had seldom or never shared. Nonetheless, my sense of myself did not seem to improve in the longer term.

The trauma that led me to first contact my therapist had begun a couple of weeks earlier in the attic of my home. I had discovered diaries that belonged to my partner. We had lived together for ten years with our two children who were then nine and seven. The diaries were from a time before we met. She had travelled quite a bit and much of the writing was from time she had spent abroad. It included intimate details of encounters with men she had met. I wasn't immune to insecurities and feelings of jealousy. If I'm honest, a voyeuristic interest probably contributed to me going on reading the diaries. But none of those responses explained the scale of the sorrow I began to feel. I could not see past what felt irrefutable. That alongside the difficult passage of a decade we had spent as a couple, the life described in the diaries made a stark contrast. Each page of my partner's words written in her own hand said that she had been a profoundly happy soul until we got together. I felt convinced I deserved my anguish. The potency of it was devastating and inescapable. The diaries made the grave confirmation that my own discontent, moods and losses of patience were the root cause of our failure to form a happier bond. I felt as though I couldn't bring contentment to her life on any front. The rawness feeling was made all the worse by the thought of how our bitter arguments and atmospheres had impacted on our children.

Among the many things I'm grateful to psychotherapy for is the way it has helped me to view the past with a more patient view of the emotional capabilities which can realistically be expected in the early stages of life. I have learnt to try to be more self-compassionate about past judgements and ways of feeling. I say this because it strikes me as significant to the way I began therapy. I can see in hindsight how my response to 'the diaries' might have been naïve. In the purer, kindlier sense of the word, it probably was. Even after a decade of living together with two kids, I couldn't see that my partner's previous adventures bore precious little relevance to the way things had turned out between us and why we made a less-than-fulfilled couple. And in psychotherapy it wasn't long before I started to discover patterns and past occurrences that were very relevant to how things had turned out between us. If anything the term *naïve* seems helpful now because I have come to understand so much about why I was exactly that.

Initially, I arrived at my psychotherapy appointments consumed by sorrowful feelings. I experienced an outpouring of grief which felt like a sudden eruption of misery. Nonetheless, even as the early appointments passed, the initial crisis seemed to feel soothed. It started to become less of a self-contained moment and more of a starting point for work with issues from further back in life. Quite early on, I think my therapist identified my need for a longer-term process. She explained, several times in the early months, how the unconscious part of the psyche can reach a moment when it has, in plain terms, had enough of living the way it does. A point where, I suppose, the amount of repressed experience becomes unfeasible or unmanageable. Working around it day in and day out and having to accommodate Lord knows what consequent anxieties becomes next to impossible. I remember feeling very moved by the compelling power of the idea and the eloquence it spoke to my experience. Like so much else that I found in psychotherapy, it felt like a true representation of what I was actually feeling. I was 45 and believed I had stumbled into what was, on the surface, an emotionally bumpy phase. But I found it was more an opportunity to examine four decades of messy and deeply settled clutter. Finding my way into psychotherapy offered a chance to begin to heal emotional wounds that had been unaddressed since my childhood.

I suppose it was around that early point that I found myself developing an implicit trust in the process. It seemed to offer more rational explanations than I had ever known for why my life had been inwardly experienced in the way it had. I had a strong desire to go on. I suspect that a sure sign that psychotherapy is working is when a client feels a certain level of awe about the process itself alongside the sense of personal benefit and development. I found a sense of something marvellous as the facility of psychotherapy dawned in those early months. It was at times a very moving experience as I started to realise that so many inner difficulties had an explanation which felt real and which I could own. While psychotherapy could do nothing to alter the past, I began to see that considering those explanations could bring a more relieved and comfortable way of living with them. In hindsight, and at the other end of a rewardingly long therapeutic journey, I can see how the critical moment that pushed me into the process tapped into fault lines and susceptibilities that had lain long in waiting.

I remember how, soon after the initial appointment, my psychotherapist recognised what she described as 'a distressed child on board'. Although I didn't mistake the kindly tone of the observation, I probably bristled slightly at the perception. Nonetheless, I suppose it said something about the trust I found in the relationship from the outset that I was more interested than offended. Something, I suppose from down in my unconscious, appeared to respond to what seemed a shrewd perception, because of the way it hinted at thoughts I'd long had about my past emotional experiences. Now I can see how my response said something about the readiness I had already stored up for therapy. My psychotherapist's support, and her gradual assimilation of what I told her, led me to understand how experiences and memories from my earlier life had been denied. How distinct phases of my childhood and subsequent development had been compromised. How, in straightforward terms, there was a distressed child inside me whilst I was trying to behave like an adult. But, more comfortingly, I was led to understand how this was okay; it wasn't any terrible crime and I was not, by any means alone or a bad person. My feelings were sometimes overwhelming as I expressed the pent-up distress I found I had held back since childhood, but I never felt judged or belittled because of this and my psychotherapist gave a strong and gentle holding in her approach to me. I started to find comfort as I began to see that my emotional struggles could be traced to childhood neglect that was often of a benign and unintended type. I began to recognise my parents' own, human vulnerabilities. Looking back now to my years as a client, I can see how I gained a sharpening of quiet curiosity and more understanding towards the behaviour I see in others.

It was intriguing how quickly the past came to seem richly alive in the conversations, as further off experiences began to mingle with talking about my current situation. In a fairly short time, my own history started to feel like the key to making the current explainable in ways that I never might have anticipated. Although it could be painful, I was absorbed by what was actually obvious about my relationship with my partner being picked up on very quickly through the lens of psychotherapy. I left each session with a bit more understanding and awareness of how an unconscious process works and how relevant this was to my understanding of myself. How things had kept on repeating themselves until I began to consciously recognise them and their importance to me. I found that I was developing a relationship of trust with my psychotherapist, which helped me to see what was in fact obvious and had really been known to me all along.

It started to be irresistibly clear that my partner and me—who had our own good reasons for it—had gone on trying to believe that a loving and workable relationship was possible between us, without properly paying attention to the issues of incompatibility which made it so difficult. I guess it was a commonplace enough situation and something that deep down we both knew. We had managed this, at least, out of commitment to our children but there was also an uncomfortable feeling of emotional dependency between us, even though the rewards of the relationship felt slim. Each week, a gradual awareness of our shared past seemed to reveal a little more about just how we had 'found' each other. How our own psychological 'backstories' made us a likely coupling—even down to the circumstances under which we met. I came to understand how we shared a compromised dependency, similar to that which both of us had known, in different ways, in our families from earliest childhood. As I talked this through each week it seemed there wasn't anywhere to hide from the reality as it emerged. It was very emotional at times, but before long, my understanding of my intimate relationship together with so much else in the present found an unstoppable sort of back-and-forth fluency with the past. That feeling of richer integration with my history, alongside a better ability to live in the present, are experiences from my time spent in psychotherapy that I treasure a great deal.

Right from the start, the makings of this psychotherapy relationship made me feel secure and as the appointments accumulated, I experienced feelings of warmth in the process they offered me. Each weekly hour, in a comfortable room suitable for reflection, felt deeply welcome. I wonder if it's not unusual for people engaging in psychotherapy to find and to recognise a long-held wish for the sort of receptive listening a good psychotherapist can provide. I certainly had that feeling and it moved me that I was being heard. I came to understand, to some degree painfully, how my early life had lacked the same consistent interest I was now finding in psychotherapy. In turn, as I explored more of the past, I started to develop more insights into how my early years and childhood had coloured my inner life. In ways that I had never really understood clearly, I could see where long-term issues with unhappiness and esteem and feelings of isolation had their origins. I began to see how my insecurity stemmed from my parents' difficulties— both within their marriage and more individually—and how these had distracted them from being able to attend to the emotional needs I had as a child and as a teenager. Despite feeling assured that their regard for me was loving, my parents were, in their own different ways, unhappy and inwardly quite lonely individuals. Both separately maintained strong and dependent ties in the relationships they had with their own parents. Psychotherapy, from the beginning, helped me, in very tender ways, to understand the muddled distractions of my parents' distress and the effect they had on me. I began to look at passages and experiences from the past that I had tended to avoid thinking about, or had even tried to disavow, out of pain or embarrassment. Here, my interest was fired by therapeutic ideas about attachment and the ways in which these seemed to speak directly to the experience of my earlier life.

I had never completely lost sight of how my mother and the memory of my father remained dear to me. Both of my parents knew how to be kindly and generous. Both of them always put myself and my brother first, where they felt it mattered, and they saw to our material needs as far as their income allowed.

Nonetheless, I found I was ready to try to talk about them as frankly as my under-standing would permit. It came as a relief to start safely to consider their troubles and the significant impact these had on the emotional life of our family home. Any happiness that my parents did share was always fragile. My mother had an unsettled temperament and often presented behaviour that was either hysterical or leaning that way. I imagine she felt it was the only way she could achieve any control in the many situations that stirred her anxieties. I guess this was, quite obviously, selfishly manipulative but she lacked the self-control to manage any better.

Psychotherapy enabled me to see how the demands of motherhood on a very young woman with the emotional vulnerability of a still younger child were more than she could handle consistently. Disagreements and arguments between my parents were rarely resolved without my mother flooding with tears and often screaming about the house. She was often and obviously very unhappy and her lack of self-containment meant a spillage of pain and troubles across the lives of those around her. Part of this unbalanced temperament meant she could show a lot of anger and physical chastisement if she was cross with me. There were exaggerated and hysterical responses to what she saw as my failure to cooperate and behave well. Even though her frequent outbursts of anger were often followed by genuine remorse and sorrow, her troubles did little to protect me from consciously feeling that I was capable of utterly hideous behaviour and therefore the cause of her distress. I often believed I was somehow wholly responsible for the long disappearances she would make routinely, about once a month, on a Sunday after-noon. I tended to believe her when she made her customary reply—in response to me asking where she had been—'walking the riverbank, looking for where it's deepest'. I came to believe that such obvious misery in my mother was a direct result of my behaviour. It was one of several misperceptions that I believe stayed with me and was at the heart of the feeling of blameful guilt that I carried into adult life. Now, I came to realise how terrified I had been at those times, when it had felt like my mother might one day go to the river bank and not come back.

I remember my psychotherapist's description of my relationship with my mother being like a small plant taken over by the rampant, unkept growth of a larger neighbouring one. One that had, in its own turn, never been properly nur-tured or contained. I became fascinated by the way that patterns seemed to show up across the generations, and our conversations considered the part played by my mother and father's own past. I came to understand and to imagine, more than I ever had done before, my mother's early life in a close-knit community of police housing in the 1950s, the way that her childhood and family life had been toned with her own mother's hysteria, mixed in with superior attitudes and pushy ideas about respectability. I could see how my grandmother's loss of her mother during the childbirth that brought her into the world, and her subsequent step-daughterhood and rivalry with her half-brother had, in their turn, diminished her capacity to support my mother's childhood development. I came to see how these events would have created a situation where my mother came to doubt her own right to be in the world. Consequently, I found that I was becoming able to fully recognise and to own my emotional inheritance, without shame, now that I had a better understanding and acceptance of the experiences which my parents and grandparents had to face. I felt more compassion for them.

I had always felt that my father understood and 'saw' me more than my mother. His obvious intelligence and the fact that he was, some of the time, emotionally observant, enabled him to make me feel more understood than was really ever the case with my mother. Nonetheless, he could be quite withdrawn and spent a lot of his time at home in his chair reading or absorbed in 1970s telly. He had a demanding job as a civil engineer, and I guess he needed his retreats from his work and the way my mother's hysteria depressed him. He was never properly able to stand up to her or help her to contain herself. His early childhood had been spent on the move with his own mother during the war whilst his father was away in the army. He was also an only child, and it wasn't difficult to recognise the powerful bond with his mother that was created in his childhood. His mother was widowed when I was about four and her presence in our home became a regular all-weekend fixture right on through the rest of my childhood and adolescence. Needless to say, whilst she may have helped in various material ways, her presence did little for my parents' marital harmony. Although my childhood family life didn't totally lack happier times, it was never long before underlying tensions broke. All of these elements created an atmosphere that I recall as often low spirited enough to be called bleak and never all that far from being filled with shouting and hysteria. I can see now that I often felt fearful because I was unable to predict what might happen next.

I think it was those details of my early family life, the way that as a child I somehow came to feel a burden of responsibility for those patterns of domestic misery, that left me to carry feelings of longer-term blame into adulthood. It took time to properly understand, but the gradual and gentle returns to the subject in psychotherapy showed how my early sense of heavy responsibility had been cropping up in my subsequent life ever since. My parents, ordinarily and benignly enough, had not been able to protect me from my magnifying feelings of guiltiness over my behaviour (childhood behaviour that might well, and unsurprisingly under the circumstances, have been difficult) into feelings of responsibility for what was far more rooted in their own background of pain and suffering. My own sense of having a responsibility for the general tone of unhappiness became very present in my perception of myself and my relations with the world beyond. As a child and really for all the time before I began psychotherapy, I had no idea about my mother's inability to take a firm emotional embrace of me or mirror back my experiences as I was developing and offer me reassurance. I could not understand it in those terms, which meant that absorption of blame characterised my inner life.

From my very early years, my attempts to reach towards the outside world always felt hampered by what I now understand was a lacking sense of worthiness. This pattern materialised continuously and I remember how, for example, I knew quite early on that I didn't seem able to properly connect with playground friends. I could never quite seem to achieve the sort of engagement that I sought, or that felt similar to the ways other young children got along. My early years at school passed with a stammer and I was a clumsy infant. As I came to learn through psychotherapy, these were both symptoms that almost certainly had their origin in the messiness and fear which characterised my emotional life at home and they persisted throughout my school years. These feelings had been magnified to points where they seemed unbearable, when I found myself in situations where I was for some reason singled out. One very difficult experience I had during school happened at around the age of 8. My teacher in that particular school year was an older man called Mr M. He had, for years, taken special pride in training his class to sing as a choir in the school Christmas concert. During practices Mr M habitually walked up and down in front of the banked arrangement of rows, cocking his ear towards the singing. I was a tall kid, and I remember being in the back row during what must have been a first rehearsal. One natural by-product of my emotional withdrawal was the sharply attuned antennae I had when any susceptibility felt as though it was facing exposure. Instinct guided me to try to cover my vulnerability, but the experience of knowing at certain times that I couldn't felt horrific. Within moments of Mr M slowing his step at the floor level two rows in front of me I knew I was facing such a moment. My toneless efforts at singing saw me plucked from the choir and pointed to a seat and never making it to the Christmas show. In spite of what I still consider to be Mr M's crass brutality, the whole situation was worsened by what it seemed to confirm to my child's understanding about me more widely. I felt that this public humiliation had exposed my private sense of shame.

Another even more memorable experience recalled in psychotherapy happened about a year later when I had moved with my parents to another part of the town we lived in. Although I could have continued at the school I had been at since the age of 4 to 5, my parents made the decision to enrol me at a more local place. Whatever slowing and failure of concentration had already happened in my schooling probably ground to a halt at this point. The whole time got off to a very difficult start on the very first morning. As in most schools, there was a full school assembly to start the year off. I remember being taken to the school by my mother and beginning to sob as we left the house. I was heaving with sorrow as my mum dragged me along the route to school and the outpouring continued very audibly on through my arrival and all the way through the assembly. I can remember, even now, how unstoppable the crying felt and how deeply the sorrow ran. Now I can see that it was strange that I was left to parade my misery like some new school exhibit, in spite of there being a full complement of staff on hand, who might have helped me. Something in me seemed to freeze, as of that point. Although I remember going some way towards settling at the school, it never felt as though I was in a comfortable place where academic progress was likely. I never quite felt as though that humiliating moment was put behind me. Psychotherapy finally enabled me to see that, although the change of schools was unfortunate in itself and there had been a damaging lack of sensitivity to my obvious distress and need for support, this experience was not the only cause of my difficulty, although it felt like it at the time. Had I been hatched from a more secure base then I may well, as some kids do, have coped better in a new school. I came to understand the occasion as another example of what happens when vulnerability which hasn't been addressed becomes exposed. I suppose such vulnerability can be inevitably counted on to face exposure at some point and the susceptibility becomes emotionally crippling when wrenched out into the open in ways such as these. The feelings of incapacity and failure seem all the more unstoppably destined to go on repeating themselves.

Although I was keen on sports in my teens, I always found I was slower to react and uncoordinated in team games. These sorts of features, together with the lethargy and depression that I experienced, saw me referred to as a 'lummox' by some of my elders. And as time moved on, I lacked both confidence and concentration in my schoolwork. I experienced significant episodes of bullying at secondary school and, despite being a bright child, I could never seem to properly express my potential. I skived and played sick to get time away from school, especially in the later years and ended up leaving with a single 'O' Level. In spite of having friends and recognising feelings of interest and sympathy towards me, the residual distractions of feeling blameful and unworthy persisted and grew. In some unknowable way, the low unhappiness only seemed to accumulate as years passed and one failure seemed to lead to another. In turn, the 'failures' seemed to make the case for believing that unworthiness was what I deserved to feel. I dropped out of sixth form college and fell into a string of jobs—manual work, shop work, low-grade office admin—that presented little stimulation or future. I could never find my way securely into an appropriate peer group and felt hampered and held back in romantic and sexual involvements with women. Again, never truly believing myself very desirable, or as though I could offer anything much.

As psychotherapy continued to address the way my parents had, in spite of doing their very best, left me prone to these inner difficulties, I began to feel that my unconscious, habitual defences were shifting. I felt a motivation which could no longer be stopped from moving me towards a more authentic way of living. It seemed like a sort of gravitational movement away from reliance on the long-standing insecurities that had seemingly been all I had known. This stage of the therapy was not always easy, as I came to realise I could make changes to the way I viewed my partner and my mother and this could bring about different actions on my part, instead of blaming them for my discomforts and frustrations. Sometimes I found this frightening, as I could not imagine having this level of influence on the mundane workings of my relationships. It was up to me to make the difference, but I didn't know what to do, and yet I couldn't turn back from the positive progress I was making. On one occasion I found myself blaming the psychotherapy itself for causing all this disruption to my emotional life and I said I was thinking of finishing. In that moment it felt as though this was the only way to resolve the stress, conflict and split loyalty between my new and my previous experience of relationship and feeling. But somehow I stuck with it and, with support,

I became able to challenge the ingrained and unsatisfactory ways through which I had avoided more honest dealings in my close relationships. By being clearer in my communication of feelings, I found that my family, rather than being wounded by this new approach, themselves seemed calmer and able to reciprocate my new intentions. This was a surprising bonus. It also had an impact on my perception of my work, and my workplace, where I had often felt resentful and unappreciated, wishing I could leave and find something better. I found that by making clearer demands and considering what would best meet my own needs, I was able to stay in the same place and realise that my colleagues, in fact, appreciated me and had higher regard for me than I had allowed myself previously to accept.

These improvements felt like the beginning of a departure, and it wasn't an exaggeration to say that I felt the process working physically, as though even my sense of time became more attuned to natural rhythms. The promise of the therapy hour revealing explanations that helped reintegrate my past life seemed to lift most of the other hours in the week. I felt more as though my life really had happened to *me*, and I gradually saw less need to feel ashamed or embarrassed by any of it. It felt like a time of tremendous reconnection with myself, as though the discoveries were allowing me to live much more in the moment. My senses began to wake up, and I started to feel more attuned to the changes in nature as each week passed. The drive to where I work includes a ten-mile stretch of countryside road, and I noticed how much more present I felt within the different weathers, colours and lights of the journey. I noticed how colleagues seemed to register a change, and it seemed as if a stronger and clearer impression of myself was finding its way into the outside world. It wouldn't be going too far to think in terms of a deep awakening, as anxiety and deeply set preoccupations began to give way, to allow more room for a recognisable sense of myself. The impact upon my family life was the most important to me. I became able to talk through and confront the difficulties with my partner, so that we could plan for changes in our future, and I witnessed the deep and positive effect this had upon my daughters. The daily round of our lives at home became easy and even enjoyable instead of being a continuous and dreary routine of chores.

Although my father had died by the time I began psychotherapy, I came to see how my relationship with my parents had been based upon a sort of shared emotional dependency that had often been deeply frustrating. But I can see that, out of need, I had kept up an unconscious desire to maintain things the way they were. A very important phase of my psychotherapy included the support I needed to challenge my relationship with my mother and to start to move away from the smothering relationship we had shared. As I did so my mother, to my surprise, became much less anxious and began to accept me as an adult with his own family. Some of this adjustment away from my parents' influence was illustrated by a series of dreams that I had at the time. In one memorably haunting dream, I found my mother in a dank, creepily silent multi-storey car park. One of the handles of a wheelchair stuck out from a lift. The sort of car park lift anyone would think twice about getting into, even in daytime. Inside the lift, my mother, apparently lifeless but with her eyes open, was sat in the wheelchair. There was a noose around her neck. She seemed too forbiddingly creepy to reach out to or to contemplate touching. I recoiled in a chilly sort of fear. The next part of the dream saw me on the concrete stairwell. It was comfortingly and brightly lit and a host of emergency workers in fluorescent uniforms were dismantling a tall vertical structure that led up to the lift where my mother was. The structure was something like a scaffold or scaffold tower. My mother was, so to speak, being 'taken down'. Everything appeared to be under the most expert control, all of the emergency workers had a very precise awareness of their role. I felt safe amid the warm, constructive atmosphere in the car park stairwell, in a way that was in complete contrast with the lift. This moment of awareness about what the dream meant to me marked the beginning of a big shift in my understanding of my prior relationship with my mother. It also remains a memorable moment in my realising the importance of the unconscious mind in our comprehension of reality, and the usefulness of dreams in communicating a fuller and deeper picture of it. Previously, and especially as a child, my experience of my mother was full of fear, inevitably influenced by the way she seemed to threaten to destroy herself. In this dream the potency of that threat was carefully being dismantled.

In another dream that came at about the same time, a figure I believed to be my father was on a beach, in front of a large deflated rubber dinghy that was hanging from a horizontal pole, which looked like a rigid version of a washing line. The floor of the dinghy had a clear gash across it wide enough to give a view of daylight on the other side. The item was, obviously enough, not seaworthy. Remarkably, the father figure seemed to be making an attempt to sell the ruptured article. On the top of the pole, three quite tatty-looking crows had perched in a row. I can see that this dream had associations with a real-life event that had happened in my childhood. My mother's parents kept a beach hut near where they lived on the coast and during one weekend visit my father (I imagine in another effort to 'escape') took the dinghy we had—it was no more than a kids' type thing—and paddled a very long way out to sea. I can remember feeling distraught as he became a tiny dot further and further out towards the horizon. The sea was like a millpond that afternoon, and he was very fortunate that it remained so as he rowed back. Nonetheless, it seemed a foolish thing to do. I suppose the ripped version of the boat that he seemed to be trying to sell in the dream, revealed some of the emotional movement I was making away from the powerful bonds I'd kept up with his memory; the dream showing more explicitly that the metaphorical boat in which I had been raised did not feel safe. And the three crows each seemed to represent one of three people I had known in adult life as long-term friends. All of them were, in a very strange coincidence, exactly 15 years my senior. Although I had close involvements with all of them, the understanding with each, in very different ways was compromised and unequal. The last of these involvements came to an end during my psychotherapy, and the dream seemed to signify how I was moving away from influences which represented significant, but unreliable attachments of an earlier self.

Psychotherapy also helped me realise how my disappointments had fostered unrealistic beliefs that I might and should have lived a different life. This had, to some degree, led to the adoption of a sort of 'false persona' based upon the need I felt for some kind of protection. I often didn't care much for the life I had lived and even, at times, felt strongly that I didn't want to be seen as associated with it. Reflecting on the past in psychotherapy led me to understand how I had created a sort of 'safety mask'. I had attempted to conceal what I saw as the mess of my more authentic identity which, I believed, was the cause of my shame and embarrassment. Again, at the source of it all, was a feeling of guilt and responsibility for all of my own failings. Right up to the point in my mid-forties when I began psychotherapy, I had persistently felt a proneness to imagining my earlier life as colourless and littered with opportunities that never seemed to materialise. I had powerful feelings of having missed out, which were sometimes nearly unbearable. In certain respects, the 'if only' constructions were a long-term activity that played a vital part in keeping me going, but without secure foundations. I fantasised continually on the theme of how I might have used my potential to far greater ends than I could realistically have achieved at the time. I believed for example that, had only things been different, I might have travelled extensively and enjoyed countless loving relationships and exotic affairs. I resented the reality of having had just one other serious involvement before meeting my partner and the fact that I hadn't flown in a plane prior to the age of 35. Now I can see how this explains my extreme reaction to reading about my partner's earlier adventures in her diaries.

I had also, since my early twenties, attempted to soothe the difficulties of my life by expansive and regularly written passages of self-therapeutic journal writing. Even though I tried to be honest about how I felt in self-reflective writing, I was still pulled along, at times uncontrollably, by a relentless and false determination to make up for lost time. The problem was that the emotional wound I never really understood, and in certain respects was blind to, continued to make me feel low about myself. Consequently, the more I seemed to not actually be making up enough of the shortfall to feel satisfied, the more spectacular became the dreams that I nursed in isolation. Needless to say, I also had to find ways of managing newly intensified feelings of failure.

One moment that might illustrate this pattern of inflated hopes occurred when I was in my early twenties. I had begun the first of several courses I took with the Open University. I remember getting an essay on *Wuthering Heights* back through the post one morning and seeing an overall mark and comments that left me elated with a sudden surge of successful feeling. It was an illumination to have my academic ability recognised by a university teacher. I had the feeling that my life was going to change very significantly. It took me only a short time to believe I might become a professor myself within ten years or so, and I did actually conceive a firm time frame for this. The same pattern of inflated ambitions followed on through my life, but nothing that I did achieve ever felt like enough. There were always points that I would look back on and chasten myself for, in hindsight, for not having found more focus to pursue my ambitions harder. In truth, although the emotional setting of my life had improved since childhood, I couldn't ever escape the insecurities and low sense of disconnection. The only chance I thought I had of escaping my painful failures was to go on believing that I could fulfil my glorious aims—aims that I didn't even really understand in terms that had much basis in reality. A similar thing happened when I began to break out of the habit of self-reflective writing and started to try to write poetry. Again, I felt a moving level of delight when editors of magazines returned my work with what were encouraging comments. Although my efforts dwindled when I fell short of having anything published, these encouragements went on prompting me to believe I was a major poetic voice in waiting. This is exaggerated only slightly, and the gist of the pattern was a lot like that.

This protective persona came out in therapy in the early sessions in other interesting ways. I began to note down reflections and memories as they occurred to me in the weeks between sessions. One quite memorable phase was a run of sessions when the fear of failure to communicate led me to read from a notebook. Whilst the habit was useful, I remember my psychotherapist gently commenting on the 'performed' style in which I read. Our rapport had taken off well and I was amused when she suggested it sounded a bit like a Victorian monologue— 'Mr Henry Irving will Read Tonight'. She suggested some time later that my reliance on reading my reflections and memories in the way I had, rather than simply talking about them, probably felt like the only safe option available to me at that early stage. I had needed to rely on a sort of performed approach, because the experience I was trying to recall and reflect on was not integrated with my sense of myself. It was too messy and jumbled, not to mention protected, to allow any easier access at that time.

As the natural progression of my therapy started to really have its positive influence on my inner life, I found I could relate far more naturally and authentically with the world around me. The most revealing step forward, and one of the most significant developments to come from the process, was the way that I did begin to write more progressively than had been the case, really, at any previous stage of my life. It was a revealing moment for me, as someone who had long harboured dreams of writing, but in distant isolation. Gradually, the challenges to different patterns within my life, and letting go of them, left me in a position and better frame of mind to write regularly. I became more naturally and calmly determined. I started to address my interests regularly, with the time I had available, and began to find satisfaction in doing so. After building pages of written material for six months or so, I overcame my fear and went to see a writing mentor who I shared my work with. It felt like an extraordinary step forward and a revealingly, real-life version of something quietly nursed for a long time. At the same time I had feelings of the long-desired breakthrough into simply and ordinarily allowing and encouraging myself towards doing what I liked most. I found that writing creatively on a real-life basis, as opposed to an imagined one, was effective in helping to dissolve the long-term prohibitive fear and guilt. As much as anything else, it felt like a key moment when I finally permitted myself to experience something near to the safety of my own authenticity and experience. The simple routine foundation of finding contentment in doing what I could, rather than judging my shortfalls according to the world around me, was important at this moment. The plain and ordinary success of such a development seemed clear when, during our first conversation and having read my work, my writing mentor suggested that it 'looked like I was writing a novel'. Until then I had only ever been able to imagine being addressed with such a comment. Now it was real. The recognition of simply doing what I wanted to do felt like a moment when all the good that I had known in the therapeutic process really had planted itself in the outer reality of my life. I haven't stopped writing since.

Then quite naturally and gradually it became obvious that my psychotherapy appointments were no longer needed and my psychotherapy was complete. I could go on using the insights I had gained because they were part of me. And even now that my psychotherapy has finished, my memories of earlier life seem to go on resolving themselves in satisfying ways and I find myself grateful for the continu-ation of the process within me. Finally, it has felt like a satisfying definition of my psychotherapy to be invited to write this case history about my experience.

Chapter 5

The shadow side of loving kindness

In this chapter I will reflect upon some of the darker experiences of clients and psychotherapists and how loving kindness can assist with these aspects of the work. If, as I have argued, loving kindness in psychotherapy is evident when a client feels witnessed and cared about through the actions of the psychotherapist, it follows that the person of the psychotherapist is a key instrument in the work being done. That work must inevitably include the capability to meet the more challenging aspects of human experience.

Rogers (1967: 39–43) suggested that 'the therapeutic relationship is only a special instance of interpersonal relationships in general'. He cited a study by Whitehorn and Betz (1954) which examined the effectiveness of young resident physicians working with schizophrenic patients on a psychiatric ward. The study found that the physicians who were able to be the most helpful in their inter-actions with patients were those who made use of active personal participation. They were much more likely to develop a relationship in which the patient felt trust and confidence in the physician. In the conclusions he drew from this study, Rogers stated: 'I suspect that similar facts would be found in a research study of almost any class of helping relationship'. And yet he had referred to 'a spe-cial instance of interpersonal relationships in general'. It is this 'special instance' which requires further examination in the setting of psychotherapy. After all, the psychotherapist is taking on a responsibility with additional challenges, when seeking to develop relationships with persons who have experienced significant damage to their sense of self. The therapeutic relationship which evolves between client and psychotherapist, especially in these circumstances, cannot therefore be simply contained within a category of 'interpersonal relationships in general', because of the challenges presented and the ethical accountability due to profes-sional relationships of this sort.

Loving kindness in psychotherapy has to be robust enough to encounter not only the potential disturbance of persons who have experienced emotional and physical trauma but must also be able to know about and confront the shadow aspects of the psychotherapist's own experience. It is not realistic for the psycho-therapist to attempt to occupy some kind of psychological and emotional high ground, as this place cannot authentically be occupied by any person. It is only as

DOI: 10.4324/9781003262114-6

a fallible human being—albeit one with a sound background in personal psychotherapy, training and consistent supervision—that a psychotherapist can function
effectively. And without active experience and acknowledgement of one's own
shadow, the inherent hazards of psychotherapy, for both client and psychotherapist, will be encountered without protection. Jung (CW11) recognised this when
he reflected, in somewhat colourful prose, upon the possibility he might discover
that he was 'the least amongst them all, the poorest of all beggars, the most impu-
dent of all offenders, yea the very fiend himself—that these are within me, and
that I myself stand in need of the alms of my own kindness, that I myself am the
enemy who must be loved'.

Jung viewed the shadow as a split-off part of a person, but one which at the
same time remains closely attached. In his description, the development of the
shadow 'runs parallel to that of the ego'. He explained how any attributes which
are not deemed useful to the ego are put to one side or repressed. Thus, the shadow
is never fully raised to conscious awareness as the ego goes about its task of maintaining the workings of everyday existence. However, Jung illuminated the way
in which psychological and emotional health depends upon our acknowledgement
of the existence of the shadow, because it can conceal attributes which are useful
to our conscious awareness and our ability to relate to others. These may include
positive qualities not yet realised or developed. Equally, they may include negative attributes, attitudes and prejudices which, if not acknowledged consciously,
may disturb thought and action to a far greater degree than they would if allowed
to enter conscious awareness. Assisting clients in developing a more collaborative relationship with their shadow side is a central function of psychodynamic
psychotherapy. And an example of the tenacity of the shadow in unconscious life
is given in Chapter 7, in the discussion about denial of mortality; where it can
be seen that even this topic can be accommodated more straightforwardly once
allowed into the conscious domain of open conversation. Jung (in Jacobi, 1973:
109–111) illustrated how the most important aspects of the shadow can thus be
correlated with the ego, leading to a stronger and more vital sense of self when
important features of awareness are no longer hidden in the darkness. He distinguished between two different forms of shadow. First, the personal shadow and
second, the collective shadow which he believed '. . . belongs together with the
other figures of the collective unconscious and corresponds to a negative expression of the 'Old Wise Man' or the dark aspect of the Self. It symbolises, as it
were, the 'back' of the prevailing *Zeitgeist*, its hidden antithesis. Both forms of
the shadow are operative in the human psyche'. Examples of these manifestations
of the shadow are provided in the two case studies which follow in this chapter.

Even where there is acknowledgement of the shadow's existence, the darker
side of psychotherapeutic work should be approached with caution and utmost
respect. It is to be expected that some of the most challenging work undertaken
by psychotherapists will concern persons who have sustained extensive injury
to both their early development and their adult life. So it is necessary, in this
chapter, to discuss some of the more sombre client experiences to be encountered

in psychotherapy practice and the considerable impact that these aspects of the work can have upon the psychotherapist. These experiences emphasise the need for the practitioner to know his or her own shadow side, in depth, in order to avoid an unconscious and unhelpful merger with difficult and potentially dangerous processes.

The shadow of narcissistic injury

I will now discuss the shadow experiences of clients where traumatic emotional and psychological experiences have caused a narcissistic injury, damaging their personal defences and sense of self-worth. Mollon (1993) has observed that the kind of damage which leads to narcissism is suffered very early, causing a profound sense of betrayal, just when the idea of the 'other' is forming. Thus, the concept of the 'other' inevitably becomes terrifying and not to be trusted. In consequence, Stiffell and Holtom (2016: 37–51) observe that the early nature of the damage and mistrust of others makes narcissism one of the most difficult disorders to work with. Persons with these difficulties can make such an impact upon the therapist that it sometimes feels almost impossible to retain an empathic stance. But it is vital to remember that they are in desperate need of therapeutic help, and with patient persistence, awareness of the other can be brought to life and some healing achieved. However, the potential cost to the therapist should not be disregarded, because the intensity of the interpersonal field in these cases is immense. Added to a propensity for somatic enactment 'the struggle can *in extremis* feel like a matter of life and death for both patient and therapist'.

Persons with narcissistic difficulties are not alone in evoking negative feelings in the psychotherapy arena. But Stiffell and Holtom make important observations about the need for psychotherapists to be especially alert to the shadows which emerge when deep work is engaged with narcissistic processes. They make particular reference to the obstacles which can beset the work, arising from the particular way in which a narcissistic client may perceive the other person in the room. A common perception of narcissism concerns the level of disregard a person with these difficulties has for others. As with Narcissus, his only object of attention seems to be his own reflection. And yet the narcissist seems to seek relatedness, but only by making seductive efforts to attract others into collusion with his needs. They state that this attitude represents a major division in the understanding of narcissistic processes: 'with the classical disregard of others being replaced by a seductive drive for their subversion'. By employing the classical myth of the sirens in which the beauty of their song lured sailors to forget their own lives and ultimately fall to their destruction, they propose that a similarly seductive lure represents the potential pitfalls of the countertransference. Such presentations have previously been thought of as movement along an axis of grandiosity, but they now propose that the concept of narcissism 'is best broadened into a two-dimensional space where a second axis defines the degree of seduction employed'.

Thus, it becomes evident that these are situations where it is especially important for the psychotherapist to avoid any symbiotic merger with the client. Where a psychotherapist has not sufficiently explored his or her own internal psychological world, vulnerability to the seductive siren call of the narcissist will be much more likely to be activated. And, at the same time, it is equally important to maintain a respectful and, wherever possible, an emotionally inclusive approach. This dichotomy presents one of the most difficult balances to achieve and to maintain in the psychotherapy relationship, especially as narcissistic behaviour in the consulting room, as elsewhere, can arouse feelings of revulsion which represent the hidden, inner world of self-loathing usually experienced by persons with these difficulties. This is why the psychotherapy trainee is required to explore the internal world of the mind in personal psychotherapy, as though it were a territory rather like that illustrated in medieval maps, showing metaphorical dragons, sea monsters and other mythological creatures representing the dangers that may be found in unexplored territories. But, perhaps surprisingly, that which is found in the shadows may also include talents and capabilities which have unconsciously been hidden or inhibited by fear of attack. Nonetheless, those shadows which are left unexplored will intensify and return in a potent and negative way, distorted by having been denied and thus gaining force. In the consulting room, the psychotherapy relationship inevitably becomes the place where such unconscious re-enactment can emerge. For example, compliments and even flattery expressed by a client may be more likely to be believed as a reflection of the psychotherapist's ego, where the psychotherapist has not sufficiently explored and questioned his or her own self-image, the substance of its foundations and the possibility of unconscious motives behind the flattery. This may lead directly into a trap of collusion which can disempower or even destroy the work being attempted.

Stiffell and Holtom were drawn to their study by reflecting on their experiences of narcissism in the consulting room. This led them to consider the fate of Echo, 'the poor disregarded worshipper of Narcissus, who gave him everything she had'. She could only repeat his words and her own qualities were rejected by him, so she wasted away, having had no independent existence. They compare this with the fate of well-intended psychotherapy with such patients. They comment on the chaos which surrounds the narcissistic personality and its dissonance with the presentation of self-assurance and aloof disregard for others which, paradoxically, seems to attract faithful admirers; observing that it is not surprising that 'the narcissistic person would crave that admiration but it is not obvious what makes many of those who come into contact with them fall into compliance with that need'. To understand how this can come about it is useful to consider the function of narcissism as a 'defensive use of the self as a primary love object' (Freud, 1905), because for the person with narcissistic difficulties, the concept of another person can seem to represent a life or death threat. On the other hand, the central function of the psychotherapeutic encounter is that of seeking to establish a relationship with another person. So it follows that this has to be approached differently in the shadowy territory of narcissism, with careful regard for the emotional and psychological safety of both psychotherapist and client. The support of clients with these difficulties has to be held within a container of reasonable emotional reserve, capable of resisting the attempted seduction. A considerable level of psychotherapeutic alertness is also necessary, because the whole defence of the siren is based on: 'intense watchfulness and immediate correction of the smallest departure of the satellite object from its orbit to avoid its escape or catastrophic impact. The siren must be constantly active to maintain the desired situation. The actions of the therapist, even when he has understood the dynamics of his own entrapment, directly feed into what is normal for the siren who will counter every move' (Stiffell & Holtom, 2016: 50).

They observe that the seductive insistence of the siren has the purpose of drawing in those who will offer continual admiration. The signals can be quite subtle but it is very important to be able to recognise them and to be quick in doing so, when formulating an appropriate response. An example might be the client's offer of soulful, lingering eye contact, which in fact engenders a creepy, unpleasant sensation in the psychotherapist, rather than the warm response experienced with other clients. It could be very easy in these circumstances to be drawn into offering a warm empathic response with the intention of giving support when, more authentically, it feels as though the client is presenting an invitation with a mixed message and a hidden agenda. For the psychotherapist to override or deny his or her authentic feeling would be to collude with the client's prior experience of betrayal and mistrust in relationship, whereas the better alternative would be to maintain a reflective and respectful distance from the seduction. In situations like this, the inner conflict and sense of unease felt by the psychotherapist will be amplified when incongruous signals are given by the client in response to reciprocal feedback: such as a false, even contemptuous, smile or an inability to remember any of the contents of previous sessions, or even things said earlier in the same session. Difficulty remembering the contents of previous encounters in the psychotherapy dialogue can signify an absence of emotional memory and a hostility to feelings, as a consequence of damaging experiences in the client's early childhood. He or she may have good intellectual capacity but may not have developed a memorable sense of emotional safety, wherein good experiences were recognised and stored for future reference and reassurance in the client's relational life. Thus, the negative impact of past experiences may be that of maintaining an emotional distance from the psychotherapist by resisting the development of a genuine therapeutic alliance. As a consequence of this Stiffell and Holtom observe that:

> In the countertransference, the therapist can feel marginalised, inadequate or idealized in turn, never sure what role they are being cast into; feeling drawn in, flattered and inflated, and for a while thinking they are doing a rather fine piece of work before coming to feel the loathing and the contempt for their pathetically inadequate capabilities. The therapist has to be able to hold their ground, firmly tied to the mast; it is so easy to collude, to be pulled into the drama. They will be helped by good supervisors who will hold them more firmly.
>
> (ibid., 43)

Given damaging early life experiences, it is inevitable that the unconscious contempt communicated to the psychotherapist is the same as that which the client feels towards others outside the psychotherapy; whilst at the same time possibly believing that he or she is a liberal, inclusive and tolerant person. This will account for breakdowns in relationship which have occurred prior to the psychotherapy. Awareness of the root cause of the psychotherapist's negative countertransference, as a response to this contempt, can assist in the formulation of appropriate responses, by not reciprocating the seductive gaze, and by recognising that the revulsion experienced probably represents the client's own denied feelings about himself, despite what his intellect believes. The narcissistic defence is an attempt to cover up a deep sense of self-loathing and disgust, the siren call of his gaze being an invitation to collude with the narcissistic 'love' of himself only as an object, instead of letting the psychotherapist see him as a wounded human being who, like any other, could potentially be worthy of love.

So the psychotherapist who has, without awareness, accepted flattery will risk entering into an unintended, unconscious contract which, in the belief of the narcissistic client, must not then be broken. As a consequence, it becomes extremely difficult to retreat from such a powerfully implied agreement. This will become obvious when the psychotherapist's feedback becomes less susceptible to the flattery, because more challenging professional responses are required in order for the work to progress. To the person with narcissistic difficulties such a change of tone, however subtle, will be perceived as deeply threatening. And inevitably, when working with the phenomenon of the narcissistic siren, it is noticeable that a client with these difficulties will take up more resources of energy than any other client and possibly more than a whole caseload, or so it feels at the time. Indeed, Stiffell and Holtom provide an example where the impact of an imagined slight by the therapist triggered such an aggressive and sustained reaction from the client that the therapist became ill, only recovering when it became clear to her that her illness might be related to her patient and her own unconscious collusion with the attacks upon her.

This issue invokes important aspects of decision making and ethical concerns in the clinical practice of psychotherapy, in both conscious and unconscious processes. One of its skills, and also one of its dilemmas, lies in the nature of interpretation of the client's unconscious experience. Unconscious processes are, by their nature, hidden from the conscious awareness of the client, but this does not mean that they are invisible to an external observer. A comical analogy might be that of a wearer of glasses who believes they are missing, when at the same time an observer can see they are being worn by the owner. Thus, unconscious processes provide the potential for an acute dissonance between the experience of the client and the experience of the psychotherapist, as they raise the question of whose reality takes precedence. Or, to use a contemporary phrase, we might ask if the interpretation offered by the psychotherapist concerning the inner experience of another person is 'fake news'. It is an essential question to be considered when working at depth with the unconscious processes of the client experience and, even more importantly, when it comes to sharing psycho-therapeutic interpretations.

This debate was opened up by Winnicott (1960: 140–152), who believed there was a need to move away from a more classical interpretive style towards what he described as a facilitating environment. He suggested that in the parallel example of healthy child development the mother needed to be present, 'but not as the other or at least not in more than a rudimentary sense'. On this view, the mother reflected the responses of the infant and did not impinge upon any sense of 'otherness'. Winnicott's 'good enough mother' was resilient, maintaining a balance: 'between her steady and firm holding in the face of love and hatred, whilst retaining the non-impingement which is so essential for the baby's development'. This created a secure foundation of good experience through which basic trust was established. What then followed would be a process of 'separating out and differentiating from the primary state of oneness'. He proposed that the survival of the hated object and its consequent recognition allowed a 'loving and mutative relationship to develop'. His use of the word survival meant that the mother stayed more or less the same and did not retaliate by rejection or punishment (Winnicott, 1969: 711–716). He applied this model to the therapeutic relationship.

This model seems to be a good fit with the experience of working with the symbiotically merged client, who may not be able to hear and receive interpretative feedback because it will seem to clash with the imagined and hoped-for experience of being one and the same as the psychotherapist. However, and importantly in a state of symbiosis, there comes a time for this to be challenged if the client is to develop the personal agency which will allow him or her eventually to become psychologically and emotionally independent. Therefore, a challenge to the symbiosis offers the potential for an important turning point in the therapy. In another case example given by Stiffell and Holtom (2016: 48), the therapist had initially followed Winnicott's approach and offered 'quiet containment, making no challenge to the grandiosity of the patient's position. This gave full scope to the patient to patronize and become increasingly inflated with the success of his domination of the therapist, who seemed to have nothing to say'. But they cite the alternative approach of Kernberg (1975), who believed that narcissistic illusions have:

> a pernicious effect upon the psychoanalytic treatment. Based upon delusions of the self-sufficiency and perfection of the grandiose self, they undercut the very basis on which the analytic process rests; the presumption that the patient may gain something meaningful from someone else. Therefore, he urges a persistent interpretation of the defensive function of grandiosity and idealization as they emerge in the transference. He considers everything else a waste of time since the narcissistic illusions systematically destroy the ground on which the treatment proceeds.
>
> (ibid.)

Thus, he proposed that the 'analyst must continuously focus on the particular quality of the transference in these cases and consistently counteract the patient's efforts towards omnipotent control and devaluation'. In this case, the therapist realised the extent to which he had been undermined, and that the feeling he was being destroyed was a direct consequence of his 'enslavement by the patient'. By employing the insights illustrated by Kernberg, he found enough courage to change the nature of the therapy. Initially, this provoked expressions of murderous rage by his client. But by consistently applying his therapeutic interpretation of what was happening, he enabled his client to become calmer, more thoughtful and reflective. Some easing of his client's condition was achieved, as the therapist's presence was brought to life.

Acquaintance with the shadow aspects of the psychotherapist's own experience provides a necessary ground of preparation, from which the practitioner may accompany a client into the territory of his or her own shadows, but not be consumed by them. In the case cited here, the therapist was withholding valuable and powerful qualities of insight which needed to be brought into the light in order for him to work more effectively. I like to think of a metaphor of the client at risk of being carried along by the current in a river, but being held onto by the therapist, who is always keeping one foot on the river bank, with the supervisor standing not far away. But addressing issues of this kind can seem, from a client's point of view, to be the exact opposite of loving kindness. It doesn't *feel* kind, if the psychotherapist will not jump into the deep water of the client's experience and indeed may feel positively cruel. It may even feel injurious, and in a sense it is injurious towards outdated and unhelpful ways of behaving, such as the clinging symbiotic relationship which draws authentic life energy away from a satisfying and creative existence and which has to be given up if life is to be lived in full. The narcissistic perspective, by its nature, can never include others and yet it represents the often desperate desire to relate to others which hides in the narcissistic shadows.

Loving kindness and the shadow of trauma

At the same time it is vital, wherever possible, not to increase the sense of injury which a client has already experienced in life. This is particularly important where the client has been subjected to significant trauma prior to therapy. In these situations, the question of 'separating out and differentiating from the primary relational state of oneness', often needs to be held back until the prior consideration of past trauma has at least to some extent been resolved. Post-traumatic effects have distinctive and potentially devastating impacts upon the body and the mind and may arise from assaults upon any or all of physical, emotional, sexual, psychological or spiritual aspects. However, the central and dominant risk factor common to all of these assaults is relational, arising from the betrayal of basic trust and loss of personal safety. Emotional safety therefore relies upon consistent feelings of trust, essential to a sense of survival in the human world and based upon the core belief that we will be protected from harm.

Gerhardt (2015: 168–169) observed that the notion of abuse has historically been associated with obvious physical maltreatment or sexual violation. It has been more difficult to appreciate that being left unattended and alone or subjected to demeaning comments are, in a child's experience, equally traumatic from an emotional and psychological perspective. 'The essential aspect of trauma is that it generates doubts about surviving—either as a body, but equally as a psychological self'. For example, one of my adult clients became able to link the source of a panic attack with a childhood event at a play venue, where his dad had booked a boat ride for him and his brother. Being only small he was not completely alert to joining the queue at the right moment, only to discover that his father and rather grumpy older brother had gone on the boat ride without him. This left him on his own; trying to figure out where they had gone, not knowing if they would come back, and acutely aware that they were angry with him, but not sure why. This was part of a pattern of emotional trauma which stood out painfully in my client's mind. The panic attack in adulthood was triggered by a work colleague mentioning that he had been on a similar boat ride. My client was able to soothe himself when he realised what had triggered the panic attack and to consolidate the soothing by telling me about the experience at our next session. An event which had been held in memory was now able to be discussed out in the open, with all of the understandable attendant feelings acknowledged.

Bancroft and Patrissi (2011: 60) conclude that at the heart of trauma 'is a sense of complete helplessness combined with feeling abandoned by those who could or should have protected him or her'. Additionally, the survivor may have no verbal capacity or coherent memory with which to express the impact of the initial trauma. Consequently, encouragement to talk about it too early in the therapeutic process could risk retraumatisation, due to the way in which the brain processes such experiences. Incapacity to verbalise trauma in post-traumatic stress disorder (PTSD) has a neurological basis. The parts of the brain which perform a primary role in the processing of memory, decision making and emotional responses such as fear, anxiety and aggression, store traumatic memories at an unconscious level which is not flexible to change. This is an adaptation which has evolved as a protective mechanism enabling the brain to respond to the remembered threat in future. Later evolutionary development has added the more rational, conscious ability to evaluate situations, update information, anticipate outcomes and verbalise experiences (Gerhardt, 2015: 166–167). These capabilities allow the subject to assess situations from both personal and shared points of view, thus widening perspectives and minimising polarised 'black and white' thinking. It is therefore vital in psychotherapeutic work with persons who have been traumatised, to gauge the most appropriate pace and extent of intervention, as these two essential aspects of brain function are becoming integrated. This can be a lengthy but very rewarding process, as illustrated in the case studies provided later in this chapter.

In PTSD there is a problem integrating traumatic experience with verbal memory. Rauch and his colleagues (1996) discovered, through observation using PET brain scans, that the brains of persons who had experienced trauma reacted in a particular way when their traumatic memories were activated by hearing their own taped account of what had happened to them. They found that blood flow decreased in the parts of the left brain concerned with verbal organising, and increased in the areas of the right brain where emotions, sense of smell and visual images were activated. This stimulated a disconnect between the two functions, causing an inability to make sense of the experience or render it into speech and coherent, narrative order. As Gerhardt (2015: 167) observes: 'This may account for the phenomenon of speechless terror—that awful moment when you are confronted with something so overwhelming that you just squeak or can't get any words out at all'. Left brain activity would normally put experiences into a context and into a time sequence. But without its involvement, traumatised feelings cannot be placed in the past, thus seeming to be ever present. This is what is known as the flashback state, which presents the subject with a fragmented jumble of memory which has not been adequately processed.

It therefore makes complete sense that therapeutic dialogue, set at the individual pace of the client, presents a constructive path towards the necessary integration of thinking, verbalising, feeling and memory, which can then be called upon in a meaningful way and put into words, as in my client's account of his childhood memory of the missed boat ride. This allowed the distressed feelings of a childhood experience to be accommodated and fully acknowledged as proportionate to the situation in which he was placed and over which he had no control. The adult brain can be capable, with support, of responding robustly to stressful situations, painful though these may be. But the infant brain and body are still in the process of development and are therefore much more vulnerable. Infants have not yet acquired adult resources and cannot survive on their own. Their dependency on adult carers is necessary until they arrive at a sufficient level of physical, emotional and cognitive development to help them encounter the challenges of adult life. So the infant brain is aware that without the care of adults there is risk, which is why, in the early years, children experience distress when their carer goes out of sight. Thus, the imprint of trauma at this point occurs at the most important stage of brain development, when the capacity to experience feelings and to be soothed when distressed would, within a secure attachment, assist the development of trusted emotional memory. Clients with a history of early trauma will have missed opportunities to develop these capabilities and, consequently, they may not initially be able to cope with very much verbal interaction, because they cannot experience feelings safely or put them into words. They may show resistance to feedback and interpretation of their experiences, which could be perceived as an attack upon them, because they cannot relate to what is being said. So what matters therapeutically, right from the start, is the establishment of a trusted and heartfelt relationship, within which feelings can gradually be experienced, identified and integrated.

The therapeutic relationship with a client who has experienced trauma may require long silences to be held and may rely upon non-verbal cues, as well as verbal dialogue, in order to gently build up a shared language between client and psychotherapist. This is illustrated in the case study of Amanda in Chapter 1. Westland describes the embodied context within which this happens:

> When psychotherapists notice both their own and the client's verbal and non-verbal communication, fuller communication is going on. . . .
>
> Verbal and non-verbal communication are usually defined in polar opposition to each other, but they are closely enmeshed. . . . Cognitive psychologists describe verbal and non-verbal communication as explicit and implicit communication. Explicit communication is conveyed in spoken language, whereas implicit communication is conveyed physically and not symbolised in words. Non-verbal communication includes the way in which verbal messages are delivered, but it goes far beyond this and includes a wide range of communications expressed by the body. Messages are carried in postures and movements . . ., gestures, facial expressions . . ., self and other touching, gazing, and personal mannerisms. Non-verbal communication includes changes in breathing . . ., changes in skin colour and hue . . ., and involuntary movements such as shivering with cold, fatigue, or fear.
>
> (Westland, 2015: 2–3)

She observes that because the body is essential to non-verbal communication, being able to see clients is usually essential in order to read the emotions being expressed and respond to them. This said, it can sometimes be surprising to find just how much is communicated during a telephone session, by attending to the tone of voice, the intervals and the speed at which a person communicates. 'Spoken words—verbal communication—provide information and content, but the way the words are spoken carries their emotional meaning. This background communication of emotions non-verbally is called paralanguage . . . such as ums, ahs, sniffs, sighs. . . . These sounds convey emotions in their intonation, pitch, and rhythms' (ibid).

By building up a psychotherapeutic conversation of this kind, a relationship of trust can be established and embodied. Trevarthen (1999) observed that the brain: 'coordinates rhythmic body movements and guides them to act in sympathy with other people's brains'. This function is derived from mirror neurons, specialised cells in the cerebral cortex, which provide the brain-to-brain links between infant and carer and between client and psychotherapist, providing the capacity for empathy and attunement (van der Kolk, 2015: 58–59). Thus, Gerhardt (2015: 237) has described how the establishment of a psychotherapeutic relationship helps people progress towards the development of 'a portable regulation system that can be used with other people to maintain mental wellbeing'. These functional aspects of the therapeutic relationship are based upon the fact that it is established solely for therapeutic purposes. It is not a personal friendship in the usual sense of the word, although it does incorporate some of those characteristics. Helping clients to recognise the difference and remembering it professionally are central, ethical features of loving kindness in psychotherapy.

For clients who are recovering from trauma, the psychotherapy relationship offers opportunities to try out different ways of being with others. This encourages the development of new approaches to relating which change habits of behaviour and feeling. Prior assumptions about other people can be challenged, and this supports the healthy development of emotional discrimination between that which is nourishing and that which may need to be avoided. This process will initially trigger old habitual responses which are laid down in existing neural networks. But with therapeutic assistance, new ways of responding to activations of this sort begin to replace reactive habits and assumptions. This process is not always easy for the client or the psychotherapist, as illustrated in the case study of Gemma in Chapter 3, when she believed for a while that the new emotional experiences were posing a threat to her health. It was only through her continuing participation in the psychotherapy process that she became able gradually to move forward into more satisfying and secure experiences of relating to others. Thus, her feelings were allowed more room, having been accepted within the boundaries of the therapeutic relationship. She became able to enjoy novel experiences of comfort and pleasure, replacing the state of fear and apprehension with which she had lived for so long.

Once this stage of psychotherapy has been reached, it becomes possible to review the prior events of a lifetime with greater equanimity and compassion. Memories of unresolved wounding, fears of loss and experiences of legitimate anger can now be accommodated without the client feeling overwhelmed. And conflicting views and experiences in the therapeutic relationship can be encountered without it breaking down, as Gemma discovered. This part of the psychotherapy process is essential because it demonstrates the capacity to face differences of opinion and conflict, knowing that these can be resolved and repaired. Repetition of these encounters gradually consolidates the new experiences, both personally and neurologically, as the capacity to be heard and to listen deepens and becomes habitual.

But given the nature of the impact of trauma, it can take a while for a traumatised client to even begin to engage in psychotherapy. This is due to the layers of psychological defence which have necessarily built up, sometimes over many years and in some cases—as I shall discuss in the following case history—for generations in one family, where trauma has itself been held within a collective shadow. As discussed earlier, people who have experienced trauma have difficulty integrating those experiences into coherent memory. Part of the way the brain attempts to make the trauma psychologically survivable is by splitting off such overwhelming experiences from each other and from a coherent sense of personal identity. As van der Kolk has stated:

> Dissociation is the essence of trauma. The overwhelming experience is split off and fragmented, so that the emotions, sounds, images, thoughts, and physical sensations related to the trauma take on a life of their own. The sensory fragments of memory intrude into the present, where they are literally

relived. As long as the trauma is not resolved, the stress hormones that the body secretes to protect itself keep circulating, and the defensive movements and emotional responses keep getting replayed. . . . They have no idea why they respond to some minor irritation as if they were about to be annihilated.

Flashbacks and reliving are in some ways worse than the trauma itself. A traumatic event has a beginning and an end—at some point it is over. But for people with PTSD a flashback can occur at any time, whether they are awake or asleep. There is no way of knowing when it's going to occur again or how long it will last. People who suffer from flashbacks often organise their lives around trying to protect against them. They may compulsively go to the gym to pump iron . . ., numb themselves with drugs, or try to cultivate an illusory sense of control in highly dangerous situations (like motorcycle racing, bungee jumping, or working as an ambulance driver). Constantly fighting unseen dangers is exhausting and leaves them fatigued, depressed, and weary.

(van der Kolk, 2015: 66–67)

Over an extended period, and without treatment, traumatic memories become embedded more deeply in the mind, creating long-term habits of thought and feeling as well as assumptions about the world as experienced by the traumatised person. Consequently:

Ordinary, day-to-day events become less and less compelling. Not being able to deeply take in what is going on around them makes it impossible to feel fully alive. It becomes harder to feel the joys and aggravations of ordinary life, harder to concentrate on the tasks at hand. Not being fully alive in the present keeps them more firmly imprisoned in the past.

(ibid.)

In some cases, clients may be struggling to resolve traumatic difficulties which have been repeated throughout the generations. Their internal working model could partly have been inherited through certain kinds of cultural expectation about what is right and good, whilst having been damaging all along. Thus, Jung (CW8) stated that individual consciousness is subject not only to the influences imposed by the immediate environment but also to those which are predetermined within a collective unconscious, which comprises the psychic life of our ancestors from its earliest origins. He asserted that this is 'the matrix of all conscious occurrences, and hence it exerts an influence that compromises the freedom of consciousness in the highest degree since it is continually striving to lead all conscious processes back into the old paths'. On this view, that which is held within the family shadow and not brought to conscious awareness continues to exert a powerful influence upon the later generations of a family, if left unchallenged. This is demonstrated in the following case study.

Case study of Olivia

Olivia came to see me during the mediation process arising from divorce proceedings in her second marriage. Her husband was highly motivated to continue their marriage, whereas she was much more ambivalent. When we began our work together, they were continuing to attend mediation sessions as a couple. Olivia had left the family home, taking her young children with her, following a long period of discord, including serious domestic violence against her. This included life-threatening actions and repeated coercive behaviour, much of which had been seen by her children. At the same time, Olivia loved her husband and was reluctant to leave him. She left when the local authority advised her that, unless she did so, her children would be removed from her care. She and the children left in secret and moved away to a new home.

When I first met Olivia she was in a state of acute fear, experiencing feelings of confusion about what to do next. She and her children sorely missed their home and their friends, who were now more than a hundred miles away. The initial stages of work with Olivia, as with any severely traumatised client, consisted of listening quietly and carefully whilst offering a kind, affirming and supportive presence, making every effort to avoid any actions or words which might, unintentionally, add to her experience of injury. Initially, she was experiencing what can be described as 'inescapable shock' (van der Kolk, 2015: 265), where the sensory experience of living in her body felt shattered and helpless. So the most important function at this point was that of encouraging her to gain at least a minimal sense of feeling grounded and present in the moment. This was extremely difficult for her, and I recall how she would throughout the sessions continually look at the clock, as if she were waiting to spring forward, ready to flee. The basic requirements for psychotherapy to thrive are at a premium when working with acute trauma. These include the consistent weekly appointment and an unambiguous understanding of when that appointment will be, as well as clear communication which does not make demands upon the client, initially even to relax, as to suggest this might draw unwanted attention to the client's difficulty in doing so. All that the psychotherapist can do at this stage is to be present, grounded, fully attentive and compassionate, without judgement. Westland (2015: 72) notices how this enables us to be aware of our own experiences, whilst making: 'heartfelt, unobtrusive, observations of clients . . . staying subjectively engaged, in a kind way'. This subjective engagement offers an initial level of emotional regulation which is outside the client's conscious awareness.

I was very aware, during the early stages of working with Olivia, that she needed plenty of space to tell me, in her own time, what had happened. I felt instinctively that I should stay well back without intervening directly, as one might do when trying to help a wounded and terrified animal. Olivia was able to give a clear account and her thoughts were in good order. She had a capable and thoughtful mind, having previously enjoyed prize-winning success as a film photographer. What had been severely damaged was her sense of self as a worthwhile person, who could own and be proud of her previous achievements and her capabilities as a mother. She had been made to feel that she had no right to any self-esteem and that, somehow, she was at risk by demonstrating who she was. Thus, she had sustained a profound moral injury which, along with the physical and verbal attacks which had been made upon her, made her feel unsafe in the world.

As our work progressed and trust built up between us, more dialogue and exploration became possible. Olivia became more able to face the terrible dilemma of still loving her husband but realising that he had not changed and that, if she returned to him, the cycle of bullying and abuse would begin once again. This began a long and painful process for her, first of all by recognising the extent of the trauma she had experienced, then gradually realising that she could influence the future events of her life and protect herself from harm. Separation from her husband was emotionally distressing, and he made efforts to persuade her to return. Difficult divorce proceedings continued during which he would always deny that there had been any wrongdoing on his part. But Olivia became more able to take support and she derived benefit from both psychotherapy and good legal advice. Although she faced financial hardship and the demands of being a single parent, she began to develop some awareness that she could build the foundations of a life lived in freedom from fear. During the necessary years of psychotherapy which followed, the main task continued to be that of supporting Olivia in building those foundations.

What also emerged during that time was an understanding of the extent to which her experiences echoed a lengthy family history of trauma. That history continued along a difficult and dangerous path, until such time as Olivia gained a sense of agency in the direction of her life, where she found that she could, through her own actions, avoid harm and build a sense of security for herself. Her capacity to do so depended upon her both discovering and acknowledging that she was worthwhile and worth protecting. She found that she could be herself, without justification or apology and so the process of grounding continued. Against considerable odds, Olivia was able to secure a home for herself and her children and to attend to their needs more effectively, in their own recovery from the trauma of domestic abuse. Subsequently, they were able to succeed at school and later at university. But their emotional scars were, inevitably, long lasting, and they needed many conversations and a deepening understanding of past events, supported by Olivia's capacity for emotional honesty, to gradually come to terms with the trauma they had experienced.

An insight which emerged during this time was the extent to which Olivia had always tried to control her eating, believing that being thin would give her social distinction and advantage. Both her parents had emphasised the importance of being thin and elegant, because it seemed so essential to their view of themselves. This became Olivia's own internal working model and that of her sister. But the impact of it was one of discord and envy in her personal relationships and a need to control the ways in which cooking and eating took place in her home. This came to a head when one of her children challenged her about the way she seemed to control the table at mealtimes. They argued angrily, but the argument opened up a conversation where they gained insight and understanding of each other, instead of Olivia trying to pretend that she did not have a problem. We then talked about the way in which Olivia had tended to try to avoid food and, consequently, the table where it was served. And she came to see how she had been critical of her children's healthy appetites. Her difficulties made sense to me, as she had told me that on a previous occasion as a teenager, when alone and alienated from her parents, she had taken herself off to a sailing regatta where she linked up with some young men and tried to pretend that she was fine and enjoying herself. In fact, she was all alone and had no money. She survived for the whole weekend on one chocolate bar which she carefully ate at intervals, in small sections. She talked about a sense of pride and achievement in doing this, which amounted to a belief that she could manage without needing anything from anybody. Her young life had been full of examples of having to manage without adult support, and so she had devised a way of not seeming to have any needs and of trying to convince herself and others of this false image of self-sufficiency. Consequently, her intimate relationships had failed, one after another, because she could not rely on a foundation of trust in another person or admit to the needs which human beings have and the necessary demands they make of one another.

Perhaps inevitably, Olivia was drawn to partners who had their own vulnerabilities which were not obvious on first acquaintance. Her first marriage was a good and loving bond, but the couple had faced the painful challenge of their first child being born with substantial physical difficulties requiring neonatal intensive care. Her daughter was in hospital for six months and Olivia described the distress, which still haunted her, of spending many days at her daughter's bedside without being able to hold her or alleviate the pain of her condition and the treatment she underwent. On one occasion she asked the treating doctor whether it was humane to go on putting her daughter through this and might it not be better to let her die? He was able to support Olivia by presenting the alternative point of view, that it was worthwhile and her daughter would be able to come through it, which she did. But the anguish of this experience remained with Olivia, compounding her sense of moral injury, in the belief that somehow she should have been able to prevent her daughter from being hurt in this way. And the effect of the cumulative stresses the couple experienced in this situation made an impact which affected her husband in the form of heavy drinking. As a teenager he had experienced bereavement through the loss of his father, and he could not seem to find a way through the challenges presented to him now, as a father himself. The couple had a second child, but Olivia described a key moment which occurred on a day when she was tackling the usual routine of household tasks and becoming acutely aware of her husband lying intoxicated on the sofa and unable to assist. At this point she made a clear decision to go it alone, because it seemed that life would be easier if she did so. There was a great deal of love in the marriage, but it could not overcome the difficulties faced by the couple in this challenging situation. Once again Olivia found that, based upon her previous experiences, the prospect of going it alone was the one on which she felt she could rely, however difficult this might prove.

Olivia's second marriage also began with great mutual attraction and affection. It promised a home for her children, material security and initially as a family they enjoyed a comfortable life together. Olivia was aware that her second husband had himself survived experiences of abuse and neglect as a child. But she did not know that, as a consequence of this, he was capable of cold and cruel behaviour. Their relationship began to deteriorate when his daughter from a previous marriage came to live with them, and he seemed to favour her over and above Olivia's children. At the same time, he became increasingly controlling of Olivia and began to use threats and violence against her in argument. During one disturbing scene, he struck her and the children saw it happen. She was afraid for their safety and did not feel she could defend them or herself. It was circumstances like this which led to her being persuaded to leave permanently, to protect them.

Following on from this, Olivia had further experiences of relationships with charming, attractive, yet abusive men and a number of fairly superficial and unsupportive friendships, within which she was often treated with disrespect, at the same time as being viewed as a rather sparkling social asset. This repetitive habit derived from her internal working model of moral injury and shame, wherein she had come to believe not only that such neglectful treatment confirmed her lack of worth but also that she must try to keep up a convincing image of cool sophistication. It was not until she began gradually to see herself as worthwhile, and deserving of love and kind attention, that she came to realise she did not have to tolerate this and that these were not really her friends in any meaningful sense of the word. Until this point, it was as though she believed that other people and their opinions were worthy of regard, but somehow she was not worthy to receive this herself. This was noticeable when she was employed as a support worker for homeless people and came to be highly respected for her work. She was so conscientious, that she would go to any length to make sure the people she was helping had the best service possible, even though she might be going a long way beyond what her employer expected, or could provide. On several occasions she became physically ill with exhaustion and had to take absence from work, during which she said she felt guilty, even though her doctor and her employer fully supported her taking time off. Finally, during one of these breaks, she began to see that she could care for herself and did not need to have permission to do so by giving such overconscientious care to others. She also came to see that she had a great deal going for her in ordinary ways. She had a number of true friends and family members who loved and appreciated her just as she was, without her having to be thin, or dressed expensively, or possessing any kind of elevated social status.

To fully understand Olivia's repetition of this internal working model, it was necessary to consider the way in which her heroic and self-denying pattern of behaviour had been repeated through past generations of her family. Olivia's parents had both experienced traumatic childhoods within which each of them was exposed to emotional injury of various kinds. In their parenting of Olivia and her sister, they repeated, unconsciously, the same kind of emotional withholding which they had themselves experienced. On the surface, both of Olivia's parents came from successful and affluent families. Both were attractive and elegant and, in her father's professional sphere, highly regarded. He was a military hero who had been awarded considerable honours for his bravery and leadership. Olivia remembered being happy in early childhood, when both her parents enjoyed the experience of being with her and her sister, living in idyllic, remote countryside. But she also recalled being expected by her father to attempt things that were very frightening like swimming unaccompanied for long distances in deep water. Later, her parents' marriage got into difficulties, and she recalled how she would see her father at parties, which her mother had worked hard to arrange, where he was obviously conducting affairs with other women. When she was sent to boarding school, she grieved the loss of her family and her home but, when her distress became obvious, she was told emphatically by the headmistress that 'this crying really has to stop'. When she was at her second boarding school, her parents told her that they were separating and she remembered this as a cold experience, which felt lacking in understanding or acknowledgement of how she and her sister might feel. She told me that on hearing of her parents' separation, she spoke to no one about this news. She stopped eating and 'just shut down'.

Olivia's initial experience of being sent away to boarding school was particularly distressing, because her early experience of childhood had included the warmth and immediacy of her family. The experience of this separation led to considerable emotional difficulties later on. Duffell and Basset (2016) have discussed the valiant attempts made by young children to deny their acute feelings of loss and sadness on separation from their families when they board at school. They make the link between these early emotional experiences and difficulties being in touch with feelings in adulthood. Young children in these situations are placed in a bind between the grief of their separation from parents, brothers, sisters and family pets, whilst at the same time believing that their parents love and want them. Their most natural states of feeling will inevitably be those of bewilderment, anger, loneliness and perhaps a sense of betrayal. But Duffell and Basset point out that at boarding school expression of these feelings is not encouraged because 'it is believed to upset and tire the child. Nor do they want to worry their customers, the parents'.

> The theory is that in the first weeks, while the child is in what is called the 'settling-in period', contact with home is inadvisable because it would upset all parties. Homesickness is seen as something that children will naturally get over; the aim is to encourage children to be self-reliant and used to what is called 'community life'.
>
> Amongst their peers, children may also discover an explicit or implicit prohibition on sharing feelings. While apparent weakness may be frowned

upon, other children do not want to see evidence of the feelings that they themselves are desperately trying to hide.

(Duffell & Basset, 2016: 32–33)

Thus, they comment that when ex-boarders present as clients, psychotherapists should not be surprised if they have serious problems with feelings. These can present as dismissal, stoicism and denial, or despising their expression by other people. There will be difficulties sharing spontaneous and authentic feelings with others and inhibition or mistrust in forming close relationships. Sometimes they will believe that they have too many feelings, imagining that 'they are sitting on an emotional volcano' fearing that if they once start to express themselves there may be no way of stopping.

> I have observed the pain in the child and indeed the parent, when that moment finally comes that each say farewell in a hallway, by the car or in a dormitory. Some don't touch, embrace or find words to say farewell, but turn away and 'don't look back'; others occasionally collapse. In some ways, it has echoes of when a child is placed in care and the struggle for child and parent to separate in such tragic circumstances. (Anonymous school counsellor).

(ibid.)

On being sent away to school, Olivia's sense of having some security within her family was damaged by the disconnection from her home and she had no alternative but to try and adapt as far as possible. When later the news came of her parents' separation, she had few resources and no support to help her deal with this blow. All she could do was shut down her feelings.

The inability of Olivia's parents to support her in her distress repeated some of the emotional themes of their own childhoods. Olivia's paternal grandfather had committed suicide, following a military catastrophe which led to the loss of many lives and through which he sustained the moral injury of self-blame, which he could not resolve. At around the same time Olivia's father, as a young boy, had also experienced the loss of his younger sister who died following a collision with a car. He had been holding his sister's hand before this happened and was responsible for looking after her. He took the blame for this accident onto himself and thus experienced his own moral injury. In adult life, he went on to a very successful military career but, during major combat, he witnessed the bombing and sinking of ships commanded by his friends, with huge loss of life of the young men under their command, many of them still teenagers. He was in command of the guns on his ship which shot down enemy aircraft, injuring and killing a number of young pilots. Whilst he was awarded for his bravery and leadership, it seems that the trauma caused by what he had witnessed was not expressed, remaining concealed behind a heroic exterior and without full acknowledgement of the complexities and shared culpability of human, political and military actions in conflict and war.

Olivia's mother was an emotionally vulnerable woman who had experienced levels of neglect and abuse in her early childhood, so severe that she and her sister were removed from their parents. Her sister was then 'given away' and she lost contact with her. Her father was another military hero, a charming but frightening man who would perform dangerous aerobatic feats, such as flying under bridges, and who was a domestic bully at home. Despite such traumatic early experiences, Olivia's mother managed to develop a successful career as an artist, but this was abandoned when she married Olivia's father. Olivia described her parents as a 'gorgeous couple' when they married and when they were young parents. But their marriage later got into difficulties, and her mother became addicted to alcohol and was later injured in a car accident, causing permanent neurological damage. Olivia would often comment that sadly, in some way, this allowed her mother finally to receive the permanent care she needed, both physically and emotionally.

There seems to have been little open acknowledgement of the trauma and neglect held within the family heritage of Olivia's parents. Within their cultural background, it was important to maintain an image which was believed to provide social status and success, but the price paid for this was the avoidance of feelings. The cost of winning the prize of success had repeatedly been that of suppressing the painful emotional realities which continued to afflict the family through the generations. Their traumatic experiences could not be owned and therefore could not be helped. And distressing events seemed to repeat themselves at random, as if from nowhere. But the common unifying thread was that of denying feelings and their importance in developing awareness and emotional capability in the world of ordinary human life, so that future harm might be avoided and feelings enjoyed. Olivia and her sister experienced a situation in which they knew things had gone terribly wrong for their parents, but as no one was talking about it, they could not fully understand what was happening to them. Both parents and children must have been in great pain but unable to share their feelings or support each other. By contrast, when children are able to understand what is happening in these situations, to express their feelings and receive comfort, they can find considerable resources of resilience, because they feel included in the relationships and in the emotions which are weathering the storm. As Holmes and Slade (2018: 80–81) have pointed out: 'Clearly, both adverse and positive life events are to an extent random and unpredictable, but their cognitive appraisal—the meanings we attribute to them—is not. . . . Chance and accident test resilience; the capacity to respond positively to adversity is contingent upon positive attachment experiences'.

In fact, Olivia and her sister had experienced some good and loving care in their early years. But their parents' marriage came under a level of strain which can be understood with compassion when placed in the context of their own family histories, the emotionally cool and superficial social culture within which they were raised, and the personal and military trauma experienced by Olivia's father, which could not be expressed out in the open. In this case history, it can be seen that it was healthy, normal, warm-blooded, mammalian feelings which were suppressed and held in the family shadows. Paradoxically, these were the feelings which could have been used as an instinctive guide to sympathetic understanding and mutual support. Where healthy feelings are perceived to be a source of shame or public humiliation, they have no outlet for expression, becoming intensified and distorted into fear, rage and guilt, of which the person learns to be even more deeply ashamed. By contrast, in having strong states of feeling and distress accepted within the psychotherapy process, Olivia slowly came to recognise that her emotions were not her enemy; instead, they were a reliable guide to meeting her own needs and recognising her value, as witnessed by others on whom she found she could rely.

Progressively, Olivia allowed herself to develop a therapeutic relationship of trust, which permitted exploration of the events leading to her traumatisation and loss of self-belief. The shadows cast by her family history had caused her to flee from the feelings generated by that darkness. The moral injury she suffered was compensated by overwork and focus on others, to assuage her imagined guilt. Johnson (1985: 63) has pointed out how such experiences can cause a consequent disconnection: 'from life processes—from the body, from feelings, from intimate others, from community, and often even from inanimate objects such as food, nature, etc.'. This would explain Olivia's flight from nourishing relationships and the avoidance of food which had generated further conflicts. When working with trauma, the psychotherapist necessarily enters the world of the shadow inhabited by her client and in doing so becomes part of its transformation. This is not easy or comfortable, but to avoid this involvement may mean that we stand in the way of that transformative process, even making it seem as though our client is contagious and untouchable, thus repeating and consolidating the moral injury. When she read this case history, Olivia told me she was moved by reading of herself as a full person, with human value, which contrasted with her past experiences of being given the status of an attractive but damaged object. In conclusion, as van der Kolk (2015:70) points out: 'Visiting the past in therapy should be done while people are, biologically speaking, firmly rooted in the present and feeling as calm, safe, and grounded as possible. . . . Being anchored in the present while revisiting the trauma opens the possibility of deeply knowing that the terrible events belong to the past'.

Loving kindness and trauma of the soul

Working in depth with persons who have experienced deep trauma brings the psychotherapist into contact with questions of meaning and belief. The concept of a human soul is controversial within contemporary culture and yet it also seems to have important application as a term in common use within both secular and religious settings. Definitions include ideas about the spiritual or immaterial parts of human experience and views about the moral, psychological and emotional nature of a person and his or her identity. Equally, the term can suggest a quality of emotional energy or intensity, displayed in a work of art or expressed in artistic performance. In this part of the discussion, the concept of a soul will be expressed as a person's belief that life has meaning and a purpose, capable of surviving even the most testing of material circumstances. An individual might only have simple reasons for believing that life is meaningful, but if trust in that belief is damaged or lost, the vitality and basis of life itself will be threatened. It is often in such circumstances that people seek psychotherapeutic help. This is illustrated in the following case study.

Case study of Coral

Coral became my client when she was completing her psychotherapy training. At that time she held a senior position at a counselling service, where she was respected for her work with vulnerable people and for her supervision of other counsellors. Part of her managerial task was that of developing and implementing up-to-date ethical and professional standards for the organisation. She was devoted to her work, and no effort was spared in keeping up a high standard of systems and values. However, during our first year of work together, Coral came under attack from a colleague who did occasional work for the organisation and wished to differ on some points of procedure. This colleague had formed an alliance with a new member of staff recently appointed to a senior position and, jointly, they took a complaint about Coral to an external adjudicator. This was done without warning or attempts to discuss the issues with Coral. It appeared that the matter was being widely discussed within the organisation and with some of her supervisees, in such a way that she sensed opinions were being formed and sides were being taken. This breached her trust and undermined her relationship with her employer. She held good professional boundaries and could not therefore discuss the matter freely within the organisation. What appeared to be an unacknowledged institutional shadow emerged more fully in the fact that the complaint contained oppressive comments, suggesting that she lacked intelligence and was not capable of studying for her psychotherapy qualification. This introduced what seemed to be an element of personal attack. Being a person of some experience, she was able to contain her distressed feelings appropriately throughout this storm and to challenge the complaint successfully, as it had no professional substance and consequently was dropped. Once the attempted complaint was challenged, the two colleagues who had made it each left the organisation quite suddenly.

In our psychotherapy sessions which ran alongside these events, the personal shadow of being persecuted came vividly to Coral's conscious awareness. Coral had been born with health deficits in the form of a cleft lip and palate, plus visual and hearing difficulties. She had been confined in hospital as an infant, and some of the surgical interventions and treatments she endured had been not only painful but were delivered in a harsh and unsympathetic manner. At school and in public, throughout childhood, Coral had been subjected to taunts and bullying about her facial appearance and people would make it obvious that, because of this, they assumed she lacked intelligence. This emotional wound was reopened by the comments made in the complaint. The taunts had continued into adulthood and on one occasion she was refused entry to a dance hall by a door attendant because, he said, 'you are too ugly'. This made her feel that her life was not worth living. Later she took a bath and put her head under the water with the intention of keeping it there until she drowned. She told me that, then, she felt a deep awareness of something more powerful urging her to continue living and she decided in that moment to listen to the instinct encouraging her to do so. That decision proved to be a solid foundation for her future life. She developed the personal resources and stoicism needed in managing her disability, becoming strong and capable in her knowledge of humane values and those actions which make a positive difference to people in vulnerable circumstances.

As the complaint process continued, Coral had an experience which signalled to her that not only was life worth living but had within it a sense of purpose for the future. During a psychotherapy training weekend, she was experiencing great inner distress because of the complaint. That evening she was having a bath, when she became aware that some kind of inner transformation was taking place. She got out of the bath and curled up on the bed, where she fell into a deep sleep. When she woke up, she felt as though some terrible burden had been taken from her. She returned to her training the following day and, from then on, became confident in her studies. Her belief in her capacity to work effectively with people was restored. She came to see much more clearly how her sense of loyalty to her employer had been exploited and that she had not been witnessed and valued. She realised that she could leave the counselling organisation and set up one of her own. After she left, and having succeeded on her new path, those ex-colleagues and supervisees whom she had been able to trust, began to get back in touch and to tell her they had missed her and wondered where she had gone. Gradually, she was able to piece back together her sense of self in the standards and values she represented to her trusted colleagues.

When we began our work together, Coral would often say that she dissociated when under pressure. Indeed, we might describe both of her transformative experiences in the bath as dissociative, in the clinical sense. However, I noticed that she sometimes used this term when just talking about ordinary forgetting, or not quite being able to keep up with the busy events of the day. It was as though she had developed an internal working model which told her there was something pathologically wrong with her and consequently the 'something wrong' would always attract punishment. Until such beliefs come out of the shadows for reappraisal, it is almost inevitable that the thing being hidden and denied, in this case fear of persecution, will draw that very thing to itself in magnetic fashion. So we could say that Coral's dissociative experiences were necessary to 'bring her to her senses'. Within this context, Kalsched (2013: 124–126) has discussed how it is that transformation, in the psychological and spiritual sense, can come from a deep descent into personal experience because this presents a moment of urgency, in which true change is possible. In such a moment the extent of the terrifying feelings which led to dissociation and deadening are faced in full. 'The challenge for the psychoanalytic pilgrim is to re-visit this hell of unthinkable trauma one step at a time, re-experiencing the unbearable affect within a window of tolerance, aided by the witnessing function, the compassion, and the interpretive under-standing of the analyst'.

Kalsched goes on to observe that, once this painful process has been negotiated, the nature of suffering changes as the client begins consciously to take responsi-bility for the self-loathing and shame. 'He or she finds his or her way through the darkness to an emerging light. This is a spiritual experience, a spirituality that inheres in reality itself, the reality of what it is to be human, something that has not been tolerable until now'. So there is acceptance of the human condition, 'made possible by the previous long journey with a witnessing partner'. Living in the reality of being human, it seems to me, makes it possible to weather the storms that life brings and to be more fully alive. The conflict that Coral confronted in her work was in effect a power struggle. Within it she believed that, although the accusations made against her were untrue, she would be persecuted anyway and even destroyed because this was her unarguable fate. But in sinking to the depths of despair something else happened; a deeper resource of awareness emerged and guided her next steps, in collaboration with a therapeutic witness. By holding her experience of persecution unconsciously, Coral was drawn into an unwanted struggle which appeared as if from nowhere but, being unconscious, it emerged as the will to power enacted by the complainants. And fear of persecution inhib-ited her capacity to trust her instincts which already knew that their actions were wrong. As Jung (CW7) understood it: 'Eros is a questionable fellow and will always remain so. . . . He belongs on one side to man's primordial nature which will endure as long as man has an animal body. On the other side he is related to the highest forms of spirit. But he thrives only when spirit and instinct are in right harmony'. Thus, by weathering the storm of the complaint made against her, by coming to awareness of her false belief that she must expect persecution, by instinctively challenging this assumption and by allowing herself to be accom-panied therapeutically on her journey, Coral regained a true sense of her value through her spirit and instinct being 'in right harmony', in the form of loving kindness extended to herself.

Coral's response to the case study, in her own words

The power in witnessing my own awakening through the words of my therapeutic witness is deep, a concerto of sounds and movement delicately played out in the arena of a well-soundproofed hall. Apart from my therapeutic witness and I, no one else was privy to the hell we descended into, nor the fields we danced in when harmony came.

As I read, I sense the holding space which was created, the respect and warmth for the distress I felt, the shame I expelled and the trauma that had bound my mind and clouded my heart. I hear the rhythm of our contact and the stillness and strength of the structure we built to hold my experience. I see the stair-case I descended into hell, and then the rise of my steps into life. Movement is everywhere—I am accepted for my skewed perspective—'of course you reacted that way—of course you did'; there is movement in the language, and in the encouragement to be compassionate to myself and let go of what is not mine. Ascending the staircase to the rhythm of the gentle concerto, I see the chains that bound me dropping away. I pass back what I cannot own because it is not mine to bear. I no longer expect to be wounded or to carry the burden of being defective, because I am not defective, I am Coral. That's it. I am who I am and I am proud of that. I witness myself standing whole in the flames, not rushing to get away, instead, standing steady and becoming associated with the true sense of who I am.

As a trainee therapist, it did not pass my attention that being written about as a client has been a very consolidating experience, not just personally but also for my own clinical practice and awareness. My therapeutic experience has been held by a therapist in the way that I hope to do in my own work with people. My therapeutic witness mirrored my own, felt, sense of what I hope to provide by way of boundaries and authentic contact. Without this genuine witnessing, I know I would have remained in part cut off from my instincts. I needed another person to see how rotten I felt about myself. My false beliefs felt real because, unconsciously, they were interrupting my better instincts and feeding my belief that I was here to be burdened, telling me that 'because I am defective, I should expect things to go wrong and be in pain'. I did not know that I was doing this to myself. I thought that it was just another case of the world treating me badly. By discovering that my true self was not a cause for punishment, I found my capacity to affirm my own presence in the world, without shame or fear.

Chapter 6

Loving kindness and difficulties of engagement with psychotherapy

In this chapter I will suggest that psychotherapy, in order to progress towards a satisfying outcome for the client, requires the shared creation of what I shall call a *therapeutic ecosystem* or collaborative therapeutic alliance. I have borrowed the term *ecosystem* from the developing field of studies in ecology, which is concerned with the set of relationships a particular living organism has with its environment. In this case, I will suggest that the particular organism in question is the human mammal, in the setting of his or her relationships and their wider terrestrial environment. The task for the psychotherapist is that of providing assistance to his or her client, by developing an ecosystem within which their shared work is likely to thrive because it is based upon trust. And where difficulties arise in psychotherapy, making it difficult for treatment to proceed, I propose that this is because a variety of factors could not support the creation of a shared ecosystem. I believe that this approach takes negative judgement out of questions concerning difficulties of engagement in psychotherapy.

Difficulties can arise because there is an insufficiently good 'fit' between client and psychotherapist, from the outset. One example could be where a client might feel more at ease seeing a psychotherapist of a different sex or gender preference to the one initially chosen. Or it might be that there is something more nebulous than that, which just 'doesn't feel right'. In these situations it is important for the psychotherapist to be open to discussion about the experience of his or her client and, if necessary, to assist them in finding a suitable alternative, when proceeding indefinitely does not appear to be helpful. Difficulties of engagement in psychotherapy can also occur during the course of an established therapeutic alliance, due to the challenging nature of the psychotherapy process. These require a depth of understanding and committed work for both parties to the relationship, for which a sufficient foundation may not yet have been established.

It is often difficult to know exactly why it is that people decide to enter into a psychotherapy encounter. Ideally, it is a matter of personal choice, but it can also be a recommended treatment in a medical setting. Where freedom of choice is concerned, persons contemplating this step often grapple with the dilemma

DOI: 10.4324/9781003262114-7

expressed by the literary critic, Frank Kermode (1996: 120), in his reflections upon a similar question of whether counselling is a worthwhile activity: 'I can on occasion remind myself that people in deep and dangerous misery do seek and get help, or that if they do not, or if help is not to be had or arrives too late, they make the incontestably true demonstration of what it is to need help and not to get it'. In his memoir, Kermode discusses his many encounters with ambivalent feelings and sadness in his personal life and in his career as a writer, critic and academic. It could be said that it was his avoidance of help which contributed to a sadness which seems never to have been resolved. But, of course, it is impossible to have such certain knowledge of another person's experience. And so it remains somewhat of a mystery as to why a natural ambivalence, for some, resolves into a decision to try psychotherapy, whereas for others it continues with avoidance.

There can be a wide range of reasons why people hold back from seeking help. Some of these concern a lack of sufficient information about what it is that psychotherapy has to offer; although there is much more open discussion about professional help for psychological and emotional distress than was possible, or approved of, even a few decades ago. Increasingly people are able to talk in public and through the mass media about difficulties they have encountered and help they have received. But at the same time, psychotherapy can seem to present a bewildering array of options when it comes to deciding how to proceed. I believe that there may be an added confusion caused by poor definition of the difference between psychotherapy and counselling. In practice, each of these options can be helpful, for various reasons, and they often look very similar. However, there are important differences between the two approaches. For the purposes of this discussion, I will say that counselling tends towards a focus upon external events and difficulties experienced in the lives of persons, with which they are trying to come to terms. This, too, can be the main focus of psychotherapy in its initial stages. However, a difference in emphasis opens up—especially where the same difficulties have recurred in a person's life over a period of time—as he or she begins to perceive that internalised patterns of behaviour and assumptions made about the world have contributed to the recurrence of those external events, which previously seemed to occur as random misfortune.

Psychotherapy is therefore equipped to recognise and address these recurrent patterns as unconscious motivations and can assist in bringing them to awareness. But it can be very challenging for clients to become aware of repeated patterns in which they have played a part; because it could seem as though an entirely different person, someone not quite like them, is being seen by the psychotherapist. By contrast, and generally speaking, it is the task of counselling to listen, to offer reflective feedback, and precisely not to go beyond Winnicott's facilitating environment (1960). Acceptance without impingement on a fragile sense of self, is required at this early stage of self-discovery. Kohut (1972a) saw that any intrusion upon a sense of oneness with the listener could interrupt the rhythms which reflect the client's need for others to be seen as an extension of the self. Within such acceptance the client will feel that their experiences are truly felt by the listener because they are sharing them and not attempting any other interpretation. This theme is addressed by Akhtar (2018b: 136–137) in his discussion of treatment considerations, which includes reflections on setting the right individual pace for the client. He refers to the observation of Amati-Mehler and Argentieri (1989: 303) that: 'The patient ought to experience for a sufficient length of time and at different levels of the soundness of the therapeutic rapport, the security of being understood'.

The initial stages of psychotherapy may rely entirely and necessarily on this approach, as we have seen in the case study of Olivia, in Chapter 5, where to intervene or to interpret her distress could have seemed as though her experience was being taken away from her, diminished, or even destroyed. This might have echoed an aspect of the trauma she experienced when the headmistress, in response to her legitimate distress, told her without sympathy, 'this crying really has to stop'. The demand made by the headmistress arose from her own need as an authority figure to maintain order in the school and had no reference point from within Olivia's feelings and experience of the situation. And much later in the psychotherapy, when Olivia became able to talk about her eating difficulties, she told me that if I had raised this issue earlier, she would have stopped me. It was therefore very important to wait until the right moment, and to be invited in, in order to have that discussion.

On the other hand, if repeated cycles of misfortune are to be avoided, and if personal change is to become possible, then something stronger than a listening presence is required. It has to be said that entering into and continuing on the path of psychotherapy requires considerable courage and determination, as can be seen in the case studies presented in this book. The challenges encountered in the deeper processes of psychotherapy are considerable and may even bring the psychotherapeutic relationship close to breaking point. This is not always so, but we saw how near the process came to it in the case study of Gemma in Chapter 3. The crisis was precipitated by Gemma beginning to see how she was being seen by me, through receiving feedback which reflected my experience of her and which made her feel extremely uncomfortable, not least because it highlighted the way in which her dependency on her mother was stifling any prospect of a truly satisfying life of her own. This crisis in the psychotherapy had to be faced and negotiated if beneficial change was to take place. And by our surviving, understanding, and repairing the crisis together, a new way of seeing things emerged for Gemma, which she felt she could own for herself. She began to explore the experience of having agency in her life and an ability to make choices which did not rely on her mother's approval.

At the beginning of a psychotherapy relationship, it can be difficult to answer the almost inevitable question about how long the treatment will take. It is almost impossible to answer it, because it is not uncommon for months and, in some cases, years of treatment to be necessary before the required level of trust develops and the roots of the difficulty are found and fully understood. Such timescales are not easily predicted at the beginning of treatment. It is also a challenge, as the deeper roots of difficulties are exposed, when clients encounter levels of distress which seem to be even more painful than the original experience. As defences dissolve—defences which may have taken a lifetime to construct and which have prevented that original pain from being felt within conscious experience—there can be very testing stages in the psychotherapy process. Understandably these can cause clients to wonder why they started out on this journey in the first place. But so often after this critical stage has been reached, real change begins to become evident, pointing the way to a life that can be better lived. Freud (1895) famously observed that much could be gained from psychoanalysis by the transformation of hysterical misery into common unhappiness. Whilst this is a very wise observation, it is also true that even common unhappiness can be transformed at least into an acceptable level of contentment.

In resolving the question of when and how to proceed from a counselling to a psychotherapy approach, it is vital to assess the unique needs and capabilities of each client as an individual. On this question Lomas (1993: 151–155) discusses the balance of responsibility between therapist and patient. He observes that, if the therapist is to help the patient towards a more manageable sense of responsibility he needs to have: 'a realistic approach to his own powers and their limits. . . . If the patient is left too much to her own devices, or if the therapist overestimates his own responsibility for the patient's life, little good will come from the endeavour'. The attitude of the therapist therefore influences the extent to which he can help his client find a balanced way of taking responsibility for herself.

Lomas emphasises the need for this balanced approach when he asserts that each new client will, in the end, need to develop a sense of personal agency and become able to take responsibility, if meaningful personal development is to emerge from the encounter. A client may arrive at the point of seeking help believing that they have no autonomy and they may seek to invest all responsibility in the psychotherapist. Sometimes this can manifest in an apparently incongruous expression of extreme emotion, the intensity of which may not fit the experiences being described nor arouse empathic feelings as a response. Of such experiences, he notices that whilst the client may emphasise her predicament she may not 'expose her vulnerability or place herself in another's power'. He comments that: 'To free such a person from a passive role in the performance of which she has become adept and which preserves her from the terror of closeness is an extraordinarily difficult task. The therapist must avoid being seduced into taking more responsibility for the patient's life yet can hardly stand back calmly observing the self-destruction as if it wasn't his business'. This theme is explored in the case study of Gemma in Chapter 3.

Referring to the work of Schafer (1976), Lomas suggests that the analyst can steadily encourage activity in the patient, as opposed to acceptance of herself as a 'victim of circumstance'. But he notices that this presents a paradox which, whilst encouraging the client to take responsibility, allows for what might be seen as irresponsible behaviour—at least in 'polite society'—such as full expression of pent-up authentic feelings and strong language to represent experiences previously denied. He suggests that this paradox can be resolved through the use of intuition and assessment of the stage the client has reached in becoming capable of greater life-affirming activity. And he observes accurately that: 'To get this right is one of the hardest arts of psychotherapy'. Part of 'getting it right' must depend on the level of security established within the therapeutic alliance. Where professional boundaries have not yet been established securely, provocative work of this kind cannot be attempted because it risks retraumatisation. In order to proceed safely, Lomas points out that the distinction between therapist and client must always be clear. If this boundary fails, there is no one available to protect the safety of these more challenging experiences. But where the therapeutic boundaries are secure, then more adventurous, collaborative work can be attempted. This can include a greater sharing by the therapist of his or her experience of the client. This may be the first time a person has had the opportunity safely to realise that they make an impact on another person, who has feelings and thoughts about them:

> . . . we could encourage the patient to recognize her effect on the therapist, to realise that her words and actions are not falling on thin air but on a real person, who may be warmed or hurt by them. It is confusing to pretend otherwise, for how else is the patient to learn this reality? It would seem that, within the limits of protecting the patient from undue anxiety and hurt, and allowing for the value of tact, we should let her know that she affects us . . .
>
> Because the patient's inability to take responsibility for her effect on others is usually so central to her psychopathology, it is important that she be given as much opportunity as possible to understand the impression that the patient and her therapist have on each other and to work out a concept of joint responsibility.

> (ibid., 154–155)

When psychotherapy doesn't seem to work

All of this being said, it is sometimes the case that people who, in Frank Kermode's phrase, are in deep and dangerous misery demonstrate what it is to need help and not to get it. And perhaps the greatest fear of all may be that of real, personal change. But the psychotherapy process when fully engaged *is* a matter of change, as demonstrated in the case studies in this book. On some occasions, resistance to personal change can emerge when psychotherapy has been entered into and seems to be proceeding successfully. When this happens it is as though, for the client, the unconscious mind has gone as far as it is willing to go in surrendering its wisdom to the conscious mind. The psychotherapist can only respect this even though, after careful discussion, it may signal the end of the psychotherapy. After all, the deep contents of a person's mind and spirit may on the one hand be the psychotherapist's business and yet on the other hand may not be their business at all. To insist upon continuing could become an intrusion and a disrespectful impingement upon the reality of another person.

So here we can consider those situations where possibly, despite the best efforts of client and psychotherapist, the psychotherapy encounter can no longer proceed. In reflecting on this I have noticed, in hindsight, where a psychotherapy relationship has not been able to continue, the sheer volume of unresolved feelings, thoughts, copious notes and queries which proliferate for the psychotherapist, prior to the final impasse. It is as though the client has, quite unconsciously, transferred all of the 'therapeutic workload' onto the psychotherapist. In these situations, it is as if the psychotherapist is coming to conscious awareness of the unconscious contents of the client's experience and yet on attempting to share this awareness as feedback, however gently and subtly, is facing denial that any of it emanates from the client. At this point the psychotherapist is left holding the split-off contents of the client's awareness, which can feel like a jumbled assortment of disconnected items incapable of being integrated into a coherent whole at that time. But where psychotherapy is able to proceed, it is just this kind of impasse which can lead into real and permanent change for the client. We saw in the case study of Gemma how affronted she felt when I communicated to her my observations about her lateness for the session and what I believed was the unconscious cause of this. This crisis could have brought about an abrupt ending to our work together, and she signalled to me that this was a possibility she was considering. But something in her seemed to know that she needed my help and could benefit from continuing to have it. Thus, the psychotherapy not only survived but continued to thrive.

The functions of mirroring and mentalisation

But we are still faced with the question of how it is, in other cases, that psychotherapy is not for everyone or, even when it seems initially to have been the right choice, does not seem to work for an individual who feels unable to face the considerable challenges involved in the process. Wilfred Bion discussed the capacity people may have to tolerate the frustration involved in learning from experience. He also identified the opposite of this capacity as 'the process that strips, denudes, and devalues persons, experiences and ideas' (in Jacobus, 2005: 192). He called these 'K' and '- K', suggesting that they equate to love and hate in the psychotherapy encounter and might become the main focus for the client, rather than any transformative knowledge the client might gain. In considering the early developmental origins of this phenomenon, he proposed that the infant mind already exists and needs another mind to assist it, in learning to tolerate and make sense of experience which can then be stored as memory, helping to build a reliable 'knowledge base'. But the capacity to have thoughts has to be called into existence, to cope with thoughts which exist prior to their realisation (Bion, 1967b: 111). This implies the presence of a carer who can engage with the mind of the infant. When this presence is lacking, the capacity to tolerate the frustration involved in learning from experience is unmanageable.

The calling of thoughts into existence is provided by the function of maternal reverie, or the carer's 'thought thinking apparatus', which can be lent to the infant, offering the container within which an increasing toleration of experience can take place (Bion, 1962a: 83). Bion believed that the mind grows in response to encounters with truth as a reality and that this is the foundation of reliable emotional experience. Failing that, he proposed that '-K', or hate, represents an 'attack on linking' (Bion, 1959: 93–109), which occurs when there has been an absence of maternal reverie, where the infant has not been borne in mind by their carer and therefore has no link through which to experience thoughts. It should be emphasised here that maternal reverie is dependent upon secure emotional conditions for the parent, and not all parents will have experienced this security themselves, in their own infancy. Support for vulnerable parents is therefore essential for both infant and parent. Enhanced awareness of this has led to the development of supportive agencies like the Parent-Infant Foundation, to help parents understand and develop their 'thought thinking apparatus' in partnership with their infants. Gerhardt (2015: 222) has highlighted the improvements in mental health made possible by this kind of support. She has also commented on the fact that, despite its proven value (Barlow et al., 2008), this support is not universally available to families who need it.

Fonagy describes the capacity to recognise others' minds as *mentalisation*, or *mind-mindedness* (Fonagy et al., 2004). Starting with the eye contact initiated between infant and carer, the possibility of attunement between maternal reverie and infant experience begins to arrive. As Winnicott explained:

> The mother gazes at the baby in her arms, and the baby gazes at his mother's face and finds himself therein . . . provided that the mother is really looking at the unique, small, helpless being and not projecting her own expectations, fears, and plans for the child. In that case, the child would not find himself in his mother's face, but rather the mother's own projections. This child would remain without a mirror, and for the rest of his life would be seeking this mirror in vain.
>
> (Winnicott, 1971: 89)

Winnicott's view was confirmed later by the neuroscientific identification of 'mirror neurons' (Holmes & Slade, 2018: 44), where the metaphor of a mirror was used to describe the findings made in reflective physiology (Rizzolati & Sinigaglia, 2010). Where mirroring communications are absent or misattuned by caregivers, Westland has observed that they remain in the body as undeveloped possibility:

> These intentional, unreceived communications from babies are primary communications and carry energetic, physiological, and emotional messages. . . . When babies receive misattuned interactions, for whatever reason, their

primary communications get physically overlaid by their responses to misat-tuned interactions, forming secondary patterning. The primary and overlaid secondary elements reveal themselves in muscle and breathing patterns, loss of vitality, and inability to regulate physiological arousal and emotions. These are the physical manifestation of the psychological aspects of baby-caregiver interactions coming into present relationships.

(Westland, 2015: 202)

The overlaid secondary patterns were defined by Reich (1927, 1949) as 'muscle armouring' and by Boyesen (1980), as 'tissue and organ armour'. Lowen (1975: 13) observed how the tensions held by body armour have a protective function for the individual: 'against painful and threatening emotional experiences. They shield him from dangerous impulses within his own personality as well as from attacks by others'. It therefore makes psychological and emotional sense that, for some, the psychotherapy relationship will trigger defences which are deeply inlaid in body and mind, so much so that the encounter may arrive at an impasse. Bion (in Jacobus, 2005: 243) described this as a *reversible perspective* or 'a par-ticular and deadly form of analytic *impasse* which defends against psychic pain'. He believed that this arises from a state wherein the patient 'reverses perspec-tive so as to make a dynamic situation static'. It is an attack on linking and 'an aspect of the potential destruction and deformation of knowledge'. Bion (in Par-sons, 2000: 200–201) understood that because maternal reverie is the capacity to sense what is going on in the infant's experience, it can be seen as an act of faith. A reversible perspective occurs where the infant's act of faith is not reciprocated and trust is broken, leading to an expectation that all such acts of faith will be futile and misplaced. Such negative expectation is at the core of low self-esteem and mental ill health.

Loving kindness, attunement and theory of mind

In the psychotherapeutic setting, it is the use of reverie by the psychotherapist which offers the client the reflections of another mind, giving back the client's mirror image and confirming that their act of faith in the relational process is meaningful and worthwhile. This is known as theory of mind, a capability which can become a new foundation of both self-awareness and self-esteem, through a mirror image which is trustworthy, loving and receptive of love. But where a person's early years and first infant attempts at attunement were not met with such mirroring, they will have been overwhelmed by the secondary patterning described by Westland; established when those primary communications were overlaid by their responses to misattuned interactions. Thus, the development of vital and positive emotional experience can be powerfully diminished in the process identified by Bion; which 'strips, denudes, and devalues persons, experi-ences and ideas'. The act of faith in communication is broken and, consequently, access to awareness becomes obstructed by fear, mistrust and anger. In the psychotherapy process, the unresolved feelings which remain behind the ensu-ing relational inhibition may be so immense—having originated at a time when the infant had no capacity to self-soothe or rationalise them—that it is easy to see how withdrawal and rejection of awareness may begin to seem like the better, or the least painful, option when disturbing memories are active.

Knox discusses the necessary processes which underpin the development of a child's growing capacity 'to be aware that other people have different ideas and beliefs from his or her own'. She names attachment as one such emergent process: 'reliably constructed in the repeated interactions between mother and baby' (Knox, 2003: 140–141). On this view, Fonagy (2001: 187) has identified the distinctive survival value of an infant's expressions of distress, which not only attract protective responses from the caregiver but also create comparable distress in the infant. 'Thus an ideal situation is created for the infant to experience con-tainment (Bion, 1962) and accurate mirroring (Winnicott, 1971), in other words, a context within which internalisation processes essential to self-development can take place'. Knox goes on to observe that:

> Fonagy has thus clarified the concept of mirroring by suggesting that it is not only the image of the emotionally containing parent which is internalized. For reflective function to develop, the infant also has to internalize the parent as someone with a mental image of the infant, a parent who sees the infant as someone with a mind and emotions. It is the parent's mental representa-tion of the infant which is internalized, allowing the infant to find him—or herself in the other. If the parent fails in this respect, the version of itself that the infant encounters in the parent's mind is that of a physical object rather than a person with a mind of his or her own. Under these circumstances, it is difficult to see how infants could experience themselves as reflective beings.
>
> (Knox, 2003: 141)

Fonagy et al. have provided empirical evidence to support the essential function of mirroring, by demonstrating that the reflective function only seems to develop in a reasonably secure attachment, and that:

> it depends on the parents' reflective capacity for events to link in a meaning-ful way for the baby . . . mothers who were highly stressed and deprived in terms of numerous social and economic factors nevertheless had securely attached children if they themselves had high ratings on a scale measuring reflective function, whereas mothers who scored low on reflective function had children who showed insecure attachment.
>
> (Fonagy et al., 1995: 233–278)

Further, Gergely and Watson (1996) found that parents who were highly attuned to the emotions of their infant did not merely imitate his or her emotional expres-sions but gave an exaggerated, playful 'pretend' response. This enabled their infant to see this as a true reflection of his or her own emotions, as distinct from what might otherwise be a parent's normal 'unmarked' emotional expression and not reflective of the infant's own emotional world (ibid.).

The negative therapeutic reaction

Freud described what he called a negative therapeutic reaction, where encouragement of a client and satisfaction with the progress of treatment is met with 'signs of discontent and their condition invariably becomes worse' (Freud, 1923: 49). To understand this therapeutically, we can refer to the observations of Westland and others, in the preceding discussion, concerning the secondary patterning which performs the defensive function of shielding persons from their own dangerous impulses and from attacks by others. Simpson (2013: 25–40) illustrates this in a case study where his patient had not been able to allow himself to really succeed in fulfilling his potential. He presented as tense, bound up and in despair and, when calm, he came across as 'distant, haughty and intellectualising'. During the initial stages of the work, he put the psychotherapist under considerable pressure by the intensity of his anxiety and despair. It was only by giving steadfast attention to the experience of the patient that the psychotherapist could discover the root of his cold distancing, which was found to have originated during his infancy, when his mother had been unable to attune to his needs. He remembered that she seemed overwhelmed by caring for him and his siblings. She suffered from asthma, and in his sympathetic response to her difficulties, he became adept at soothing her anxiety and was fearful of being separated from her. Simpson observes that as a consequence of this he became 'trapped by his devotion to his maternal object', which held him in a long-term state of inhibition, from which he was 'unable to penetrate the world with real passion'. His patient believed that he could neither recover nor succeed 'until he felt his object could be restored'. It was only when the analysis progressed that it became possible to get behind this defence, by addressing his guilt and despair about his mother. Then he began to identify with his analyst as a positive figure.

Gerrard (2015: 349) reports a sense of overwhelming hopelessness sometimes, when working with negative therapeutic reactions, describing a process where: 'Frequently it is difficult to think. When I challenge, I feel as if I should not have challenged. When I don't challenge, I feel as if I am like one of those nodding dogs in car windows'. But she writes of the support she found in the work of Betty Joseph, who similarly described 'a very malignant type of self-destructiveness' when patients are more and more absorbed into hopelessness (Joseph, 1982: 127–128). Joseph was influenced by Bion, in understanding the immense difficulty involved in working with the sense of hopelessness engendered when the patient's defences try to draw the analyst towards something less painful. The patient attempts this because the new insights brought about by psychological change cause disturbance and, therefore, a wish to maintain the *status quo* to avoid it. The attempted avoidance causes a countertransferential sense of futility and weariness, as Joseph observed: 'a powerful masochism is at work and these patients will try to create despair in the analyst and then get him to collude with the despair or become actively involved by being harsh, critical or in some way or another verbally sadistic to the patient'. When the analyst loses his or her balance, the patient seems to 'triumph'. But 'there is real misery and anxiety around . . . and what is important is to distinguish whether the patient is communicating real despair, depression, fear, persecution for which he wants our help, or whether he is unconsciously creating a masochistic situation in which we can both become caught up' (Gerrard, 2015: 349).

By remaining steadfast in the face of insights such as this, the psychotherapeutic ecosystem can offer the potential for surprising levels of real change. In Coral's response to my case study, in Chapter 5, she writes of the staircase she 'descended into hell', and then the rise of her steps into life. But fear of those initial downward steps, and of viewing clearly their own personal hell, can cause some clients, understandably, to try and avoid them altogether. Because as Kalsched (2013: 125) points out: 'Accepting the human condition has not been possible for the trauma survivor, because its realities—which are difficult enough even in a 'facilitating environment'—have shocked and overwhelmed the survivor's capacities to metabolize unspeakably painful affective experience, thus requiring dissociative defenses'. But in psychotherapy the patient is offered the opportunity to be slowly introduced to the unbearable pain of trauma which divided them from the rest of their personality. The pain for Coral, on being told that she was 'too ugly' to be allowed into the dance hall, led to her staircase of descent, at the bottom of which lay the original pain of being bullied and mistreated because of her facial disfigurement. And yet, in that descent, she chose to accept her human condition and was transformed by that choice. This allowed her to move from a state of dissociation to one of association with her true self.

The fact that some clients feel unable to take these steps is not due to any lack on their part. Dissociation can offer an essential defence against unbearable pain. However, in the long term, there is an internal cost involved, arising from what Jung (CW16) described as 'feeling-toned complexes' or autonomous inner beings which can be represented, especially in dreams, as enemies. The experience for the patient is that of being attacked by something imposing itself upon the conscious mind. The feeling-toned complex is unable to be controlled by the will and the experience of it can therefore be terrifying, because dissociation of this kind involves aggression against the psyche by one of its own parts. This can manifest as attacks, whether verbal or physical, upon the self or upon others. Kalsched (1996: 13–14) observes that 'it is as though the normally integrative tendencies in the psyche must be interrupted by force. Splitting is a violent affair—like the splitting of an atom. . . . Contemporary psychoanalysis recognises that where the inner world is filled with violent aggression, primitive defenses are present also. More specifically, we now know that *the energy for dissociation comes from this aggression*'.

This point is developed further by Johnson, who suggests that resistance is not only concerned with the surrender of the defensive 'manoeuvres' which control id impulses. He proposes that it also represents a clinging to a 'primitive ego adaptation, which covers a serious ego deficiency' and literally allows the person to function. If it were to be taken away before the underlying ego dysfunctions were repaired, or another more evolved adaptation could be reached, a decompensation could well occur. He cites the example of a primitive ego adaptation in those individuals who hold rigidly and defensively to an inflexible, moralistic, fundamentalist, often religious position:

> Typically, these people have swallowed whole a very simplistic, dogmatic, and punitive moral position which is obviously low in the hierarchical development of moral sense. Frequently, they believe that when people do not hold similar views, they are possessed by evil and threaten the very fabric of society. Essentially, this is a projection. These people need such a belief system in order to control their own primitive impulses, and their defense of this position is completely in the interest of themselves and the community. This is not to say, of course, that these individuals cannot achieve a higher level of moral development. It is merely to illustrate the point being made here and to caution against attempts to remove primitive adaptations before the underlying deficits are repaired.
>
> (Johnson, 1985: 246)

Working therapeutically with the splitting effect

A manifestation of the splitting effect is illustrated in the case study of a patient of Patrick Casement (1985: 191–215), where he identifies her efforts to divide the therapeutic input through engagement with other sources of help which were alien to the analysis. The initial referral concerned an eating disorder and in the analysis which followed, his patient made concerted efforts to test him, by acting out with alternative helpers when he would not engage with her provocative efforts himself. He was also tested in trying not to control his client in ways that she had previously experienced. As the analysis proceeded, Casement was able to gather enough unconscious clues to help him understand what she needed therapeutically. These emerged in the account of her past life and the way her acting out represented this. Her experience of family life and relationships had been one of blurred boundaries. Her eating disorder had introduced a therapeutic interest in her body, which was later emphasised in the relationship with her treating doctor, who sometimes saw her in the sitting room of his own home, where he would stroke her body as a 'treatment'. Her brother-in-law, a doctor, also became involved in the management of her eating difficulties. But by steadfastly refusing to be caught up in his patient's efforts to breach the therapeutic boundaries, Casement was able to discover that she was searching deeply for something. By his tolerating her acting out, he was able to derive a deeper understanding of what that might be, but at times he felt 'analytically impotent' with the therapy at times seeming chaotic. However, he observes that what emerged:

After many months of this near annihilation of the analysis, was that it was in my non-retaliatory survival of this testing by the patient that the potency of the analysis ultimately lay. She came to discover that the analysis continued to offer her an unbiased relationship space in which she could begin to become her 'own version of herself'. . . . She did not have to offer a compliance to please. Neither did she have to maintain, indefinitely, her protest against the pressures that had always been upon her to comply.

Having found this neutral space in the analysis, Miss K. began to use it in preparation for how she would be later. For the first time in her life, she was able to own herself and find an independent life apart from the family's expectations of her . . . the progress has been maintained since.

(Casement 1985: 192)

This case study confirms that, because psychotherapy is a relationship of attachment, injuries sustained in the early relational lives of patients can be revisited within its containment towards a different outcome.

Acceptance and reparation through loving kindness in psychotherapy

The process of reparation is reflected in neuropsychological changes which take place as therapeutic and relational progress is made. Due to the plasticity of the human brain, established neural networks which have been 'wired in' to form defensive patterns can be repaired and reconfigured. Openness of communication between therapist and client thus facilitates affectively focused treatment, which tunes in to the dissociative gaps and places where the connection with the patient might otherwise have broken down. As Kalsched (2013: 13) states: 'What has been broken relationally must be repaired relationally'. Of this reparative process, Johnson comments (1985: 246) that: 'A deep appreciation of the client's level of ego functioning requires time and experience with the client's coping mechanisms over the course of treatment. Usually, inexperienced therapists tend to overestimate rather than underestimate the client's level of emotional development'. And as Edinger points out:

Individuation is a process, not a realized goal. Each new level of integration must submit to further transformation if development is to proceed. . . . Out of this state there emerges a more or less continuous dialogue between the conscious ego and the unconscious, and also between outer and inner experience. A twofold split is healed to the extent individuation is achieved; first the split between conscious and unconscious which began at the birth of consciousness, and second the split between subject and object. The dichotomy between outer and inner reality is replaced by a sense of unitary reality. It is as though original unconscious wholeness and oneness with life, in which we began and out of which we had to emerge, can now be recovered in part on a conscious level.

(Edinger, 1972: 96–97)

It seems to me that this is what Coral describes in her response to my case study of our work together, in Chapter 5:

> Movement is everywhere—I am accepted for my skewed perspective—'of course you reacted that way—of course you did'; there is movement in the language, and in the encouragement to be compassionate to myself and let go of what is not mine. Ascending the staircase to the rhythm of the gentle concerto, I see the chains that bound me dropping away. I pass back what I cannot own because it is not mine to bear. I no longer expect to be wounded or to carry the burden of being defective; because I am not defective, I am Coral. That's it. I am who I am and I am proud of that. I witness myself standing whole in the flames, not rushing to get away; instead standing steady and becoming associated with the true sense of who I am.

Nathan (2018) speaks of the way in which therapeutic acceptance means: 'demonstrating a curiosity about the patient's internal world, implying what they consider hateful, even repulsive, can be tolerated and thought about'. This is theory of mind in action which, in its deeper mirroring, can see beyond the negative internal working model imposed by traumatic experience, and towards the emergence of an authentic self. He goes on to say that:

> Such acceptance requires a capacity to adopt an analytic neutrality predicated on a maternally affective attunement to the patient. *In extremis*, even self-harm may be an appropriate response to intolerable psychic despair. . . . The patient can begin to have an experience of a therapist who has the capacity to think about the patient's experience: as Fonagy and Target (1996) put it, *a mind able to think about another mind*. In this way, Sandler and Sandler (1983) suggest the patient may begin to internalize and continue to develop their own capacities for toleration, curiosity and thought, where the self-hating 'pathetic' cries of the vulnerable infantile self, may also come to be seen as an expression of a longing to be protected and loved.
>
> (Nathan, 2018: 67–68)

Loving kindness, mentalisation and epistemic trust

This viewpoint is explored in depth by Fonagy & Campbell (2015) and Bateman & Fonagy (2016) and has particular relevance for persons whose trust in others has been severely damaged by prior experiences of neglect, abuse or exploitation. Fonagy and Campbell confirm the central importance of mentalising, which they define as the capacity to understand ourselves and others in terms of intentional mental states. It involves an awareness of mental states in oneself or in other people, particularly when it comes to explaining behaviour. Mentalising provides a comprehensive map of social cognition:

> As the human mind has been required to respond to ever more challenging, complex and competitive conditions, the exact nature and content of social knowledge cannot be fixed by genetics or constitution; it must be optimised through a prolonged period of development by a group of kin, that is, attachment figures. Mentalization exists not only to permit superior adaptation to the physical environment through facilitating social collaboration and well-functioning kinship groups, but also to support competition for survival when social groups are at odds. Evolution has charged attachment relationships with ensuring the full development of the social brain. The capacity for mentalizing, along with many other social-cognitive capacities, evolves out of the experience of social interaction with caregivers.
>
> (Fonagy & Campbell, 2015: 237–238)

They go on to identify another important function of attachment relationships, which is that of 'the development of epistemic trust and the enabling of social learning in an ever-changing environmental context'. Bateman and Fonagy (2016) explain that this theory is based upon the fact that our reliance on the information we receive from others, about our social world, develops within a significant social and emotional context and in the ways in which we are able to consider social knowledge as genuine and personally relevant to us. Csibra and Gergely (2011) developed this concept through their study of the evolutionary importance of human infants' capacity to learn from their primary caregivers. Human beings have evolved to both teach and learn new and relevant cultural information, through their sensitivity to forms of communication which signal opportunities for this kind of learning. Within this process of communication, a caregiver signals to the infant that what they are conveying is relevant and useful cultural knowledge. In doing so, the caregiver uses *ostensive cues* to which human infants are attuned with particular responsiveness. These include eye contact, turn-taking contingent reactivity and the use of a special vocal tone (*motherese*), all of which appear to stimulate a particular mode of learning in the infant. This occurs because the cues indicate that the caregiver recognises the child as an individual, and as a mentalising (thinking and feeling) 'agent'. Sensitive responding to the child's need fosters not just confidence that he or she matters as a person but opens his or her mind more generally to receive new information as relevant, to adjust his or her beliefs and consequently to modify his or her behaviour (Bateman & Fonagy, 2016: 23). When this theory is applied to the setting of psychotherapy, Fonagy and Campbell state that 'the reopening of epistemic trust may be at the heart of all therapeutic interventions', the first stage of which involves:

the transmission of substantive content to the patient about the nature of their state in a way that is coherent and credible enough for the patient to accept. . . . The patient has the experience of their agentive self being understood through a therapeutic form of marked mirroring. As well as providing a form of relevant social communication, the very process of applying and transmitting this knowledge involves a subtle and rich process of ostensive cueing on the part of the therapist. It requires the therapist to be able to mentalize the patient effectively, to be able to understand the patient's state well enough to be able to respond with the right forms of ostensive cues and to formulate the model—the social knowledge of the intervention—in a manner that fits with the patient's own experiences of their own mental state. The actual content of this form of social knowledge can provide extremely valuable ways for the patient to understand—to mentalize—themselves and their reactions to others. But the generic value of communicating this social knowledge, which falls across different models of treatment, lies in the patient's experience of being recognized. This is what skilful, sensitive therapeutic mentalizing involves, and it results in a relaxation of epistemic mistrust.

(Fonagy & Campbell, 2015: 243–244)

Thus, when Mark—in his account of his experience in Chapter 4—speaks of 'finding his way into psychotherapy', he says that the experience gave him a true representation of what he was actually feeling. This allowed him to develop epistemic trust with another person and to later apply it to his own social world outside the psychotherapy. In a different context, this theme is developed by Salaam Abdel-Malek (2022: 457–469), in her reflections about the personal impact of multiple, complex trauma upon her work as a psychoanalyst in Lebanon, during the Covid pandemic. She writes about her need as a psychoanalyst to restore her internal setting and to do her own personal trauma work. This restored her capacity 'to think and listen to my patients so that they could subsequently do their own trauma work and discover their subjectivity'. It was not the ground rules, setting or technique of the psychoanalytic frame which allowed this but rather the: 'unconscious ability to use another person's mind . . . when traumatic events attack the setting, it is the presence of a psychoanalyst who is capable of thinking and creating that is important'. Such work needs to take time, especially where trauma has generated complex mental disorders. According to studies cited by Sekechi and Chiesa (2022: 495–496), long-term psychodynamic therapy is significantly more effective than shorter forms of psychotherapy in these cases (Leichsenring & Leibing, 2003; Leichsenring & Rabung, 2008; Munder et al., 2019). The capacity of the therapist to mentalise and share social knowledge depends upon the qualities observed by Rogers when he stated that:

personal change is facilitated when the psychotherapist is what he *is*, when in the relationship with his client he is genuine and without 'front' or façade, openly being the feelings and attitudes which at that moment are flowing *in* him. We have coined the term 'congruence' to try to describe this condition. By this we mean that the feelings the therapist is experiencing are available to him, available to his awareness, and he is able to live these feelings, be them, and able to communicate them if appropriate. No one fully achieves this condition, yet the more the therapist is able to listen acceptantly to what is going on within himself, and the more he is able to be the complexity of his feelings, without fear, the higher the degree of his congruence.

(Rogers, 1967: 61)

I propose that in order for attunement to be made possible within the psychotherapy relationship and, indeed, within the parent–infant bond, a certain sort of feeling needs to be experienced. I suggest that it is loving kindness, as a steadfast quality, which generates the congruent ostensive cues that trigger a special mode of learning in the infant. The same mechanism is evident in the functioning psychotherapeutic alliance. This support allows ostensive cues to be embodied and trusted, making them useful for further reference and storage in emotional memory. Loving kindness forms experiences which are physiologically and psychologically recognisable, believable and able to be safely absorbed by the subject. Thus, the subjective experiences of persons form the basis of reliable social knowledge when shared, witnessed and acknowledged. They enable authentic social networks to be constructed. Fonagy and Campbell (2015: 239) have observed that 'the attachment system was 'captured' by evolution to provide a platform for the transmission of cultural knowledge across generations, most particularly understanding about the nature of subjectivity and the symbolic functioning of the human mind'. I suggest that loving kindness, as a subjective experience, allows the emergence of the client's own subjective and unique perspective, as seen in the case studies and discussed in the final chapter of this book. In respecting the subjective experience of each individual client, it becomes possible to see how those who experience difficulty within the psychotherapy relationship are the same as all other clients, because they demonstrate how they have established their own particular way of adapting and surviving despite, in some cases, extreme levels of emotional deprivation and harm. Thus, in developmental terms, it can be seen that the attachment style of each individual is 'an adaptive learning outcome concerning what might be the most appropriate method of social survival in a complex interpersonal world' (Belsky, 2006; Mikulincer & Shaver, 2007; Simpson & Belsky, 2008, in Fonagy & Campbell, 2015: 241).

Understanding why some clients are hard to help

Holmes and Slade (2018: 75) have pointed out that 'insecure patterns are not to be conceived as unhealthy or undesirable in themselves, rather as *resilience-promoting adaptations* to specific environments, enabling survival under adverse circumstances'. That a client may experience difficulty or even extreme challenge in psychotherapy is to be expected, where early memories include a significant prior betrayal of epistemic trust. On this view, it makes sense that even serious personality disorders, such as borderline personality disorder (BPD), whilst clearly dysfunctional within social norms, can represent adaptive benefits for persons living in a state of emotional emergency, such as that arising from interpersonal violence (Fonagy & Campbell, 2015: 241–242). In such conditions, there will be an increased need for protection, so that highly charged, intense emotional relationships may be able to generate some kind of support very quickly, due to the urgency of the situation. 'The mentalizing strengths that have been noted in many individuals with BPD—a tendency to be able to make quick inferences of other people's mental states on the basis of their immediate visual and emotional cues, a hypersensitivity to facial expressions, hyper-reactivity to positive and emotional stimuli—are all suggestive of a mentalizing profile that may be an adaptation to functioning in a threatening or high-risk environment'.

A central factor standing in the way of developing a reliable therapeutic alliance is a fundamental loss of trust in other people, once that trust has been damaged or broken. By contrast, a person who has experienced a secure attachment will have viewed their primary attachment figures as dependable sources of knowledge, both truthful and authoritative in their understanding of the surrounding social world (ibid., 240). Where this has been lacking in the life experience of a client, resistance to treatment can arise from their 'high levels of epistemic mistrust, or outright epistemic freezing', wherein social adversity, trauma or maltreatment have destroyed 'the individual's trust in incoming social knowledge of all kinds'. Here, it becomes difficult for that individual to accept that new information is applicable to them at an interpersonal level and across social contexts. For example, the kind of rigidity and 'unreachable' quality which is found in cases of borderline personality disorder, 'which has historically made this patient group so hard to help (often causing intense feelings of frustration in therapists), is caused by an inability to trust what they hear' (ibid., 243).

By contrast, the communication of social knowledge in an attuned psychotherapy relationship encourages the development of agency, through authentic responsiveness to the feelings of the client. This opens up the client's capacity to believe in social communication from reliable attachment figures, which had previously been lost 'for reasons of environmental adversity, genetic propensity or both. By effectively mentalising the patient, the therapist is modelling how they mentalise in an open, trustworthy and relatively low-arousal environment' (ibid., 244). Thus, the therapeutic alliance can become a joint exploration and learning experience for both client and psychotherapist.

Creating a psychotherapeutic ecosystem

Whilst considering the myriad experiences brought to the psychotherapy encounter, it also has to be borne in mind that neither counselling nor psychotherapy are the answer for everyone. Richard Mabey (2005) speaks of his recovery from depression in his book, *Nature Cure*, in which he describes the devastation he felt when he lost connection with that which had previously sustained him in nature, and how this connection was restored through friendship and love. Nature writers, in particular, seem to lead us back to our love of that which really matters and makes a difference. The environmentalist Roger Deakin illustrated this throughout his *Notes from Walnut Tree Farm*, published posthumously by his friends, Alison Hastie and Terence Blacker, who, in their editors' foreword, describe the way the entries in his notebooks reflected the events of his inner and outer life. Deakin communicated to the reader his love of the place where he chose to live, in a small moated farmhouse on a Suffolk grazing common, and how on coming back to it he experienced the same kind of relief he imagined a badger would feel, returning to its sett after a foraging expedition. His writing shared a mental image of a real place, with its chimney showing above a spinney of ash, maple, goat willow, holly and gnarled thorn trees (Deakin, 2008: 204–207). He noticed how a song thrush went on singing beautifully from the top of an ash tree, even when the wind was blowing it about, and in these sounds he heard the music of the uilleann pipes.

Ronald Blythe, another seasoned observer of countryside matters on the Suffolk/Essex border, also described the way in which nature, even when cultivated and altered by man, mirrors our human roots and our elemental need of it:

> My neighbour John who has the loveliest fields in Wormingford, with their surprising heights in what is popularly known as a flat country, has given me the obituary of a farmer who died in 1930. This obituary is in the form of one of his fields saying farewell as the cortege passed, the coffin on a flowery waggon, the Suffolk punches be-plumed.
>
> 'I have been a field for nigh on a thousand years, and I know men. Some are clever, some are kind, but very few are clever and kind, but he was, and I am sorry that all the other fields of England—who need him so much these days—will have to go on without him'.
>
> (Blythe, 2005: 261)

These passages of writing evoke something of the power of nature in providing solace, through reminders of that which lends comfort and companionship to the human state. Mabey expresses his need of this when he reflects on how he cannot do without wild creatures. He suspects that our species cannot do without them either, and that to lose contact with them is to lose contact with our origins and with the wellsprings of life.

The concept of the ecosystem was introduced by the botanist Arthur Tansley, in 1935, to draw attention to the importance of transfers of materials between organisms and their environment. And in 1973, the philosopher Arne Naess proposed the concept of deep ecology. He believed that only a deep transformation of modern society could prevent an ecological collapse. He criticised one-sided technological approaches to environmental problems, believing that the design of a sustainable world should be seen not only as a question of environmental technology and economy but also as an issue of world views and attitudes towards life. Diehm (2012: 22) comments that Naess, in his sensitivity to the world of nature and its environment, emphasised an 'awakening to the precariousness of the other'. Similarly,

Roger Deakin (2008: 60) wrote about consideration being at the heart of all true conservation, out of fellow feeling for other living things. These words can equally be applied to loving kindness in psychotherapy. And as Diehm has observed: 'A world in which myriad others follow their own trajectories appears to be one in which there are myriad possibilities for ethical encounter, innumerable occasions for realising that we ought to arrange our lives such that we do not leave others in disarray'. This way of thinking about the environment of human experience, whether from an internal, psychological perspective or that of the external, the social and the environmental, echoes the thought of Emmanuel Levinas, his concept of alterity and his sensitive awareness that 'the precariousness of the other' is of paramount importance, as discussed in Chapters 2 and 8 of this book.

In ecology, an ecosystem is understood to consist of all the organisms and the physical environment with which they interact. Ecosystems, as dynamic entities subject to periodic disturbance, and always in the process of recovering from some past disturbance, are controlled by both external and internal factors. The tendency of an ecosystem to remain close to its equilibrium, despite disturbance, is termed its resistance. The capacity of a system to absorb disturbance and reorganise while undergoing change, so as to retain essentially the same function, structure, identity and feedback, is termed its ecological resilience. It seems inescapable at this point to notice that this description bears a striking resemblance to central aspects of the psychotherapy process. Thus, we could say that human attachment has an unrivalled capacity to attempt to 'remain close to its equilibrium, despite disturbance', and that the resistance sometimes encountered in the psychotherapy relationship can therefore be understood as a core environmental need of the client and not a perverse intransigence designed merely to thwart the psychotherapist. Equally, the capacity of a client 'to absorb disturbance, and reorganise while undergoing change' could describe the recovery process in which a person discovers their resilience.

Thus, nature writers and deep ecologists, like Naess, regard human life and experience as being part of nature and the natural world and not some separate and superior entity. They also propose that myriad 'other-than-human entities' can be valued intrinsically, including species, populations and their habitat, in rivers, landscapes and ecosystems (Diehm, 2012: 19). On this view it is not just mistaken but hazardous to separate human life from its deeper identity in nature. Merchant describes the difficulties posed by this separation in thinking, which corresponded with the development of the nation-state in Europe:

> As European cities grew and forested areas became more remote, as fens were drained and geometric patterns of channels imposed on the landscape, as large powerful water-wheels, furnaces, forges, cranes and treadmills began increasingly to dominate the work environment, more and more people began to experience nature as altered and manipulated by machine technology. A slow but unidirectional alienation from the immediate daily organic relationship that had formed the basis of human experience from earliest times was occurring.
>
> (Merchant, 1990)

Of these developments, the philosopher Susan Bordo (1987: 59) describes an enforced rupture from the organic world, imposing a culture where 'precision, clarity and detachment' became dominant. In this new phase, humanity became 'a decisively separate entity, no longer continuous with the universe with which it once shared a soul'. Here again, the parallel with the psychotherapy process is striking. When people bring their concerns to a psychotherapist, it is so often the case that, whatever their presenting difficulties, the core of the distress they experience is located in a sense of separation and alienation from a true sense of identity and origin. Thus, the psychotherapist, in 'awakening to the precariousness of the other', brings a sense of responsibility to an ethical encounter with the client, with a motive of reintegration between the life of that person, their origins and their soul. A wider sense of shared human precariousness has been brought home more forcefully in the contemporary encounter with climate change and the Covid pandemic, which represent urgent and immediate concerns for all humanity. These events emphasise the fact that humans, in order to survive and to thrive, share the same need to maintain the stable state necessary to all forms of earthly life. However, the psychotherapeutic ecosystem has to accommodate the fact that some will find psychotherapy is not for them, or they cannot proceed with it beyond a certain point.

Chapter 7

Loving kindness and the question of suffering in pandemic times

This book discusses the fact that the creation and maintenance of the therapeutic relationship, through loving kindness, arises from a steadfast focus upon the client as its object of attention. But psychotherapy is by no means alone in its application of loving kindness to processes of reparation, because it is a potential which can respond to all aspects of human life. This includes the fact of mortality, which can also generate fears about the body and its imperfections, especially concerning the ageing process, despite contemporary evidence that older people can, and often do, live fulfilling and creative lives. Many apparently mundane fears, and even some phobias, may conceal a deep-rooted fear of human impermanence. The needless struggle to deny this fact of human life is the theme of this chapter, which will present a case for the way in which a full encounter with the reality of human mortality, rather than being negative or destructive, can be transformative and life-affirming when support, through loving kindness, is present. I will therefore discuss applications of the term loving kindness not only to psychotherapy but also to the work of other caring professions and its beneficial use in the field of palliative care medicine.

Loving kindness in the contexts of human suffering and denial

Loving kindness can be expressed through the fundamentals of effective psychotherapy as identified by Holmes and Slade (2018: 135), which are the building of trust and a capacity to help people who are exploring pain and unhappiness. These fundamentals are also found in the practice of other caring professions and, of course, in human behaviour more generally. The need for loving kindness becomes most obvious at times and in places where pain and unhappiness are likely to be found, especially in those settings where people are faced with the fact that suffering is an unavoidable part of human life. At other times and in different circumstances, kindness may not seem to be so necessary. This presents the practitioner with a common feature of human perception and behaviour, that when all is well and we have full health and strength, it is possible to believe that suffering is not our personal lot and only happens to other people. Thus, it becomes a taboo, a subject personally to be avoided, for fear of bringing it too near. This can be a

DOI: 10.4324/9781003262114-8

powerful reason why people may delay or forever put off the idea of consulting with a psychotherapist, to avoid admitting that this taboo has visited them and may bring with it some perceived stigma or sense of failure.

The nature of denial

The capacity for human denial and repression of such uncomfortable realities was described by Freud (in Wolheim, 1971: 157–176), as something occasionally necessary for the psychological survival of brutal realities and responses to fear. As Akhtar has observed:

> The fact that fear is ubiquitous in the animal kingdom suggests that it is a "needed emotion", . . . one that is important for the organism's survival and functioning. For all living beings, including humans, the emotion of fear serves as a protective device; it warns them that some danger is approaching and they had better take measures to avoid it. This could be in the form of actively combating the "enemy" or rapidly escaping from it, meaning the well-known "fight-or-flight" response to threats.
>
> Some fears are widespread over the animal kingdom and seem "hard-wired". Others are the result of developmentally unfolding, epigenetic sequence of fantasies that are specific to human beings. Among the former are fear of loud noises, sudden and jerky movements, looking down from heights, and animals that have fangs, claws, sharp teeth, and can jump or move at great speed (Abraham, 1913a; Akhtar & Brown, 2005). Present from birth onwards and persistent throughout life (even if in attenuated forms and at a preconscious level), these fears give testimony to man's essential kinship with animals since their function is self-protective and oriented towards survival. Among the latter are the developmentally derived fears of loss of love objects, loss of love, and castration (Freud, 1926d); fear of death joins this list somewhat later during the course of psychic development.
>
> (Akhtar, 2018b: 4)

Thus, it can be seen that developmentally derived fears, such as fear of one's own death, are relatively sophisticated concepts from an evolutionary and cognitive-developmental point of view, when compared with more primitive survival instincts, because they require the ability to conceptualise a sense of living selfhood. Equally, it is perfectly possible for the human mind to repress what seems to be personally unthinkable, that the life of an individual is not a permanent state.

Personal denial

The intense power of denial, of which human beings are psychologically capable in such circumstances, is movingly illustrated by Rachel Clarke (2020) in the context of palliative medicine. In the following dialogue, she describes her responsibility and ethical motivation as a clinician, in sharing honest information with a 36-year-old man whose untreatable condition means that his life is approaching its end. She accompanies her patient, as he traverses the terrifying emotional journey from denial to conscious acceptance of the fact that his life is soon to be taken from him and from his family:

'I don't want to be here. I need to get home as soon as possible,' Joe declared when I entered his room. 'I need to be building up my strength, get some weight back on, be strong enough for the girls and my immunotherapy'. Beside him, Angie sat with her eyes to the floor, tugging at threads on the sleeve of her jumper.

Joe's oncologists, I knew, had already concluded he could no longer withstand further treatment. His seizures had recurred, his tumours were spreading, his body was too frail to take any more. They had transferred him from their ward to the hospice to die, yet neglected to discuss this with their patient. I had been waiting all day for them to come and talk to him, the team he relied on and trusted.

'How soon before I'll get started?' asked Joe, almost childlike in his urgency. 'If it goes well with the immunotherapy, I'm going to get some more gamma knife too. But I have to start now. There's no time to waste'.

Angie, a slight young woman half the size of her husband, began to cry softly. I could see she did not believe a word of it. 'I've really got to get back to the girls,' she told me. 'I just can't wait here any more for Joe's oncologist.'

Two pairs of eyes were locked on mine, one full of hope, the other of tears. I longed with every fibre to be anywhere but here, pinned down by the weight of a life and its extinction. I could only imagine what filled Joe's mind in this moment. Perhaps his youngest's first day at school, his oldest's head teacher's award, the future mermaid birthday parties, the first battle over boyfriends, the summers spent in sand dunes, the snowball fights at winter—all of this life to come, to savour, moments dancing like charms on a string, yet unspooling without him, a father lost to cancer.

The temptation to leave this conversation to others almost overpowered me. I could frame any number of justifications in my head, pretending my abdication was in my patient's best interests. Instead, I steeled myself to prise a young father away from the life he still yearned for, the future he clung to so fiercely.

I took a deep breath and sat down. The external world fell away into shadow. Four eyes, out of time, were waiting and staring. We had arrived at the point where everything hangs in the balance.

The words you choose, in these moments, could not matter more. A misstep may spell irreparable damage. Gently, calmly, without pity or drama, I embarked on the task of cleaving my patient from his future, while striving to preserve something he could still believe in. It is a delicate dissection, the tallest of orders. But it can be done—because the life we have left is still life in all its loveliness, if only we can inhabit the present.

'Joe,' I began, 'the oncologists have seen how much weaker you've become in the last few weeks -'

'Yes,' he interrupted, 'but that's why I'm here. To build myself up again. To get strong enough for immunotherapy.' Even as he spoke, I could see how hard he was fighting to resist his exhaustion. I had to be blunt, choosing words without ambiguity.

'I'm sorry Joe. That's not what they've told us. Immunotherapy can be really tough on the body, and we don't think you are strong enough to take any more of it.'

'You can fix that, though. You can get me stronger. That's what I'm here for. You can give me decent food, physiotherapy. I'll get better. Tell her, Angie. Tell her.'

I turned to Angie, whose head was in her hands, weeping quietly. I needed both of them to know she was in no way responsible for these decisions being made by her husband's doctors.

'Joe,' I continued, 'Angie wants you to live as much as you do. But there comes a point when we know you're too weak for treatment. You're too exhausted. It wouldn't work for you.'

'You don't know that,' he insisted. 'You can't say that for certain. Let me try. Please don't take away my chances.'

I steeled myself to go on. 'Joe, if we tried more treatment now it would make you feel rotten. It might even shorten the time you have left. We can't cure your cancer or slow it down any more. But we can help you feel as well as you possibly can, to give you the best chance of enjoying every day as it comes with the girls and Angie.'

There was silence, the longest, darkest pause. All the advice for these conversations is that you must, without fail, use the word 'dying', but in Joe's case this felt like unnecessary bludgeoning. Like me, Angie waited quietly. The room felt very still. I wondered if Joe were starting to fall asleep in his bed, but behind closed eyes he was thinking, adapting, perhaps, even, accepting. Finally, as though dredging himself back from the underworld, he spoke in a voice little more than a whisper.

'Is there any chance at all of me getting out of here alive?'

I met his gaze without flinching. 'If you would like to spend your time at home then, yes, Joe, absolutely. We are here to try and help you live the time you have left on your terms, the way you want to. We can't stop your cancer, but we will do everything we can to support you, including going home, if you'd like to.'

I knew this was not what he meant. He wanted his whole future, a glimmer of life untruncated. But time was short, so few moments to cherish, and Joe was tortured by the desire to prolong them, chasing round after round of futile treatment. I did not want to crush all his hope. My job was to disillusion Joe sufficiently that he might find acceptance, while not completely devastating him.

'I'm dying,' he said at last.

'Yes, Joe,' I said softly, 'you are. But you still have time with Angie and the girls. That is precious, and we want to help you make the most of it. What really matters to you in the time you have left?'

Recalibrating your hopes—setting achievable goals such as reaching a child's birthday or a final Christmas—can bring great comfort. In Joe's case, his aims were simple: to spend as much time as he could with his wife and daughters. The conversation ended when his fatigue overwhelmed him. Angie and I retreated outside where, to my surprise, she thanked me. 'It had to be said,' she told me bluntly. 'He couldn't enjoy anything. He was so obsessed by treatment.' She paused for a moment. 'Would you talk to the girls tomorrow? They want to ask you some questions too.'

(Clarke, 2020: 201–205)

Denial in communities

Clarke (2021) revisits the realities of this kind of journey of realisation about death and dying in her reflections upon the Covid pandemic which arrived in 2020. She describes the dawning awareness of its potential impact upon all of humanity, placing her observations within their wider social and historical context. Up to the beginning of the twentieth century, witnessing death was a common occurrence for families and communities, including the deaths of children, given the infant mortality rates of those previous times. But in developed, industrialised countries, the fact of dying became increasingly hidden away in hospitals and care homes, making it possible to live an entire life without seeing death. Thus, it evolved in the public mind, from a natural, domestic occurrence, into something fearful and foreign from which many now recoil, and where 'even some doctors have a habit of tiptoeing away from the daunting business of their patients' dying'. However, in 2020, Covid made it impossible to ignore the fact that death and its impact upon the bereaved will always be universal human experiences.

Denial illustrated in literature

Quite uncannily, the ways in which a human community approaches its collective fear of mortality are accurately represented and paralleled in the observations made by Albert Camus in his novel *The Plague*, which Clarke mentions. Apparently, Camus used a nineteenth-century cholera epidemic in Algeria as the source material for this novel which he set in the twentieth century, describing a community trying to contain the fear of an approaching threat to its life.

The narrator of the emerging story is Bernard Rieux, a doctor in the town, who begins to admit to himself the possibility of an epidemic. He notices how the ordinariness of the town and its inhabitants rely upon habit and a foundation of daily routines; life may not be particularly exciting, but in the main it seems to be predictable. Consequently, the community has no reason to believe that any threat to its security is approaching, because this would be so much out of the ordinary. And even when the word *plague* is uttered for the first time, Dr Rieux is himself reluctant to act upon the evidence of his eyes. Like everyone else he is taken by surprise, because it is difficult to accept that this could happen in their town, and so he fluctuates between a state of anxiety and a belief that all will be well. He comments on the general tendency to continue being preoccupied with mundane concerns and to consign fears to the realms of a bad dream, because it is hard to conceive of the enormity of an epidemic in everyday human terms. And so the townspeople continue to make their usual arrangements, believing themselves to be free from any worries over and above those accepted as normal.

Even when the news begins to circulate that there is an infection in the town, it is consigned to the realms of unreality. For as long as the town continues to look the same, the possibility of threat can be ignored and any slight unease dismissed. Dr Rieux continues to rationalise the emerging reality by relying on his medical common sense. He reasons with himself on the basis that whatever is coming can be confronted and solved with logical planning. There is no point in worrying as long as he does his job conscientiously. But gradually the news of the epidemic becomes more public. A few references find their way into the local papers, and official notices advising the townspeople to stay calm begin to appear around the town, but in places where they do not attract attention and written in language which does not cause anxiety. The contagious potential of the infection is not advertised. However, as it takes hold, the narrator finally has to confront the reality of the epidemic because, in his medical role, he can no longer ignore the facts of what he is witnessing. In this novel Camus illustrates the way in which denial of painful experiences, in the end, has to be transformed into an encounter with reality in order to cope with it effectively. And he reflects on the fact that life itself can achieve real substance and authenticity when rooted in an acceptance of its materiality.

The courage of despair

In everyday thinking it seems paradoxical, possibly even repellent, to finally agree with Camus's narrator that part of the substance of vital living is found in the capacity to experience and fully comprehend suffering. In describing the way in which people will for a time, and we might say quite naturally, try anything but face a painful reality, he illustrates how they can be deprived of potential inner resources in so doing. Rachel Clarke's patient—Joe—valiantly attempted this, until he found that his more achievable aim was the simple one of comfort, in spending as much time as he could with his wife and daughters once he was enabled, with sensitive support, to admit that he was dying.

This path of realisation has direct application to psychotherapy, wherein denial of realities can go on depriving a person of their encounter with a more authentic self. But the question remains, of how human beings can possibly be expected to address the apparently incongruous and counterintuitive idea of becoming more rooted in their distress, and how this is distinct from a masochistic kind of self-abnegation. Woodhouse (2009) explores this question in discussing the *courage of despair*, a concept used by the twentieth-century theologian, Paul Tillich. As he explains:

> We may think of courage and despair as opposites, and assume that we have to choose one or the other. . . . A person threatened by despair may determinedly walk forward into the future, refusing to acknowledge their despair in the fear that, if they do, they will be undone. All is well and all shall be well. This is their courage. They may for a time win out over their despair, but they will remain a brittle person, haunted by the fear that the despair may return. . . . Or alternatively a person may surrender to despair and become overwhelmed by it, and curl up in a corner and wish to die, feeling that nothing can be changed and all is hopeless.
>
> It would seem that the choice is either courage *or* despair. But what does it mean to put these words together and speak of 'the courage *of* despair'?
>
> This gives courage an altogether deeper meaning. It is 'the courage to be' *in spite of* death, fate, meaninglessness, or despair. It is about affirming life in the face of what seems unalterable in your situation. You do not pretend that despair is not there. You acknowledge it: it is part of you. *But, by living courageously in the face of it, you rob it of its power.* This is the courage of despair. To live with this kind of courage is immensely challenging. It is the challenge of becoming an integrated and fully human person.
>
> (Woodhouse, 2009: 149–150)

Woodhouse takes as his example the life of a 27-year-old Dutch Jewish woman named Etty Hillesum, who in 1941 was living in enemy-occupied Amsterdam. As a member of the Jewish Council, she went, at her own request, to work in the euphemistically named department of 'Social Welfare for People in Transit' at Camp Westerbork in the east of the Netherlands, where the Nazis aimed to place all Dutch Jews prior to their deaths in the extermination camps. From there she was transferred to Auschwitz, where she died in 1943. But quite extraordinarily Woodhouse describes how, in her letters and journals, she 'invites us to look whatever difficult situations we may face straight in the eye, whether they are personal or much wider, and to engage with them, seeking *life* through that engagement' (ibid., 148). He observes the way in which she steadfastly refuses to deny the reality of the horror she is witnessing and consciously carries the sorrow, loss and hopelessness it brings. In facing up to her situation, and integrating herself with it, she is released to 'face the present with courage, and to believe in the future with hope' (ibid.). This presents her with the demand of an impossibly difficult and courageous struggle but one through which she gains the transformation of becoming fully herself.

In her writing, Etty Hillesum describes the experience of everything important being carried within her, providing for everything she needs, so that she can encounter all the events she witnesses with astonishing equanimity, in the knowledge that she continues to have love for life and for people. She writes about the everyday sensations of sitting on a wooden bench and looking at the wild flowers on the heath beyond the barbed wire of the wooden barracks. She is involved in the daily round of tasks: making coffee, giving out bread and scrubbing the toilets. She reads and shares poetry with a nervous young girl. She comforts a weeping woman with a small child asleep nearby. And among all of this, she pays attention to her own need to be alone sometimes. Woodhouse notices that her writing shows her: 'gently and without any drama, caring, serving, listening, and—in this place of death—giving out life. Punctuated with gentle irony and humour, it is full of warmth and compassion. . . . The despair is not denied: it exists, *but it is entirely swallowed up in courageous living*' (ibid., 152).

Tillich was born and raised in Germany, where he developed a teaching career as a philosopher and theologian, so he was deeply conscious of what the Holocaust meant. And in one of his sermons, he summed up the courage manifest in Etty's life, as the power and triumph of love:

> It is love, human and divine, which overcomes death in nations and generations and in all the horror of our time. . . . Death is given power over everything finite. . . . But death is given no power over love. Love is stronger. It creates something new out of the destruction caused by death; . . . It is at work where the power of death is strongest, in war and persecution and homelessness and hunger and physical death itself. It is omnipresent and here and there, in the smallest and most hidden ways as in the greatest and most visible ones, it rescues life from death. It reaches each of us, for love is stronger than death.
>
> (ibid., 152–153)

Denial and therapeutic avoidance

If we were to transpose Tillich's concept of the courage of despair into the psychotherapy setting, this could raise questions about whether a perceived lack of courage makes psychotherapy seem inaccessible to people who feel unable to find this power within themselves or, even if they can find it, do not feel 'strong enough' or 'good enough' to engage in an exploration of deeper self-awareness. We have seen in the case study of Coral, in Chapter 5, how lengthy and painful her journey was towards awareness and healing. But not everyone has the inner resources to take such a path, and it could seem unintentionally oppressive to assume that they can. We also saw in the case study of Olivia, in the same chapter, how a continuing inherited history determined the way in which members of her family who were suffering did not reach out for help, probably from a belief that to do so would expose them as weak. Consequently, family tradition meant that when Olivia experienced a torrent of feelings about the separation and loss involved in being sent away to boarding school, and her feelings were disallowed, she felt that she was sitting on an 'emotional volcano', fearing that, if she once started to express her emotions, there might be no way of ever stopping. The only option that seemed to be left to her was that of shutting down her feelings. But it is easy to see that it was not courage she lacked; in fact, she needed immense courage just to keep going and to continue to be.

Myths, stigma and fantasies which perpetuate denial of emotional pain

For some, talking about painful experiences can be associated with being seen as not only weak but possibly mad, bad or dangerous to know. Although taboos about mental ill health are declining, they still exist and can prevent people from seeking the help they need, for fear of being seen in a prejudicial light which, even nowadays, can impact upon a person's perceived capacity to sustain employment and to engage in social and community life. As Jacqueline Hopson observes: 'The loss of reason called madness provokes perhaps the greatest human fear, for it is reason that dignifies humanity and separates us from beasts'. She writes of her personal experience as a psychiatric patient undergoing hospital admissions and a variety of treatments, prior to a positive experience of psychotherapy which gave her 'a recovery story to tell' (Hopson, 2019: 241). In an article for the *British Journal of Psychotherapy*, Hopson explores the way in which the psychiatric professions are portrayed in British and American fiction and film, and how stigma and fear influence these portrayals:

> Overall, these depictions are malign: the reader/watcher/player is encouraged to fear the mad, the madhouse and the mad-doctor. Choosing to use less abrasive vocabulary to name the condition of madness makes no difference to the terror the condition arouses, for the content of many books and games aims to inspire fear. In spite of considerable efforts over many years, the stigma which attaches to mental illness remains firmly in place for patients, while psy (sic) professionals also carry their share of 'some of the discredit of the stigmatised' and join patients in a stigmatised group. Popular belief often equates the psy professions with madness . . . and the stigma which clings to sufferers and their professional carers, is perpetuated by a constant stream of popular cultural artifacts.
>
> (Hopson, 2019: 233)

Such oppressive stereotyping of the professionals responsible for the treatment of persons experiencing mental and emotional distress is, of course, unable to accommodate any reflective understanding of the skills and capabilities required in the delivery of effective treatment. These capabilities include the capacity for the professional to engage with his or her own state of mind, whilst being able to distinguish it from the mind of another. And further, for the psychiatric practitioner, Saayman (2021) has observed that the experience of working with some of the most fragile states of mind can require engagement with his or her own 'countertransferential disturbances in a manner that may be frightening, unsettling, and at times overwhelming'. The therapist's own subjectivity can even be eclipsed by that of the psychotic patient, making it very difficult to track their own experiences and responses (Kernberg, 2016).

> The psychotherapist, confronted with what is essentially an obliteration of their subjectivity, can in these instances be thrown into situations where they have to tolerate high levels of anxiety and discomfort, while trying to construct a preliminary version of the patient's subjectivity (Brazil, 1988; Searles, 1966; Yerushalmi, 2018). In these instances, the possibility exists that the psychotherapist may hold the patient responsible for the negation of their subjectivity, providing the therapist with what might be viewed as a reasonable alibi for disengaging from a disturbing experience (Ivey, 2013). Yet engaging with disturbance is, to a large extent, the psychoanalytic task; for the psychotherapist to follow their patient's projections however deep they may penetrate, to hold and render thinkable the resultant disturbance, to separate out their own disturbance from that of their patient, and to give back to the patient an understanding that can be used to construct and validate the patient's subjectivity, perhaps for the very first time (Brazil, 1988; De Masi, 2015; Kernberg, 2016; Long, 2015).
>
> (Saayman, 2021: 48)

Thus, within the relationship of psychotherapy, the psychotherapist must call upon his or her own human experiences as points of reference. Saayman observes that the clinical application of the psychotherapist's own countertransference 'makes up a crucial part of psychotherapy' (Lee, 2017; Long, 2015), because it helps the psychotherapist to keep a hold on his or her mind and to track what is happening in their own experience, even when being disturbed by the transference (Jakes, 2018). Furthermore 'the psychotherapist's deep and nuanced awareness of how they experience their psychotic patient . . . forms part of the structuring of a coherent representation of the patient, made up of all the fragmented self-experiences, undifferentiated part-objects, confusion and pain that the patient fails to cohere on their own' (Jakes, 2018; Lee, 2017).

So the psychotherapist is required to remain focused upon the patient as his or her object of attention and, in so doing, to be thought about by someone else with a thinking mind (Bion, 1957), however disorganised that thinking mind may seem to be, whilst not objectifying the person who is the patient nor completely merging with their individual subjectivity. What has to be tolerated in this intricate process is the inevitable anxiety which is generated, allowing it to be transmuted into a validation of the patient's experience.

Facing mortality in professional settings

In a very different clinical arena, this 'coherent representation of the patient' runs parallel with Rachel Clarke's ability to 'steady the ship' with her patient, Joe, as the end of his life approaches, by holding fast to her task of communicating the most challenging facts to him about his situation, whilst at the same time comprehending, respecting and sympathetically supporting his subjective reality. In her book *Dear Life* (2020), she writes about her own encounter with loss and bereavement, when her father died, and how this deepened her understanding and capability in palliative care medicine. She demonstrates how necessary it is for persons with professional responsibility towards those facing suffering to be able to face their own humanity in all its variety. By doing so and by applying the learning derived from this personal experience to her clinical work, Clarke illustrates how, far from being a negative aspect to be avoided, her practice was enhanced by these courageous steps into a deeper and wider dimension, which extended beyond the usual limits expected of medical practice. And she shows, in her practice with Joe, how these steps can be taken without letting go of necessary professional boundaries. She opened up a substantial and meaningful, if only fleeting, collaboration with Joe and his wife, enabling them to take their next steps in ways chosen and fully understood by them both.

Satoshi Handa (2021: 70–71), a psychiatrist working in Japan, has written about the importance and the difficulty for a therapist 'in accepting his mortality and the finality of things'; matters which represent a deep experience of the human state. He discusses his work with two cases of once-weekly psychotherapy, during which he had to take a three-month period of sick leave. These experiences began a process through which, in coming to face his own mortality, he deepened his understanding of the internal world of his patients. In his writing, Handa illustrates the paradox that, whilst it is natural to deny death, we need to face it if we are to face life. He shows how this paradox generates a 'perpetual oscillation between acceptance and denial of our mortality and the finiteness of things. . . . Time never stops and we will certainly have to depart and say farewell to everything we value someday. However, there is an enormous gap between understanding it intellectually and accepting it emotionally'.

Handa poses a question about why it was that an aphorism—*You will die, too*—which was posted on the front wall of a Buddhist temple in Japan became popular on social media. He wonders why this phrase captured the imaginations of so many people. In answering his own question, Handa concludes that:

> Of course, I never think that I have fully accepted my own mortality and finiteness of things or that someday I will. It is against human nature, and therefore, it is an omnipotent delusion if we think we can reach a point of complete acceptance. . . . Kitayama often talks about Japanese people's love for cherry blossoms. . . . We Japanese enjoy them every spring because we all know how transient they are. They are all the more beautiful because they

fall very quickly. And yet, we would not be able to enjoy them if cherry trees never flowered again. Paradoxically, we can relish the transience of cherry blossoms because we believe that they will come back in the next spring . . .

Our minds accept and deny at the same time and never stop oscillating between the two.

(ibid., 81)

Therapeutic avoidance as fear of personal change

Perhaps the greatest fear of all, therefore, is that of real and personal change. As demonstrated by the case studies in this book, the psychotherapy process when fully engaged is, in and of itself, a question of change. It could be said that because this is also true of life in general, psychotherapy only amplifies the fact and, by allowing this awareness to come to consciousness, makes it possible for people to gradually relinquish the unconscious structures of denial which can prevent it from being acknowledged. However, we are creatures of habit and may choose to live with denial and the discomfort and pain it can cause. That discomfort may include a realistic fear of losing relationships with loved ones, even where those relationships are neglectful or even abusive. This is so often the case in matters of domestic violence, where the abused partner is reluctant to leave, for fear of losing the relationship. Where there is such strong resistance to change, then psychotherapy may not realistically be able to proceed, even though there can be some merit in providing a supportive function; but this can be difficult to do without being drawn into collusion with an abusive pattern and a negative model of relationship.

Understanding the function of denial in institutional settings

In comprehending further the function of denial in the face of suffering, it can be helpful to examine this phenomenon within institutional settings. A study conducted in the late 1950s found that the nursing service in a general teaching hospital carried the full impact of stresses arising from the provision of continuous care for patients, but this was not enough to account for the level of anxiety and stress the nurses experienced (Menzies, 1959: 97–117). Menzies observed that:

> The situations likely to evoke stress in nurses are familiar. Nurses are in constant contact with people who are physically ill or injured, often seriously. The recovery of patients is not certain and will not always be complete. Nursing patients who have incurable diseases is one of the nurse's most distressing tasks. Nurses are confronted with the threat and the reality of suffering and death as few lay people are. Their work involves carrying out tasks which, by ordinary standards, are distasteful, disgusting, and frightening. . . . The work situation arouses very strong and mixed feelings in the nurse: pity,

compassion, and love; guilt and anxiety; hatred and resentment of the patients who arouse these strong feelings; envy of the care given the patient.

(ibid.)

An attempt was made to understand the ways in which the nursing service provided for the alleviation of anxiety, to identify its 'social defence system' and to consider in what respects it failed to function adequately. The conclusion reached was that the social defence system represented the institutionalisation of very primitive psychic defence mechanisms, the main strategy of which was the evasion of anxiety. Clearly, this contributed little towards its modification and reduction.

Menzies concluded that the avoidance of recognising the impact of legitimate anxiety upon trainee nurses, given the nature of the tasks required of them, led to excessive staff turnover and failure to train nurses adequately for the realities of their future roles. Some 30 years later, in my own research within a hospital-based school of nursing (Reeves, 1989), prior to the transfer of nursing training to the university sector, I found that the capacity to retain nurses had remained unaltered and the significant factors governing this pattern appeared to be the same since a study conducted by Birch in 1979. In his role as divisional nursing officer for the Gateshead area health authority, he found that the level of anxiety experienced by student nurses increased significantly after two years of training. The nurses identified the following as stressful factors they encountered during the two-year training period reviewed: being shown up on the wards in front of patients and staff by more senior personnel, dealing with patients with cancer, care of the terminally ill, care of the dying, dealing with bereaved relatives, last offices, dealing with patients on cardiac monitors and with cardiac arrest, anticipation of night duty and progress reports by the ward sister or charge nurse.

In 2020, some 40 years after Birch made his findings, the *Nursing Standard* reported on the recurrent theme that one in four nursing students were failing to complete their degree programmes, despite recent government efforts to reduce the dropout rate. For the fourth consecutive year, a *Nursing Standard* investigation found that almost a quarter of UK nursing students on three-year programmes left their studies before graduation. Across the UK, the attrition rate was 25% in England, 23% in Scotland, 12% in Wales and 10% in Northern Ireland. Whilst it is not within the scope of this book to provide more recent data on this question, it seems reasonable to speculate that there has been a continuing lack of resolve in addressing fundamental questions about the stresses imposed by the real tasks of nursing. This factor has probably continued to be a deterrent to the significant minority of students of nursing who choose not to continue their training or leave the profession soon after qualifying.

Further, citing a study by Revans (1959), Menzies had connected the recovery rates of patients directly with the morale of nursing staff. She found that the social structure of the nursing service was faulty, not only as a means of handling anxiety but also as a method of organising its tasks. She stated that these two aspects could not be regarded as separate, as the inefficiency was an inevitable consequence of the chosen defence system. Thus, she concluded that the success and viability of a social institution were intimately connected with the techniques it used to contain anxiety. She referred to the work of Freud, and the central position given to anxiety and the defences in personality development and ego functioning proposed by Melanie Klein (1948b), suggesting that an understanding of the functioning of a social institution is an important diagnostic and therapeutic tool in facilitating beneficial, institutional change. She noted that Bion (1955) and Jaques (1955) had stressed the importance of understanding these phenomena, relating difficulties in achieving social change to problems in tolerating the anxieties which are released when social defences are restructured. Menzies observed that:

> This appears closely connected with the experiences of people, including many social scientists, who have tried to initiate or facilitate social change. Recommendations or plans for change that seem highly appropriate from a rational point of view are ignored, or do not work in practice. One difficulty seems to be that they do not sufficiently take into account the common anxieties and the social defences in the institution concerned, nor provide for the therapeutic handling of the situation as change takes place. Jaques (1955) states that 'effective social change is likely to require analysis of the common anxieties and unconscious collusions underlying the social defences determining phantasy social relationships'.
>
> (Menzies, 1959: 118)

The continuing absence of focus concerning the impact of the work carried out by nurses, since Menzies completed her study, indicates that their psychological needs are still not acknowledged and that this is implicated in the consistent dropout rate. The needs of medical and other frontline staff are similarly neglected, and the Covid pandemic emphasised an inherent problem which remains unaddressed. The overwhelming number of deaths from Covid and the lack of support in dealing with the anxiety caused left a legacy of moral injury amongst health care personnel, feeling that they should have done more, when in fact they did everything they possibly could to save lives. As Menzies recognised, this of course has a direct impact on the future capacity to deliver care. Current figures indicate that, with a growing and ageing population, at least another 475,000 clinical staff will be needed in the next decade (*Guardian* newspaper, 26.07.22). These figures reflect the impact of the high dropout rate of doctors and nurses since the pandemic. As suggested by this discussion, the ability to retain frontline health care personnel is not merely a matter of economics, vital though such considerations are. If staff are to be enabled to carry out the tasks of health care, then serious attention has to be given to their emotional and psychological needs as human beings. Institutional denial of the inevitable anxieties associated with the care of people facing the end of life stands in the way of progress in understanding the needs of staff.

Supportive factors in resolving denial

When supporting people in situations where legitimate fear can naturally trigger avoidance and denial, it is important for psychotherapists, and other professionals working with similar issues, to offer an authentic and accessible emotional structure which feels strong enough for difficult conversations to proceed. This takes the form of therapeutic listening, as described by Akhtar (2007: 4–22). He observes that 'a maternal sort of holding of the psychically banished elements has to precede a meaningful examination of them with the aim of deeper self-understanding'. And he notices how this capacity for empathy with another does not grow by virtue of reason. Instead, it grows in a response to the needs of patients which demonstrates an affective awareness of their unique, individual nature. 'This kind of basic recognition and inherent legitimisation allows the patient to regard the other, to see the other without relinquishing or losing the vitality of herself'.

An example which illustrates the use of this collaborative empathy is given by Rachel Clarke, when she asks a patient in the hospice what his wishes would be if he became infected with coronavirus.

> 'There's something I need to have a chat with you about, John,' I begin, choosing my words with care. 'Have you been following the news about coronavirus?'
>
> He grimaces in response. 'Awful. I hope they find a vaccine soon.'
>
> I nod in agreement. 'We're having to think ahead about something important, which is what happens if patients here catch the virus. That's what I want to ask you about, John. I need to know your views on that. There's no reason why you should catch it, but if you did, do you have a sense of whether you would want to go to hospital to be treated or stay here with us?'
>
> To my surprise, John smiles without hesitation. 'No hospital for me, Rachel. I know I don't have long. I'd like to stay here if I can. But—now, this is important—if it's better for the other patients for me to go to hospital, then you send me in. I wouldn't want anyone else to catch it because of me, so you send me in if you're worried about that.'
>
> (Clarke, 2021: 69)

Clarke observes how her patient, fully aware of the serious implications of what he is saying, prioritises the needs of others. His first instinct is to consider them with kindness. She reflects on how she has made this request of a man already close to death, to rearrange his thinking around the needs of others, and she concludes that 'it is easy to forget, amid the frenetic business of living, that most people try to be good'. Here, she demonstrates Akhtar's 'maternal sort of holding' of a subject which could escape, as a 'psychically banished element', through avoidance of a perfectly natural fear of death and dying. She allows a meaningful examination of the issue with the aim of deeper understanding. She does so by opening up an apparently ordinary conversation but on one of the most challenging topics imaginable. Her therapeutic approach allows her patient both to be heard and to employ his own resources in coming to an important decision. Thus, loving kindness, as steadfastness in its focus upon our object of attention, is also a collaborative art, which can be used in support of people facing dark and difficult realities. The need for denial becomes less urgent, and may even dissolve, when such realities can be discussed with authentic emotional support. Akhtar (2018b: 33) concludes that courage is a particular variety of response to fear, 'as are counterphobia and cowardice . . . all of us are capable of reacting to fear in all three ways. Which one predominates, when, and with what consequences ultimately gives shape to our adaptation to inner and outer reality, our overall character, and the direction our life takes'.

And that adaptation to inner and outer reality depends upon the support and understanding made available to us. Therapeutic listening provides the possibility of a collaborative experience which, as discussed earlier, must be able to take the question of suffering seriously and 'not simply dismiss it as a symptom of so-called 'negative thinking' or 'biological failure'—there is wisdom in our pain, thus it may be a symptom of something healthy within us' (Davies, 2012: 173).

Intelligent kindness

Campling (2015) observes that the kind of fear which inevitably exists as anxiety in health care settings, due to the nature and the demands of the work involved, can be modified by what she has named *intelligent kindness*.

> Kindness has its roots in the old English word *cynd*—meaning nature, family, lineage—kin. Kindness implies the recognition of being of the same nature as others, being of a kind, in kinship. It implies that people are motivated by that recognition to cooperate, to treat others as members of the family, to be generous and thoughtful. The word can be understood at an individual and at a collective level, and from an emotional, cognitive, even political point of view. Adding the adjective 'intelligent' signals, first that it is possible to think in a sophisticated way about the conditions for kindness, and second that clinical, managerial, leadership and organisational skills and systems can be brought to bear purposively to promote compassionate care. Intelligent kindness, then, is not a soft, sentimental feeling or action that is beside the point in the challenging, clever, technical business of managing and delivering healthcare. It is a binding, creative and problem-solving force that inspires and focuses the imagination and goodwill. It inspires and directs the attention and efforts of people and organisations towards building relationships with patients, recognising their needs and treating them well. Kindness is not a 'nice' side issue in the project of competitive progress. It is the 'glue' of cooperation required for such progress to be of most benefit to most people.
>
> (Campling, 2015: 5)

Loving kindness in psychotherapy offers therapeutic kinship, which can be seen as a vital component within all caring professions. It is able to support individuals and groups by the reduction of anxiety, and it allows for the possibility of denial being transformed into reality, however tough, as long as this foundation is available. As discussed in Chapter 2 of this book, a lack of self-kindness and warmth is central to many states of mental suffering (Gilbert, 2013: ix). But on the other hand, as Gilbert has observed, the experience of receiving kindness, gentleness, warmth and compassion tells the brain that the world is safe and that other people can be helpful rather than harmful.

Chapter 8

A philosophical basis for loving kindness in psychotherapy

In this book I have proposed that loving kindness in psychotherapy is based upon a steadfastness of focus upon the unique and subjective experience of the client as our focus of our attention. This focus is influenced by the experience of the psychotherapist who, similarly, is a warm-blooded human being with his or her own separate and subjective nature. As discussed in Chapter 2, we can refer to this activity of mind and body as *alterity*, defined by Emmanuel Levinas as: 'otherness, or an awareness of our being the 'other of two' (Levinas, 1981, 1989).

This concluding chapter will therefore provide a brief synopsis of ideas which have influenced psychotherapy theory from the nineteenth century onwards, and which are reflected in the humanistic philosophy of Levinas. These ideas support the concept of loving kindness in psychotherapy and the central importance of feelings. Therefore, I discuss the notion of the mind/body split in philosophy and medical science, with reference to Descartes (1641), and how this thinking has met a challenge in the development of affective neuroscience in the twentieth-century work of Damasio (1994, 2000), Panksepp (1998, 2010) and Panksepp & Biven (2012). I apply the concept of intersubjectivity to an understanding of attachment, relational attunement and mentalisation, as proposed by Fonagy, Gerhardt, Holmes and Slade, and the development of contemporary views of mental illness as discussed by O'Keane (2021). Finally, I draw a connection between the development of psychotherapy and the previous cultural heritage of thought within the world religions, concerning ideas about 'good', as discussed by Black (2015) and MacKenna (2002) and in the philosophical writing of Iris Murdoch. Examples of ways in which psychotherapy has developed a special way of listening, also relevant to other caring professions, bring the book to its conclusion.

The relevance of alterity to psychotherapy and supervision

Referring to the work of Schwaber (1981: 378), Akhtar has commented that 'the analyst's task is to seek the inner world of the patient and there is no better way to do so than to listen from the patient's perspective' (Akhtar, 2018a: 12). Such listening forms the basis of the alliance between psychotherapist and client, which

DOI: 10.4324/9781003262114-9

I have described in Chapter 6 as a psychotherapeutic ecosystem. The construction and continuing reliability of this ecosystem, through the experience of being the 'other of two', requires the psychotherapist to be supported by self-awareness, which is a matter of continuing personal and professional development. Consequently, alterity is also central to the psychotherapist's relationship with his or her supervisor. Here, the psychotherapist—as supervisee—becomes the focus of attention of the supervisor. And there is a third side to this supervisory relationship, making up a 'triangle of supervision'. This is the fantasy relationship between the client and the supervisor, wherein: 'Supervisors may have all sorts of fantasies about their supervisee's clients, even though they have never met them. The client may also have fantasies about the supervisor of the person who works with them. . . . These fantasy relationships complete the triangle and like all triangular processes are laden with conflict and complexity' (Shohet and Hawkins, 2006: 96).

Thus, within the interwoven dialogue between individual clients, psychotherapists and supervisors, the focus of each upon the other is subjectively experienced. And inevitably, this triangular network of seeing and being seen gives rise to many engaging discussions in psychotherapy and supervision about whose reality is the most real. As a way of thinking, this method links contemporary psychotherapy with prior discussions of the Enlightenment, on the question of how we know what we know and the epistemology of self-knowledge proposed by Montaigne (Hartle, 2005: 198).

The history of ideas which have influenced psychotherapy

It has been noted in Chapter 2 that ideas about the necessary interdependence of persons, and the inherently social view of humanity which can be seen in psychotherapy theory and practice, were matters of discussion during the period of the Enlightenment in the seventeenth and eighteenth centuries. At that time, philosophical discourse concerning the nature of human experience and the pursuit of knowledge, by means of reason and the evidence of the senses, became dominant. Its origins lay in the development of humanism, which played a central role in European culture from the fourteenth century to the seventeenth century. Renaissance humanism can be defined as: 'a broad intellectual and cultural movement, which contributed to, or at any rate engaged with, disciplines such as biblical studies, political thought, art, science and all branches of philosophy' (Kraye, 1996: xv). Hence the affinity I have highlighted between the thought of Renaissance humanism and ideas which have influenced the development of psychotherapy.

The importance of language

For example, in psychotherapy practice the use of language is essential as it provides the necessary conceptual and emotional grasp of events which have occurred in the personal history of the client. It is necessary for clients to express, as far as they are able, the concerns which have prompted them to seek this form of assistance and, for some, this may turn out to be the first time they have encountered the experience of being properly heard. Then comes the task, for both psychotherapist and client, of developing a common, shared language. This is a development which can take time to evolve, as illustrated in the case studies of Amanda in Chapter 1, and Olivia in Chapter 5. For the psychotherapist, it includes the introduction of concepts which a client may not have encountered before. This is particularly important in situations where there has been a history of emotional or physical abuse, resulting for the client in moral injury and self-blame. Here, it is necessary to point out that, as an infant, a person could not have had sufficient psychological or emotional capability to understand that they were not the cause of the difficulties or the blame being assigned to them. This is demonstrated in the case studies, which offer examples of the emotional and psychological benefits to be gained from such awareness.

An example of a useful concept in psychotherapy

An example of a useful concept which benefits from verbal articulation is that of the *drama triangle* proposed by Karpman (1968). His thinking was influenced by Berne (1964), who asserted that human insight could be discovered by analysing the social transactions between persons. Karpman proposed that a drama triangle is a form of interaction which can develop between people who are in conflict with each other, however hidden or unconscious that conflict may be. The triangle consists of each actor taking the part of either persecutor, victim or rescuer. Each respective role can be used fluidly and can be exchanged between the actors, in ways which achieve unconscious objectives and agendas. This has the effect of allowing important issues to be concealed and left unresolved within the triangular relationship. The drama triangle provides a smokescreen which conceals the avoidance of other, more fundamental, problems. So it is helpful in such cases for clients to know that, having been raised in a family or community where the drama triangle represented the characteristic manner of relating, they would not have had the emotional capability as children to understand or influence this dynamic or the role assigned to them within it. This awareness can assist recovery from trauma and moral injury. It allows clients to acknowledge that now, as adults, they have agency in their own lives and can use their conscious awareness to influence events, by making positive choices to sustain a sense of safety and self-confidence. This is especially helpful where clients are distancing themselves from exploitative and abusive relationships.

The historical impact of humanistic thought

Within the historical context, the evolution of ideas and the ability to communicate and disseminate them more widely were central concerns of Renaissance humanism. These developments were accelerated by technological advances, such as print and the production of books:

> There was no humanism without books. They were the prime material on which the movement was founded and the natural medium through which it

was transmitted. All humanists were consumers, and usually also producers, of books in manuscript. Many humanists first gained a reputation by seeking out and accumulating books. Humanists early associated themselves with the printing press when it came into being in the mid-fifteenth century and provided authors, editors and market for its products.

(Davies, 1996: 47)

Davies observes that by the end of the fifteenth century 'the raw material of humanism—the written word—was available in manuscript and print in greater quantity and more cheaply than ever before' (ibid., 59). Consequently, translators like Erasmus were able to widen their knowledge of ancient texts and variant readings, through an exploration of Greek and non-Christian sources. This enabled them to explore new ideas and suppositions based upon 'experience, knowledge and sensibility' (Hamilton, 1996: 110). New translations opened up the possibility of a wider view of knowledge and its acquisition. Thus, humanist cultural criticism challenged the established political and religious order, because the existence of alternatives undermined the chief support of any traditional society and its 'inability to recognise the value and the possibility of other ways of doing things':

The humanists' 'culture war' turned that inability into possibility, even actuality. Their intimate knowledge of another culture, their habit of comparing that culture with their own age, their realism and their habit of arguing both sides of a question led in the end to an incipient form of cultural relativism. This is perhaps most obvious in the writings of the late humanist writer Michel de Montaigne. . . . A major lesson of cultural relativism, of course, is that what one is in the habit of thinking of as a given of nature may in fact be a product of culture. And what belongs to culture, not nature, is within human power to change. Applied to the sphere of high culture, the will to reject tradition and embrace change can lead to a renaissance.

(Hankins, 1996: 127–128)

And in the sphere of modern psychotherapy, it can equally be said that the ability to reject prior assumptions and embrace change is central to the kind of personal renaissance of which persons can become capable within the therapeutic process.

The thought of Michel de Montaigne

Montaigne said of himself that he was 'no philosopher'. Langer (2005: 1–7) states that Montaigne understood a philosopher to be someone 'indifferent to pain and pleasure', whereas, on the contrary, he was notable for his attention to the influence of the human body and the human element upon behaviour and thought. There are characteristically individual features in his thought and writing, such as his scepticism about universal statements and his preference for particular cases. But whilst he was distinctive and resolute in his personal perspective, he acknowledged that what might be right for him might not be so for another person. His goal was the study of himself and his *Essays* are 'the recordings of the thoughts of a particular man living a particular life', who could see that human beings are capable of making critical, ethical judgements based upon their own experiences. Montaigne rejected the view that morality was derived from the position human beings occupied in a hierarchy, because he saw how similar we are to creatures deemed inferior within such a structure. He insisted that we practice a moral life and not simply theorise it. Similarly, modern psychotherapy can be said to be concerned with 'particular people living particular lives', and it relies upon a level of self-awareness which begins, for the practitioner, with the study of him or herself. This way of thinking later emerged in ideas about psychotherapy, which became current in the latter half of the twentieth century. For example, Rogers (1967: 23–24) stated that experience was, for him, the highest authority: 'The touchstone of validity is my own experience. No other person's ideas, and none of my own ideas, are as authoritative as my experience. It is to experience that I must return again and again to discover a closer approximation to truth as it is in the process of becoming in me'.

The importance of feelings as self-knowledge

From this perspective, Rogers (ibid., 111–112) validated individual human experience as a reliable source of knowledge. He believed that the experience of having feelings represented a potential discovery of unknown elements of the self, too often inhibited by those distractions of everyday life which divert us away from experiencing them in full, or consciously owning them. He saw that the therapeutic relationship provided the conditions within which they could safely be encountered to their fullest extent 'so that for the moment the person *is* his fear, or he *is* his anger, or he *is* his tenderness, or whatever'. And he noticed that the ability to express feelings could be deeply satisfying, whereas it might once have seemed destructive. This was in direct contrast to the experience of living behind a false persona, where unexpressed feelings could build up to explosion point and were liable to be provoked by some apparently unrelated event which was incoherent to others. He asserted that therapy could break this kind of vicious circle, as a client became able to express 'all of the accumulated anguish, fury, or despair'. Consequently, in life outside the therapy, there was less emotional overload from the past; feelings could be expressed more appropriately and were more likely to be understood. 'Gradually the individual finds himself expressing his feelings when they occur, not at some much later point after they have burned and festered in him' (ibid., 318). Hence, Montaigne's reflections on self-knowledge are recognisable and significant in the sphere of psychotherapy, because of his ease with the notion that persons inhabit physical bodies within which their experiences lend them agency in their awareness of self and others. Also, the subjective experience of the individual, which he emphasises, has validity and takes priority in the psychotherapy relationship when reflected back to the client as the focus of the psychotherapist's attention.

Effectively, as Langer points out, Montaigne 'was a philosopher, in a way', calling himself a naturalist, or someone interested in natural causes, not divine ones. For Montaigne this meant the study of causes and effects, as opposed to the analysis of means and ends (Langer, 2005: 3–6). Contemporary psychotherapy also relies upon an understanding of causes and their effects upon personal experience, relationships and the potential for reparation of harm caused by a traumatic or neglectful childhood. This is evident in the field of attachment theory which emerged in the mid-twentieth century, as discussed in Chapters 1 and 6 and in the case studies. It is interesting to see the origins of this perspective, where Montaigne positioned himself within a developing philosophical tradition which sought explanations for natural phenomena without the customary reliance upon the theology of his time. His position could not yet be described as scientific, but it shifted the grounds of inquiry wherein 'this most congenial of writers of philosophy and least seriously regarded philosopher in his own right initiated the first recognisably psychological study of human nature' (Hoffman, 2005: 177). And whilst Montaigne did not see moral philosophy as a wholly theoretical enterprise, his thought contained a central, ethical component. As Schneewind (2005: 225) has commented: 'If Montaigne did not create philosopher's answers to the questions of ethics, he did more. He shaped the questions we are still asking'.

Montaigne's historical context

The distinctiveness of Montaigne's thought is emphasised by its historical context. He was born in 1533 and during his lifetime witnessed some of the violent upheavals of the wars of religion in Europe. Although these were motivated primarily by differences in religious faith, the civil and military context was more complicated, as noble landowning families themselves began to develop religious differences which put them in conflict with each other. Thus, Montaigne was part of a society which was exposed at times to catastrophic change (Langer, 2005: 4–10). Perhaps reflecting the heightened instability of the time, some of the religious belief systems which gained influence viewed human nature as corrupted by 'original sin' and vulnerable to the worst excesses. Given the robust language which seems to have been a particular heritage of the wars of religion in Europe, it is necessary to remember the context within which these beliefs developed; generated as much by competing military powers and landowning interests, as by any theology (Phillips & Taylor (2010: 23–24). Any notion of loving kindness was modified by conflicting attitudes to the nature of the human body and its feelings. This is evident in the thought of Descartes and others, standing in contrast to that of Montaigne.

Descartes on thought and feeling in human experience

In the seventeenth century, Descartes proposed that there were great differences between the human body and the mind, which he saw as quite distinct from each other. His claim to certainty is generally summed up in his statement 'I am thinking, therefore I am' (Markie, 1992: 141). He proposed that the universe contained two radically different kinds of substance: the mind or soul defined as thinking, and the body defined as matter and unthinking (Dicker, 2013: 86). Thus, whilst Descartes believed that a human being was a composite entity of mind and body, he gave priority to the experience of the mind and proposed that it could exist without the body, but the body could not exist without the mind. This view raised an ongoing debate about the relationship between the two (ibid., 303). He stated that:

> The human body, in so far as it differs from other bodies, is simply made up of a certain configuration of limbs and other accidents of this sort; whereas the human mind is not made up of any accidents in this way, but is a pure substance. For even if all the accidents of the mind change, so that it has different objects of the understanding and different desires and sensations, it does not on that account become a different mind; whereas the human body loses its identity merely as a result of a change in the shape of some of its parts. And it follows from this that while the body can very easily perish, the mind is immortal by its very nature.
>
> (From the Synopsis to Descartes's *Meditations*, in Cottingham, 1992a: 239)

The influence of Descartes's ideas upon modern thinking has been substantial. He is widely regarded as the first to emphasise the use of reason in the development of the natural sciences, making him one of the greatest natural scientists of the seventeenth century (Grosholz, 1990 & Gaukroger, 1992: 113). However, an argument of his, that animals are incapable of reason or intelligence, is disputable (Waddicor, 1970: 63). He proposed that whilst animals do not lack the capacity for sensation or perception, this can be explained mechanistically. Sensory stimulation does not, in his view, correspond with activity of the mind. According to Descartes, human beings possess a soul, or mind, and are thus able to feel pain and anxiety, whereas animals do not, and therefore cannot experience these sensations and do not suffer (Parker, 2010). Gaukroger (2002: 180–214) asserts that this view which became prominent in Europe and North America, sanctioned by laws and societal norms, has permitted the mistreatment of animals. However, Charles Darwin proposed that the evolutionary continuity between human and other species indicated that animals are not dissimilar to humans in this respect (Workman, 2013: 177). He conducted an extensive study of the expression of emotion in different cultures and species, and although he thought of human emotions as 'vestiges from previous stages of evolution, he respected the importance of the phenomenon' (Damasio, 2000: 38–39). More recently, the fact that animals are sentient has been confirmed in unexpected and moving ways in Rosamund Young's intriguingly named book *The Secret Life of Cows*. She writes from the perspective of her long experience managing a dairy herd on a family farm. This has enabled her to make the following observations:

Watching cows and calves playing, grooming one another or being assertive, takes on a whole new dimension if you know that those taking part are siblings, cousins, friends or sworn enemies. If you know animals as individuals you notice how often older brothers are kind to younger ones, how sisters seek or avoid each other's company, and which families always get together at night to sleep and which never do so.

Cows are as varied as people. They can be highly intelligent or slow to understand; friendly, considerate, aggressive, docile, inventive, dull, proud or shy. All these characteristics are present in a large enough herd and for many years we have been steadfast in our determination to treat our animals as individuals . . .

Cows are individuals, as are sheep, pigs and hens, and, I dare say, all the creatures on the planet however unnoticed, unstudied or unsung. Certainly, few would dispute that this is true of cats and dogs and horses. When we have had occasion to treat a farm animal as a pet, because of illness, accident or bereavement, it has exhibited great intelligence, a huge capacity for affection and an ability to fit in with an unusual routine. Perhaps everything boils down to the amount of time spent with any one animal—and perhaps that is true of humans too.

(Young, 2017: 1–2)

However, as Turner (2000) has pointed out, living a social life as humans involves a degree of sensitivity and responsiveness to others, which other animals do not necessarily need. Basic emotions, such as anger or fear, may work in the defence of territory, but they do not promote sociability in the human species. Thus, he observes that in humans, basic emotions have evolved into more refined states, such as sadness or shame. These promote the ability to control behaviour in order to engage with more sociable goals. Turner states that the basic emotion of satisfaction has expanded to allow more intense feelings of love, pleasure and happiness, through which people can form bonds with each other. Correspondingly, these more complex and interactive emotions are represented in the physiological structure of the human brain, which has evolved from reptilian beginnings, on top of which has developed a mammalian emotional brain and finally a human neocortex. In tracing the progression of this development, Morrison (1999) has likened it to 'an old farmhouse, a crude patchwork of lean-tos and other extensions that conceal entirely the ancient amphibian-reptilian toolshed at its core', where the most basic functions of life are found. The emotional reaction systems develop above this core and around them the prefrontal cortex and cingulate, which have been thought of as the 'thinking part of the emotional brain' where emotional experience is held, enabling alternative courses of action to be considered (Gerhardt, 2015: 51).

As the emotional brain has developed, human beings have become capable of greater emotional complexity and sophistication. This has opened up a range of alternative possibilities and choices in our interactions, requiring the social capability of reflection upon our emotions and their impact upon others. Correspondingly, the prefrontal area of the cortex has expanded in a manner unique to humans, enabling the identification and prioritisation of sensory and motor information coming from a complex environment, so that decisions about our responses can be made. The prefrontal cortex is so well connected neurologically that it can therefore cope with the immense task of organisation required in responding to the events of everyday life and our interactions with others (Gerhardt, 2015: 51–52). Thus has emerged the human capacity to mentalise; by having a mind able to think about another mind, 'which can be seen as that which defines humanity and separates us from other higher-order primates. . . . Seeing oneself and others as agentive and intentional beings driven by mental states that are meaningful and understandable creates the psychological coherence about self and others that is essential for navigating a complex social world' (Bateman & Fonagy, 2016: 4–5).

Mind-mindedness and mental health

This is further confirmed by the work of O'Keane (2021) in the context of psychiatry. She has used her clinical experience to develop an understanding of how the brain functions and develops throughout the human life cycle. She reflects upon her personal discovery of the way in which her prior studies, in the theoretical classifications of psychology and clinical classifications of psychiatry, somehow blinded her to the importance of subjective experience. She offers a new approach, which turns away from theory, intellectual explanations and classifications of memory, 'to follow the journey of memory from sensory experiences of the world and inner feeling states to neural memory lattices' (O'Keane, 2021: 9–10). She states that, in forming memory, the human brain is essential to the establishment of our sense of self. This approach is opening a door to better-informed perceptions and attitudes towards persons experiencing severe and enduring mental ill health, inviting a more inclusive view of their essential humanity. She places an understanding of their subjective human experience at the centre of her work.

Through an understanding of the wider processes involved in the organisation of memory, O'Keane incorporates the experiences of individuals with mental illness into the body of knowledge in neuroscience and the community at large. This new knowledge of wider memory organisation indicates that psychiatric illness 'probably involves disruptions in integrative brain processes, in network brain function, which we are only coming to understand now through network neuroscience and connectomics' (O'Keane, 2021: 228–229). Connectomics is the study of comprehensive 'maps of connection' within the nervous system of an organism. She describes the 'infinite jostling and flarings of neurons in a vast, pervasive connectivity of present experience interacting with memory networks'. All this microscopic synaptic activity has 'a whole-brain effect and it is the whole-brain effect that presents itself as a conscious experience'. She explains how the brain develops an increasingly complex way of understanding the inner and outer worlds of experience, throughout the life cycle. This is reflected in corresponding changes in overall brain anatomy (ibid., 152).

As a psychiatrist, O'Keane also reflects upon having personally lived through a historical period in medicine, during which it developed better-informed views about brain activity and the nature of mental illness. She remembers that medical students used to be taught about the brain in terms of separate, functionally defined pathways, with psychiatry located 'somewhere in the black hole of the emotional-memory circuit', whereas now we are seeing the beginnings of a scientific understanding of the connected brain. She recalls that:

> There were no neuroscience departments in the 1980s and few in the 1990s— all this brain knowledge is new and has happened in the blink of an eye in historical terms. I have learned about the brain as this knowledge has unfolded, but my reference points for this new knowledge, my foundational memories, are rooted in personal experiences, in the experiences of my patients and in the great creative thinkers who intuited what we are now coming to understand scientifically—great artists who, immersed in introspection, wrote about the experience of memory before we could name the processes involved. I have learned, as we all do, through both knowledge and experience. Foundational memories may be based in established scientific knowledge or in the collective wisdom of the unmodified fairy tale, or the genius of highly creative observers.
>
> (ibid., 227)

She concludes that the benefit to all of us which arises from this new knowledge is gained through the potential it has discovered; that of our ability to merge knowledge and experience and integrate them with skills stored in our memory. The complicated neurological networks of the prefrontal cortex integrate our current experiences with memory. And at its most complex, memory can be consciously manipulated in our imagination, where it works without external sensory input. This enables the formation of new patterns of thinking, imagination and creativity which modify our understanding of the world. This facilitates the potential development of self-awareness and an appreciation of others being similarly self-aware. Importantly, from the point of view of psychotherapy and psychiatry: 'Through this we come to accept the singular human state, common to everyone, of existential aloneness and inseparability from others. The appreciation of others as being mirrored humans is the neural basis for the virtue of human kindness' (ibid., 228).

As these continuing advances in knowledge progress, the possibility of more accurate investigation and understanding of mental health difficulties could herald a time when the stigma associated with them becomes a thing of the past. And now, equipped with this new knowledge, it is possible to understand more explicitly the central importance of emotional life in processes of healing, for example, through the dialogue and deep listening offered in psychotherapy. Gerhardt (2015: 6) comments that this acknowledgement of the significance of emotions would have 'come as a shock to the Enlightenment philosophers and scientists . . . whose attempts to assert the power of rationality involved splitting emotion off as a thing apart—not because they were uninterested, but largely because there was no way of understanding it scientifically at that time'.

She states that there also were pragmatic reasons to split mind and body into separate territories, so that the powerful religious authorities could be persuaded to allow the scientific dissection of bodies: 'Desacralising the body was an important turning point for both medicine and religion. This deal made it possible for a more rational, free-thinking culture to emerge'. This enabled later developments which could offer technical fixes for many aspects of human life. However, emotions could not be fixed in this way and became a sideline in this enterprise.

The continuing debate about mind and body

This debate remains active, enhanced by our increasing understanding of the importance of sensory experience and the communication of feelings in the practice of caring professions, such as psychotherapy. Writing in the late twentieth century, Antonio Damasio, a neuroscientist and neurologist, discussed the fact that by the close of the nineteenth century, Charles Darwin, William James and Sigmund Freud were writing extensively on different aspects of emotion and were giving emotion a 'privileged place in scientific discourse'. Referring to the work of Hughlings Jackson, an English neurologist (1835–1911), Damasio identified the first steps taken towards the idea of 'a possible neuroanatomy of emotion', stating that the right cerebral hemisphere of humans was dominant for emotion and the left dominant for language. But he commented that, despite increasing understanding in the field of brain sciences throughout most of the twentieth century, emotion was not trusted in the laboratory because it was believed to be too subjective, elusive and vague. It was seen as the opposite of reason, which was thought to be free from emotion. 'This was a perverse twist on the Romantic view of humanity. Romantics placed emotion in the body and reason in the brain. Twentieth-century science left out the body, moved emotion back into the brain, but relegated it to the lower neural strata. . . . In the end, not only was emotion not rational, even studying it was probably not rational' (Damasio, 2000: 39).

Damasio believed that, in consequence of this view, there was a lack of evolutionary perspective in the study of the brain and the mind and a disregard for the notion of homeostasis as a basic requirement for maintaining their stability. He noticed that mind and body were still not seen to belong to an integrated whole: 'The mind remained linked to the brain in a somewhat equivocal relationship, and the brain remained consistently separated from the body rather than being seen as part of a complex living organism'. This lack of perspective demonstrated the difficulties posed by the Cartesian split between mind and body, homeostasis being essentially a physiological process which impacts upon all aspects of their functioning. It is a system of coordinated and largely automated physiological reactions necessary to maintain steady internal states. Damasio noticed that scientific progress in understanding the neurophysiology of homeostasis, the neuroanatomy and the neurochemistry of the autonomic nervous system and the complex interrelations between the endocrine, immune and nervous systems, whose interactions produce homeostasis, seemed not to have had much influence on prevailing views of how mind or brain worked. Damasio on the other hand asserted that emotions 'are part and parcel of the regulation we call homeostasis. It is senseless to discuss them without understanding that aspect of living organisms and vice versa'. Thus, he proposed that homeostasis is a key to the biology of consciousness (ibid., 39–40).

Damasio and the somatic marker hypothesis

By 2000 Damasio was able to begin answering the following question posed by Rorty (1992) concerning the Cartesian view of the emotions experienced in the body and the exercise of reasoning:

> What difference, if any, does the specific character of an individual's body make to the way that individual thinks, to his thoughts and to the sequence or association of his thoughts? What must the body be like, so that its contribution to thinking is reliable, and perhaps even useful? . . . Although Descartes did not himself ask these questions in just these terms, answering them is central to the success of his enterprise. In any case, he provided the materials for addressing those issues.
>
> (Rorty, 1992: 371)

Recognising that a new generation of scientists was interested in investigating the connections between emotion and reason, Damasio pursued his own research with patients who had sustained neurological damage in specific sites of their brains, causing a selective reduction of emotion. He found that this was 'at least as prejudicial for rationality as excessive emotion'. This became known as the *somatic marker hypothesis*, in which he proposed that emotion probably assists reasoning, especially concerning personal and social matters involving risk and conflict. He suggested that certain levels of emotional processing were associated with the part of the decision-making area in the brain where reason operated most efficiently. However, he did not suggest that emotions are a substitute for reason or that they make decisions for us, emphasising that emotional upsets can lead to irrational decisions. But he offered neurological evidence to suggest that the selective absence of emotion is a problem in reasoning. He concluded that: 'Well-targeted and well-deployed emotion seems to be a support system without which the edifice of reason cannot operate properly. These results and their interpretation called into question the idea of dismissing emotion as a luxury or a nuisance or a mere evolutionary vestige' (Damasio, 2000: 41–42).

Damasio's findings established the physiological foundations of subjective experience in matters of lived and felt human reality and the capacity to reason. He shed light on the way that, in order for a person to experience another as their focus of attention, there has to be a subjective and felt awareness of oneself to facilitate that experience. The way one person feels about another is a physical experience which can be reflected upon in the mind. Loving kindness in psychotherapy therefore requires a subjective awareness of self in the psychotherapist, in order to experience a focus upon the client as his or her focus of attention, whilst acknowledging and seeking to engage with the subjective experience of her client, as a separate being. Thus, Damasio's hypothesis, that well-targeted and well-deployed emotion seems to be a support system without which the edifice of reason cannot operate properly, is central to psychotherapeutic awareness.

Embodiment, mirroring and epistemic trust

The witnessing of the subjective experience of another is the same as that which forms the basis of a secure attachment in infancy. This is manifested in the phenomenon of mirroring, as discussed in Chapter 6. Referring to the work of Iacoboni (2005, 2009) and Kohler et al. (2002), Gerhardt (2015: 49) discusses the neuroscientific discovery of mirror neurons, which connect people to each other through the interplay of communication, from the outset of infancy. Infants have a capacity to recognise, understand and respond to the behaviour of others and to sense their emotions; hence their focus of attention upon the facial expressions and bodily gestures of those around them, which they imitate. They have this capacity before the cerebral cortex is fully developed. Iacoboni states that their 'observations' introduce infants to social and emotional interaction and help them to comprehend the intentions of others. If they find, through their experiences, that those intentions seem beneficial to them and are consistent and trustworthy, this provides the foundation of *epistemic trust* as identified by Bateman and Fonagy. This term describes 'the social and emotional significance of the trust we place in the information about the social world that we receive from another person—that is, the extent and ways in which we are able to consider social knowledge as genuine and personally relevant to us' (Bateman & Fonagy, 2016: 23).

The embodied nature of reason

Damasio (1994: xv) validated the central importance of feelings in the human capacity to reason, which develops in adulthood. He stated that each feeling has a specific content relating to the particular state of the body at a given time, and its specific neural systems, in the peripheral nervous system and the brain regions which integrate signals connected to body structure and regulation. He observed that 'because the sense of that body landscape is juxtaposed in time to the perception or recollection of something else that is not part of the body—a face, a melody, an aroma—feelings end up being "qualifiers" to that something else'. Thus, he saw that the qualifying body state, positive or negative, is accompanied and rounded up by a corresponding thinking mode: 'fast moving and idea rich, when the body-state is in the positive and pleasant band of the spectrum, slow moving and repetitive, when the body-state veers towards the painful band'. Feelings equip human beings to match their nature with the surrounding context and circumstances, to make appropriate responses and to sense discrepancies, as circumstances require at any given moment. By the term *nature* Damasio meant both that which is inherited as 'a pack of genetically engineered adaptations' and the nature we acquire through individual development and interactions with our social environment. Feelings, and the emotions which give rise to them, are the parts of our nature which act as an internal guide, to assist communication with others and to signal our intentions. Thus, he concluded that: 'Contrary to traditional scientific opinion, feelings are just as cognitive as other percepts. They are the result of a most curious physiological arrangement that has turned the brain into the body's captive audience'.

Damasio believed that the idea of this curious physiological arrangement is important because the body, as represented in the brain, may provide the frame of reference for the neural processes that we experience as the mind, wherein 'our very organism rather than some absolute external reality is used as the ground reference for the constructions we make of the world around us and for the construction of the ever-present sense of subjectivity that is part and parcel of our experiences' (ibid., xvi). Thus, he asserted that: 'the mind exists in and for an integrated organism; our minds would not be the way they are if it were not for the interplay of body and brain during evolution, during individual development, and at the current moment. The mind had to be first about the body, or it could not have been'. This assertion negates the Cartesian idea of the mind/body split, so that it becomes possible to say that loving kindness in psychotherapy is a rational response to the other, made upon the basis of authentic feelings.

The contribution of psychotherapy

Given the developments in thought following the Enlightenment, and the clinical application of ideas concerning the resolution of psychological and emotional distress since then, it becomes possible to define the contribution of psychotherapy. Holmes and Slade refer to a description of psychoanalysis by Freud (1937) as an *impossible profession*, in that its outcomes are impossible to predict. But they observe that, in order to be fully understood, the complexity of psychotherapy needs to be accommodated. They modify Freud's idea by suggesting that psychotherapy, far from being impossible:

> can be more usefully seen as an *improbable* profession. But what exactly do we mean by that? For us psychotherapy is the 'art of the improbable' in the mathematical sense of creating conditions—unlikely under normal

circumstances—which catalyse psychic change. Psychotherapy subverts 'normal circumstances'. The format of therapy and the skills of the therapist facilitate the uncoupling of entrenched sequences of expectations and actions which, in non-psychotherapeutic life, perpetuate patterns of unhappiness and self-defeatingness. 'Improbably' surprising revelations and new configurations thereby emerge.

(Holmes & Slade, 2018: 148)

In comprehending the 'improbable' nature of psychotherapy, Miller et al. (2013) suggest that the key to therapeutic success lies in 'deep, domain-specific' understanding, rather than theoretical knowledge as such. This understanding has to accommodate the fact of O'Keane's 'singular human state, common to everyone, of existential aloneness and inseparability from others', wherein the appreciation of others as being mirrored humans is the neural basis for the virtue of human kindness. This is the centrepiece of effective psychotherapy. And it explains how it is that the psychotherapy relationship is both mutual, as regards expression of feeling, and asymmetrical, because the therapist is involved but also to some extent non-attached. As Hobson (1985: 37) suggested, the psychotherapist 'should enjoy himself and yet not seek gratification at the expense of his client. He is open in relation to this particular person now, at this moment, and his responses should be congruent with the goals of therapy, the agreed problems. He does not express what he does not genuinely feel. But that is not to say that he gives vent to every fleeting emotion' (Hobson, 1985: 37, 280). Feeling involves balanced judgement. Even in the mirroring offered by loving kindness, the existential aloneness of the other will always be present as part of the human state. Thus, he notices that 'without tenderness the noise of our talk does harm', and he proposes that the psychotherapist needs to discover a language 'in which we can go out to meet and to respond to our patients with honest respect and quiet tenderness'. Quite simply, one person is trying to help another (Lomas, 1993: 172).

The cultural heritage of psychotherapy

It is noticeable that O'Keane's observations concerning the 'neural basis for the virtue of human kindness' are recognisable in a heritage traditionally held by religion, where loving kindness is a central concept. The novelist and philosopher, Iris Murdoch, observed that the significance and unity of a moral ethic had consoling power, often evident in the nineteenth-century novel where it could represent a set of profound beliefs. She noticed the shift in twentieth-century thinking, when notions of God and the soul seemed to disappear, leaving the individual to figure out his or her own code of morality, based upon subjective experience and willpower alone, rather than a shared sense of inherent human values. And she suggested that concurrent technological advances and remedies were in that regard superficial, belying a deep loss of personal reference points and generating an anxious modern consciousness (Murdoch, 1998: 222–224). As MacKenna has observed:

> the idea of God has traditionally been one of the chief symbols by which Western people have expressed themselves into existence (maybe this applies more generally, but I am only competent to speak of the Judaeo-Christian tradition); the very boundlessness of God being an expression of the fact that human being is not fixed and static, but a constant process of becoming. Once society lost this unifying image, there was no common container into which individual and collective aspirations could be poured.
>
> (MacKenna, 2006: 326–327)

He notices a psychological contrast between early Christian development and 'the nineteenth-century death of God with its unconscious deification of man. Far from turning the Christian man or woman into a super person—Nietzsche's vision, so terrifyingly fulfilled in the twentieth century—the sense of divine indwelling made it safer for the individual to accept the limitations of mortality and the frailty of human imperfection' (ibid., 330–331). He points to a parallel between the early Christian revolution and the possibilities opened up by psychotherapy, both of which in different ways offer a container wherein persons can engage in a 'constant process of becoming'. In this, he refers to Jung's distinction between ego and self:

> Jung's ego is the semi-constant, semi-fluctuating awareness I have of myself; but it is not, and never can be, the whole of myself. At any given moment there are more things I know about myself than can be held in consciousness. The ego, like a beam of light, can only focus on so much at one time. Beyond the realm of things able fluently to inform my consciousness, there is a vastly greater realm of human possibility: everything I have it in me to be or to become, which Jung calls self.
>
> (ibid., 331)

In order for things fluently to inform consciousness during the psychotherapy process, a therapeutic container is required, as illustrated in the case studies offered in this book. Given the fragility and transience of all human life, that container is at best offered in a spirit of loving kindness. Through this we can: 'recognise goodness because we are moved by it when we encounter it; we recognise it directly, we don't deduce it from some reported statement of God's will or commandments' (Black, 2015: 521). This supports Iris Murdoch's assertion (2001: 100) that love, 'when it is even partially refined . . . is the energy and passion of the soul in its search for Good, the force that joins us to Good and joins us to the world through Good'. This allows the possibility of what Levinas described as an epiphany, which he saw as transcendent of ordinary vision:

> or the world of natural science, in which I might see the literal face of the other and shrug my shoulders;. . . I might think the other is nothing to do with me; I might see nothing wrong with murder or genocide.
> This notion of the 'face of the other', which evokes in me the awareness of my responsibility, is very remarkable. It is not a mythological notion, like the gods or demons of a religion, but nor is it an abstraction like the concepts of philosophy. It is a notion that derives directly from felt experience, not from theory, and theoretical ideas are not allowed to intrude, to criticize, diminish, or 'interpret' it. . . . The face of the Other, therefore, is a notion that carries both emotion and obligation.
>
> (Black, 2015: 517)

The process of becoming fully human requires the presence of loving kindness, in order for it to be refined into a secure and satisfying experience. Each individual attachment process, and its impact upon the individual, demonstrates that a life has either been able to develop in this way or, as can so often be found in the psychotherapy consulting room, has been impeded and damaged. Loving kindness in psychotherapy offers an opportunity for this to be put right, by acknowledging what has been missing. Through steadfast and compassionate attention to the client, it gives structure and form to a process within which emotional and psychological experiences can be understood and repaired. But the foundations of this process need to be consistently maintained and supported and they depend upon the values of society. As Black has observed:

> we cannot take for granted that a society's highest values will survive in the long term as effective motivators within that society. By 'highest values' I mean values such as justice, concern for members of weak and minority groups, and respect for promises and for the attempt to speak truthfully. . . . If they are to survive and to be effective, two things may be necessary: firstly, unpredictable 'epiphanic' moments in which the power of these values is emotionally experienced by individuals, and secondly, institutions and a vocabulary in which these values can be remembered, discussed and affirmed in emotionally and imaginatively impactful ways.
>
> (ibid., 510)

He concludes with the reflection that when Philip Larkin the poet, 'an unbeliever, embarrassed to have strayed into a church, took off his cycle-clips 'with awkward reverence', he was recognising the values embodied in his surroundings. When later, somewhat reluctantly, he tried to spell out the significance of the experience, he wrote: 'A serious house on serious earth it is' (Larkin, 1988: 97–98). And psychotherapy is, after all, a serious business.

Conclusion

In this book I have explored the topic of loving kindness in psychotherapy with clinical and reflective applications to case studies from my practice, psychotherapy theory, biographical examples and themes from literature. I conclude that loving kindness regards the psychotherapy client as its focus of attention because this is a fundamental expression of humanity. I have discussed the nature of infant attachment, its central role in emotional development and the essential place of mirroring in the nurture of infants, which facilitates the development of an emotional brain and the capacity to mentalise. The discussion has required analysis of the foundations of human communication, in the interplay between the subjective nature of human experience and the presence of another.

I propose that loving kindness in psychotherapy provides the basis of a relationship which helps to integrate the subjective experience of the client, when he or she is seen as the object of kind attention by the psychotherapist. Erikson (1958: 75) named this process, not as a matter of objective knowledge, but one of disciplined subjectivity in which the therapist, 'in order to discover the patient's unconscious and refrain from imposing unconscious assumptions of his own, must listen in a special way, waiting for the gradual emergence of the themes which signal the patient's message. The material ought not to be subsumed under existing categories. The patient is a 'series of one' who must be understood in terms of the unique *experiences* of his life'.

By listening in a special way, loving kindness allows us to 'open our tent flaps to the suffering other, without too many preconceptions about what will come in or what will be given or taken, we can take some satisfaction in being used, in surrendering to the otherness of the other. We need not worry about doing it perfectly, understanding perfectly, or any of that' (Orange, 2016: 42).

Bibliography

Abraham, K. (1913a). Restrictions and transformations of scoptophilia in psycho-neurotics: with remarks on analogous phenomena in folk-psychology. In *Selected Papers on Psychoanalysis* (pp. 169–234). New York: Brunner/Mazel.

Akhtar, S. (Ed.). (2007). *Listening to others: Developmental and clinical aspects of empathy and attunement*. Plymouth: Jason Aronson.

Akhtar, S. (2018a). *Psychoanalytic listening: Methods, limits, and innovations*. Abingdon: Routledge.

Akhtar, S. (2018b). *Sources of suffering: Fear, greed, guilt, deception, betrayal and revenge*. Abingdon: Routledge.

Akhtar, S. (2022). *Tales of transformation: A life in psychotherapy and psychoanalysis*. Bicester: Phoenix.

Akhtar, S., & Brown, J. (2005). Animals in psychiatric symptomatology. In: S. Akhtar & V.D. Volkan (Eds.), *Mental zoo: Animals in the human mind and its pathology* (pp. 3–38). Madison, CT: International Universities Press.

Amati-Mehler, J., & Argentieri, S. (1989). Hope and hopelessness: A technical problem? *International Journal of Psychoanalysis, 70*, 295–304.

Ashton, R. (1996). *George Eliot: A life*. London: Hamish Hamilton.

Baldwin, J. (1955). *Notes of a native son*. Boston: Beacon Press.

Ballatt, J., Campling, P., & Maloney, C. (2020). *Intelligent kindness: Rehabilitating the welfare state*. Cambridge: Cambridge University Press.

Bancroft, L., & Patrissi, J. (2011). *Should I stay or should I go? A guide to knowing if your relationship can—and should—be saved*. New York: Berkeley.

Baraitser, L. (2008). Mum's the word: Intersubjectivity, alterity, and the maternal subject. *Studies in Gender and Sexuality, 9* (1), 86–110.

Barber, L. (2011). *An education*. London: Penguin Books.

Barlow, J., McMillan, A., Kirkpatrick, S., Ghate, D., Smith, M., & Barnes, J. (2008). Health-led parenting interventions in pregnancy and early years. Research Report No. DCSF-RW070.

Barnes, H., Hurley, R., & Taber, K. (2019). Moral injury and PTSD: Often co-occurring yet mechanistically different. *Journal of Neuropsychiatry and Clinical Neurosciences, 31*, A4.

Bateman, A., & Fonagy, P. (2004). *Psychotherapy for borderline personality disorder: Mentalization-based treatment*. New York: Oxford University Press.

Bateman, A., & Fonagy, P. (2016). *Mentalization-based treatment for personality disorders: A practical guide*. Oxford: Oxford University Press.

Belsky, J. (2006). The development and evolutionary psychology of intergenerational transmission of attachment. In C. Carter, L. Ahnert, K. Grossman, S. Hardy, M. Lamb, S. Porges & N. Sacher (Eds.), *Attachment and bonding: A new synthesis*. Cambridge, MA: MIT Press.

Berne, E. (1964). *Games people play: The psychology of human relationships*. New York: Grove Press.

Bion, W. (1954). Notes on the theory of schizophrenia. *International Journal of Psychoanalysis, 35*, 113–118.

Bion, W. (1955). Group dynamics: A review. In M. Klein, P. Heimann & Money-Kyrle (Eds.), *New directions in psychoanalysis*. London: Tavistock Publications, pp. 440–477.

Bion, W. (1957). Differentiation of the psychotic from the non-psychotic personalities. *International Journal of Psychoanalysis, 38*, 266–275.

Bion, W. (1959). Attacks on linking. *International Journal of Psychoanalysis, 40*, 308–315. Reprinted in *second thoughts: Selected papers on psycho-analysis*. London: William Heinemann.

Bion, W. (1962a). *Learning from experience*. London: William Heinemann.

Bion, W. (1962b). A theory of thinking. *International Journal of Psychoanalysis, 43*, 306–310.

Bion, W. (1965). *Transformations*. London: William Heinemann.

Bion, W. (1967a). Notes on memory and desire. *Psychoanalytic Forum, 2*, 271–280.

Bion, W. (1967b). *Second thoughts: Selected papers on psycho-analysis*. London: William Heinemann.

Bion, W. (1970). *Attention and interpretation*. London: Tavistock.

Birch, J. (1979). The anxious learners. *Nursing Mirror, 148* (6).

Black, D. (2015). Religion as the affirmation of values. *British Journal of Psychotherapy, 31* (4), 510–523.

Bloom, H. (Ed.). (1987). *Michel de Montaigne*. New York: Chelsea House.

Blythe, R. (1978). 'Far from the madding crowd': Introduction to the Penguin English Library edition of Hardy, T. (1874). *Far from the madding crowd*. London: Penguin.

Blythe, R. (2005). *Borderland: Volume 111 of the Wormingford trilogy*. Norwich: Black Dog Books/Canterbury Press.

Boadella, D. (1974). Stress and character structure. *Energy and Character: International Journal of Biosynthesis, 5*, 41–83.

Bordo, S. (1987). *The flight to objectivity: Essays on Cartesianism and culture*. Albany, NY: University of New York Press.

Boutcher, W. (2005). Montaigne's legacy. In U. Langer (Ed.), *The Cambridge companion to Montaigne* (pp. 27–52). Cambridge: Cambridge University Press.

Bowlby, J. (1969). *Attachment and loss: Volume 1: Attachment*. London: Hogarth Press and the Institute of Psychoanalysis.

Bowlby, J. (1973). *Attachment and loss: Volume 11: Separation, anxiety and anger*. London: Hogarth Press and the Institute of Psychoanalysis.

Boyesen, G. (1980). *Biodynamic psychology: The collected papers (Volumes 1 & 2)*. London: Biodynamic Psychology Publications.

Brazil, H. (1988). On questioning the psychotherapy of psychosis: Discussion of 'Care and Confidence' by Paivikki Viinisalo. *American Journal of Psychoanalysis, 48* (4), 320–7.

Bromberg, P. (2006). *Awakening the dreamer: Clinical journeys*. Mahwah, NJ: The Analytic Press.

Campbell, D., & Groenback, M. (2006). *Taking positions in the organization*. London: Karnac.

Campling, P. (2015). Reforming the culture of healthcare: The case for intelligent kindness. *British Journal of Psychiatry Bulletin, 39* (1), 1–5.

Camus, A. (1947). *The plague.* (Published in translation (1960) by Penguin Books, in association with Hamish Hamilton). London: Penguin.

Casement, P. (1985). *On learning from the patient.* Hove: Routledge.

Clarke, D. (2006). *Descartes: A biography.* Cambridge: Cambridge University Press.

Clarke, R. (2020). *Dear life: A doctor's story of love and loss.* London: Little, Brown.

Clarke, R. (2021). *Breathtaking: Inside the NHS in a time of pandemic.* London: Little, Brown.

Cobb, M. (2020). *The idea of the brain.* New York: Basic Books (Edited extract, *The Guardian* Journal, 27 February 2020), p. 10.

Corpt, E. (2009). The importance of analytic generosity in the treatment of intergenerational trauma. Paper presented at the Conference on Intergenerational Trauma, Dublin/ London.

Cottingham, J. (1992a). *The Cambridge companion to Descartes.* Cambridge: Cambridge University Press.

Cottingham, J. (1992b). Cartesian dualism: Theology, metaphysics, and science. In J. Cottingham (Ed.), *The Cambridge companion to Descartes* (pp. 236–257). Cambridge: Cambridge University Press.

Coxon, P. (2018). Hardy's loving-kindness. *The Hardy Society Journal, 14* (2), 56–60.

Cozolino, L. (2007). *The neuroscience of human relationships: Attachment and the developing brain.* New York: W.W. Norton.

Crittenden, P. (1990). Internal representational models of attachment relationships. *Infant Mental Health Journal, 11* (3), 259–277.

Csibra, G., & Gergely, G. (2011). Natural pedagogy as evolutionary adaptation. *Philosophical Transactions of the Royal Society of London. Series B, Biological Sciences, 366,* 1149–1157.

Cunning, D. (Ed.). (2014). *The Cambridge companion to Descartes' meditations.* Cambridge: Cambridge University Press.

Damasio, A. (1994). *Descartes' error: Emotion, reason and the human brain.* New York: Avon Books, Inc.

Damasio, A. (2000). *The feeling of what happens: Body, emotion and the making of consciousness.* London: Vintage.

Davies, J. (2012). *The importance of suffering: The value and meaning of emotional discontent.* Hove: Routledge.

Davies, M. (1996). Humanism in script and print in the fifteenth century. In J. Kraye (Ed.), *The Cambridge companion to renaissance humanism* (pp. 47–62). Cambridge: Cambridge University Press.

De Masi, F. (2015). Delusion and bi-ocular vision. *International Journal of Psychoanalysis, 96* (5), 1189–211.

Deakin, R. (2008). *Notes from Walnut Tree Farm.* T. Blacker & A. Hastie (Eds.). London: Hamish Hamilton.

Descartes, R. (1641). *Meditations.* In *The philosophical writings of Descartes.* (Translated by J. Cottingham, R. Stoothoff, and D. Murdoch (1984). Cambridge: Cambridge University Press.

Dickens, C. (1850/1991). *David Copperfield* (New Oxford Illustrated edition). London: Everyman's Library.

Dickens, C. (1857/1985). *Little Dorrit*. John Holloway (Ed.). London: Penguin Classics.

Dickens, C. (1861/1996). *Great expectations*. London: Penguin Classics.

Dicker, G. (2013). *Descartes: An analytic and historical introduction*. Oxford: Oxford University Press.

Diehm, C. (2012). Alterity, value, autonomy: Levinas and environmental ethics. In W. Edelglass, J. Hatley & C. Diehm (Eds.), *Facing nature: Levinas and environmental thought* (pp. 11–24). Pittsburgh, PA: Duquesne University Press.

Duffell, N., & Basset, T. (2016). *Trauma, abandonment and privilege: A guide to therapeutic work with boarding school survivors*. Abingdon: Routledge.

Durkheim, E. (1964/1915). *The elementary forms of religious life*. London: George Allen & Unwin (via Project Gutenberg (2012). Translated by J.W. Swain).

Edinger, E. (1972). *Ego and archetype: Individuation and the religious function of the psyche*. Boston, MA: Shambala Publications.

Eliot, G. (1860/1964). *The mill on the floss* (Everyman paperback edition). London: J.M. Dent.

Erikson, E. (1958). The nature of clinical evidence. In D. Lerner (Ed.), *Evidence and inference*. Glencoe, IL: The Free Press of Glencoe.

Fairbairn, R. (1952). *Psychological studies of the personality*. London: Tavistock Publications & Routledge & Kegan Paul.

Feldman, R. (2015b). The adaptive human parental brain: Implications for children's social development. *Trends in Neuroscience*, *38*, 387–399.

Fliess, R. (1942). The metapsychology of the analyst. *Psychoanalytic Quarterly*, *11*, 211–227.

Ferenczi, S. (1949). Ten letters to Freud. *International Journal of Psychoanalysis*, *30*, 243–250.

Fonagy, P. (2001). *Attachment theory and psychoanalysis*. New York: Other Press.

Fonagy, P., & Campbell, C. (2015). Bad blood revisited: Attachment and psychoanalysis. *British Journal of Psychotherapy*, *31* (2), 229–250.

Fonagy, P., & Target, M. (1996). Playing with reality: 1. Theory of mind and the normal development of psychic reality. *International Journal of Psychoanalysis*, *77*, 217–233.

Fonagy, P., & Target, M. (1997b). Research on intensive psychotherapy with children and adolescents. *Child and Adolescent Psychiatric Clinics of North America*, *6*, 39–51.

Fonagy, P., Gergely, G., Jurist, E., & Hepworth, M. (2004). *Affect regulation, mentalization and the development of the self*. Hove: Routledge.

Fonagy, P., Steele, H., & Steele, M. (1991). Maternal representations of attachment during pregnancy predict organization of infant-mother attachment at one year of age. *Child Development*, *62*, 891–905.

Fonagy, P., Steele, M., Steele, H., Leigh, T., Kennedy, R., Mattoon, G., & Target, M. (1995). Attachment, the reflective self, and borderline states. In: S. Goldberg, R. Muir & J. Kerr (Eds.), *Attachment theory: Social, developmental and clinical perspectives* (pp. 233–278). London: Analytic Press.

Fonagy, P., & Target, M. (2003). *Psychoanalytic theories: Perspectives from developmental psychopathology*. London: Whurr Publications.

Forster, J. (1872). *The life of Dickens (Volume 1)*. London: Chapman Hall.

Frame, D. (1965). *The complete essays of Montaigne* (Translated by Donald M. Frame). Stanford, CA: Stanford University Press.

Frank, A. (1969). The unrememberable and the unforgettable: Passive primal repression. *Psychoanalytic Study of the Child*, *24*, 48–77.

Frankl, V. (1946/2006). *Man's search for meaning*. Boston, MA: Beacon Press.

Freud, S. (1895). *Studies on hysteria*. (Translated from the German and edited by James Strachey (1955)). *The standard edition of the complete psychological works of Sigmund Freud* (Volume 2, pp. 1–335). London: Hogarth.

Freud, S. (1905). Three essays on the theory of sexuality. In *The standard edition of the complete psychological works of Sigmund Freud* (Volume 7, pp. 125–244). London: Hogarth.

Freud, S. (1915). Thoughts for the times on war and death. In *The standard edition of the complete psychological works of Sigmund Freud* (Volume 14, pp. 273–300). London: Hogarth.

Freud, S. (1916). On transience. In *The standard edition of the complete psychological works of Sigmund Freud* (Volume 14, pp. 303–307). London: Hogarth.

Freud, S. (1923). The ego and the id. In *The standard edition of the complete psychological works of Sigmund Freud* (Volume 19, pp. 1–66). London: Hogarth.

Freud, S. (1926d). Inhibitions, symptoms and anxiety. In *The standard edition of the complete psychological works of Sigmund Freud* (Volume 20, pp. 87–172). London: Hogarth.

Freud, S. (1937). Analysis terminable and interminable. In *The standard edition of the complete psychological works of Sigmund Freud* (Volume 23, pp. 211–253). London: Hogarth.

Gaukroger, S. (1992). The nature of abstract reasoning: philosophical aspects of Descartes work in algebra. In J. Cottingham (Ed.), *The Cambridge companion to Descartes* (pp. 91–114). Cambridge: Cambridge University Press.

Gaukroger, S. (2002). *Descartes' system of natural philosophy*. Cambridge: Cambridge University Press.

Gergely, G., & Watson, J. (1996). The social biofeedback model of parental affective mirroring. *International Journal of Psychoanalysis, 77*, 1181–1182.

Gerhardt, S. (2004). *Why love matters* (1st edition). Hove: Routledge.

Gerhardt, S. (2015). *Why love matters* (2nd edition). Hove: Routledge.

Gerrard, J. (2015). Hopelessness in the analysis. *British Journal of Psychotherapy, 31* (3), 348–359.

Gilbert, P. (2013). *The compassionate mind: A new approach to life's challenges*. London: Robinson (An imprint of Little, Brown Book Group).

Gilbert, P. (2020). Compassion: From its evolution to a psychotherapy. *Frontiers in Psychology: Review, 11*, 1–31.

Gilbert, P., Basran, J., MacArthur, M., & Kirby, J. (2019). Differences in the semantics of prosocial words: An exploration of compassion and kindness. *Mindfulness, 10* (11), 2259–2271.

Green, A. (2000). Commentary. *Journal of the American Psychoanalytic Association, 48* (1), 57–66.

Greene, B. (2021). *Until the end of time: Mind, matter, and our search for meaning in an evolving universe*. London: Penguin Books.

Grosholz, E. (1990). *Cartesian method and the problem of reduction*. Oxford: Clarendon Press.

Grotstein, J. (1981). *Splitting and projective identification*. New York: Jason Aronson.

Grotstein, J. (1984). Forgery of the soul. In M. Nelson & M. Eigen (Eds.), *Evil: Self and culture*. New York: Human Sciences Press.

Grotstein, J. (1995). Orphans of the 'real': Some modern and postmodern perspectives on the neurobiological and psychosocial dimensions of psychosis and other primitive mental disorders. *Topeka, KS: Bulletin of the Menninger Clinic, 59* (3).

Hamilton, A. (1996). Humanists and the Bible. In: J. Kraye (Ed.), *The Cambridge companion to renaissance humanism* (pp. 100–117). Cambridge: Cambridge University Press.

Handa, S. (2021). Mortality and finiteness. *British Journal of Psychotherapy, 37* (1), 70–83.

Hankins, J. (1996). Humanism and the origins of modern political thought. In J. Kraye (Ed.), *The Cambridge companion to renaissance humanism* (pp. 118–141). Cambridge: Cambridge University Press.

Hardy, T. (1874/2012). *Far from the madding crowd.* London: Penguin English Library.

Hardy, T. (1886/1997). *The mayor of Casterbridge.* London: Penguin.

Hartle, A. (2005). Montaigne and skepticism. In U. Langer (Ed.), *The Cambridge companion to Montaigne* (pp. 183–206). Cambridge: Cambridge University Press.

Hertzman, C. (1997). The biological embedding of early experience and its effects on health in adulthood. *Annals of the New York Academy of Sciences:* 85–95.

Hobson, R. (1985). *Forms of feeling: The heart of psychotherapy.* London: Tavistock Publications.

Hoffman, G. (2005). The investigation of nature. In U. Langer (Ed.), *The Cambridge companion to Montaigne* (pp. 163–182). Cambridge: Cambridge University Press.

Holmes, J. (1993). Attachment theory: A biological basis for psychotherapy? *British Journal of Psychiatry, 163,* 430–438.

Holmes, J. (1998). The changing aims of psychoanalytic psychotherapy: An integrative perspective. *International Journal of Psychoanalysis, 79,* 227–240.

Holmes, J. (2014). *John Bowlby and attachment theory* (2nd edition). London: Routledge. (1st edition published 1993).

Holmes, J., & Slade, A. (2018). *Attachment in therapeutic practice.* London: Sage.

Hopson, J. (2019). Stigma and fear: The psy professional in cultural artifacts. *British Journal of Psychotherapy, 35* (2), 233–244.

Iacoboni, M. (2009). *Mirroring people: The science of empathy and how we connect with others.* London: Picador.

Iacoboni, M., Molnar-Szakacs, I., Gallese, V., Buccino, G., Mazziotta, J., & Rizzolati, G. (2005). Grasping the intentions of others with one's own mirror neurons. *PLoS Biology, 3* (3), e79.

Ignatieff, M. (2022). *On consolation: Finding solace in dark times.* London: Picador.

Ivey, G. (2013). Cognitive therapy's assimilation of countertransference: A psychodynamic perspective. *British Journal of Psychotherapy, 29* (2), 230–244.

Jacobi, J. (1973). *The psychology of C.G. Jung: An introduction with illustrations.* London: Yale University Press.

Jacobs, T. (1991). *The use of the self: Countertransference and communication in the analytic situation.* Madison, CT: International Universities Press.

Jacobs, T.J. (2005). Discussion of forms of intersubjectivity in infant research and adult treatment. In B. Beebe, S. Knoblauch, J. Rustin & D. Sorter (Eds.), *Forms of intersubjectivity in infant research and adult treatment* (pp. 165–189). New York: Other Press.

Jacobs, T.J. (2007). Listening, dreaming, sharing: On the uses of the analyst's inner experiences. In S. Akhtar (Ed.), *Listening to others: Developmental and clinical aspects of empathy and attunement* (pp. 93–112). Lanham, MD: Jason Aronson.

Jacobus, M. (2005). *The poetics of psychoanalysis: In the wake of Klein.* Oxford: Oxford University Press.

Jakes, S. (2018). *Loss of self in psychosis*. New York: Routledge.

Jaques, E. (1955). Social systems as a defence against persecutory and depressive anxiety. In *New directions in psychoanalysis*. London: Tavistock Publications.

Johnson, S. (1985). *Characterological transformation: The hard work miracle*. New York: W.W. Norton.

Joseph, B. (1982). Addiction to near death. *International Journal of Psychoanalysis, 63,* 449–456. Reprinted in: *Psychic Equilibrium and Psychic Change* (1989) pp. 127–138. London: Routledge.

Jung, C.G. (1910/1946). *The collected works of C.G. Jung (Volume 17). The development of personality*. Princeton, NJ: Princeton University Press.

Jung, C.G. (1912/1943). *The collected works of C.G. Jung (Volume 7). Two essays on analytical psychology*. Princeton, NJ: Princeton University Press.

Jung, C.G. (1913/1936). *The collected works of C.G. Jung (Volume 6). Psychological types*. Princeton, NJ: Princeton University Press.

Jung, C.G. (1922/1950). *The collected works of C.G. Jung (Volume 15). The spirit in man, art and literature*. Princeton, NJ: Princeton University Press.

Jung, C.G. (1928/1950). *The collected works of C.G. Jung (Volume 11). Psychology and religion: West and east*.

Jung, C.G. (1928/1954). *The collected works of C.G. Jung (Volume 8). The structure and dynamics of the psyche*. Princeton, NJ: Princeton University Press.

Jung, C.G. (1929/1951). *The collected works of C.G. Jung (Volume 16). The practice of psychotherapy*. Princeton, NJ: Princeton University Press.

Jung, C.G. (1934/1955). *The collected works of C.G. Jung (Volume 9). The archetypes and the collective unconscious*. Princeton, NJ: Princeton University Press.

Kalsched, D. (1996). *The inner world of trauma: Archetypal defenses of the personal spirit*. Hove: Routledge.

Kalsched, D. (2013). *Trauma and the soul: A psycho-spiritual approach to human development and its interruption*. Hove: Routledge.

Karpman, S. (1968). Fairy tales and script drama analysis. *Transactional Analysis Bulletin, 26* (7), 39–43.

Katz, C. (2013). *Levinas and the crisis of humanism*. Bloomington, IN: Indiana University Press.

Kazdin, A.E. (2009). Understanding how and why psychotherapy leads to change. *Psychotherapy Research, 19,* 418–428.

Keats, J. (1899). *The complete poetical works and letters of John Keats*. Boston, MA: Houghton, Mifflin and Company.

Kermode, F. (1996). *Not entitled: A memoir*. London: Harper Collins.

Kernberg, O. (1975). *Borderline conditions and pathological narcissism*. New York: Jacob Aronson.

Kernberg, O. (2016). New developments in transference focused psychotherapy. *International. Journal of Psychoanalysis, 97* (2), 385–407.

Khan, M. (1996). *The privacy of the self*. Abingdon: Routledge.

King, D.B., Woody, W., & Viney, W. (2013). *A history of psychology: Ideas and context*. New York: Pearson.

Kitayama, O. (1998). Transience: Its beauty and danger. *International Journal of Psychoanalysis, 79,* 937–942.

Klein, M. (1946). Notes on some schizoid mechanisms. In J. Mitchell (Ed.), *The selected Melanie Klein* (pp. 175–200). New York: Free Press.

Klein, M. (1948). The importance of symbol formation in the development of the ego. *Contributions to psychoanalysis* (1921 to 1945). London: Hogarth Press and Institute of Psychoanalysis.

Knox, J. (2003). *Archetype, attachment, analysis: Jungian psychology and the emergent mind.* Hove: Routledge.

Knox, J. (2019). The harmful effects of psychotherapy: When the therapeutic alliance fails. *British Journal of Psychotherapy, 35* (2), 245–262.

Kohler, E., Keysers, C., Umilta, M., Fogassi, L., Gallese, V., & Rizzolati, G. (2002). Hearing sounds, understanding actions: Action representation in mirror neurons. *Science, 297* (5582), 846–848.

Kohut, H. (1972a). *The selected writings of Heinz Kohut: Volume 2: 1958–1978.* New York: International Press.

Kohut, H. (1972b). Thoughts on narcissism and narcissistic rage. *Psychoanalytic Study of the Child, 27,* 360–400.

Kramer, R. (1995). The birth of client-centred therapy: Carl Rogers, Otto Rank, and "The Beyond". *Journal of Humanistic Psychology, 35* (4), 54–110.

Kraye, J. (Ed.). (1996). *The Cambridge companion to renaissance humanism.* Cambridge: Cambridge University Press.

Kubler-Ross, E. (1969). *On death and dying.* New York: Scribner.

Langer, U. (Ed.). (2005). *The Cambridge companion to Montaigne.* Cambridge: Cambridge University Press.

Larkin, P. (1988). *Collected poems.* London: Marvell Press with Faber and Faber.

Lee, E. (2017). Working through countertransference: Navigating safety and paranoia for a client with complex trauma history and borderline personality organization. *Psychoanalytic Social Work, 24* (2), 75–95.

Leichsenring, F., & Leibing, E. (2003). The effectiveness of psychodynamic therapy and cognitive behaviour therapy in the treatment of personality disorder. A meta-analysis. *American Journal of Psychiatry, 160,* 1223–1232.

Leichsenring, F., & Rabung, S. (2008). Effectiveness of long-term psychodynamic psychotherapy. A meta-analysis. *Journal of the American Medical Association, 300,* 1551–1565.

Levinas, E. (1981). *Otherwise than being or beyond essence. The Hague and Boston Hingham.* Boston, MA: M. Nijhoff and Kluwer Boston.

Levinas, E. (1989). Ethics as first philosophy. (Translated by S. Hand & M. Temple). In: S. Hand (Ed.), *The Levinas reader* (pp. 75–87). Oxford: Blackwell.

Loewald, H. (1960). On the therapeutic action of psycho-analysis. *International Journal of Psycho-Analysis, 41,* 16–33.

Loewald, H. (2000). *The essential Loewald: Collected papers and monographs.* Hagerstown, MD: University Publishing Group.

Loewenstein, R. (1951). The problem of interpretation. *Psychoanalytic Quarterly, 20,* 1–23.

Lomas, P. (1993). *Cultivating intuition: An introduction to psychotherapy.* Northvale, NJ: Jason Aronson.

Long, C. (2015). The use of a concept: Projective identification and its theoretical use in supervision. *Psychoanalytic Psychology, 32* (3), 482–499.

Lowen, A. (1974). A hierarchy of character structure. *Energy and Character, 3.*

Lowen, A. (1975). *Bioenergetics.* New York: Penguin.

Lowy, M., & Sayre, R. (2002). *Romanticism against the tide of humanity*. Durham, NC: Duke University Press.

Mabey, R. (1987). *Gilbert White: A biography of the author of the natural history of Selborne*. London: Century Hutchinson.

Mabey, R. (2005/2015). *Nature cure*. London: Penguin Random House. (Reissued in Vintage Books).

MacKenna, C. (2006). Self images and god images. *British Journal of Psychotherapy*, *18* (3), 325–338.

MacLean, F. (1970). The triune brain emotion and scientific bias. In F. Schmitt (Ed.), *The neurosciences second study program*. New York: Rockefeller University Press.

Mahler, M. (1968). *On human symbiosis and the vicissitudes of individuation*. New York: International Universities Press.

Mahler, M. (1972). Rapprochement subphase of the separation-individuation process. *Psychoanalytic Quarterly*, *41*, 487–506.

Mahler, M., Pine, F., & Bergman, A. (1975). *The psychological birth of the human infant*. New York: Basic Books.

Markie, P. (1992). The cogito and its importance. In J. Cottingham (Ed.), *The Cambridge companion to Descartes* (pp. 140–173). Cambridge: Cambridge University Press.

Masterson, J. (1976). *Psychotherapy of the borderline adult*. New York: Brunner/Mazel.

Meares, R. (2001). *Intimacy and alienation: Memory, trauma, and personal being*. Hove: Routledge.

Menzies Lyth, I. (1959). The functions of social systems as a defence against anxiety: A report on a study of the nursing service of a general hospital. *Human Relations*, *13*, 95–121. London: Tavistock Institute of Human Relations.

Merchant, C. (1990). *The death of nature: Women, ecology, and the scientific revolution*. San Francisco, CA: Harperone.

Mikulincer, M., & Shaver, P. (2007). *Attachment in adulthood: Structure, dynamics, and change*. New York: Guilford Press.

Miller, S., Hubble, M., Chow, D., & Seidel, J. (2013). The outcome of psychotherapy: Yesterday, today and tomorrow. *Psychotherapy*, *50*, 88–97.

Mitchell, S. (1988). *Relational concepts in psychoanalysis*. Cambridge, MA: Harvard University Press.

Mollon, P. (1993). *The fragile self*. London: Whurr.

Morrison, R. (1999). *The spirit in the gene*. Ithaca, NY: Cornell University Press.

Munder, T., Fluckiger, C., Leichsenring, F., Abbass, A., Hilsenroth, M., Luyten, P., Rabung, S., Steinert, C., & Wampold, B. (2019). Is psychotherapy effective? A reanalysis of treatments for depression. *Epidemiology and Psychiatric Sciences*, *28*, 268–274.

Murdoch, I. (1998). *Existentialists and mystics: Writings on philosophy and literature*. London: Allen Lane.

Murdoch, I. (2001). *The sovereignty of good*. Abingdon: Routledge Classics.

Naess, A. (1973). The shallow and the deep, long-range ecology movement. A summary. *Inquiry: An Interdisciplinary Journal of Philosophy*, *16*, 95–100.

Naess, A. (1995). The deep ecology movement: Some philosophical aspects. In G. Sessions (Ed.), *Deep ecology for the twenty-first century*. Boston, MA: Shambala.

Nathan, J. (2018). The use of benign authority with severe borderline patients: A psychoanalytic paradigm. *British Journal of Psychotherapy*, *34* (1), 61–77.

O'Keane, V. (2021). *A sense of self: Memory, the brain, and who we are*. New York: W.W. Norton.

Oliver, M. (2016). Of power and time. In *upstream: Selected essays*. London: Penguin.

Orange, D. (2006). For whom the bell tolls: Context, complexity, and compassion in psychoanalysis. *International Journal of Psychoanalytic Self Psychology*, *1*, 5–21.

Orange, D. (2016). *Nourishing the inner life of clinicians and humanitarians: The ethical turn in psychoanalysis*. Abingdon: Routledge.

Osborne, C. (1994). *Eros unveiled: Plato and the god of love*. Oxford: Oxford University Press.

Panksepp, J. (1998). *Affective neuroscience*. Oxford: Oxford University Press.

Panksepp, J. (2010). *The archaeology of mind: Neural origins of human emotion*. New York: W.W. Norton.

Panksepp, J., & Biven, L. (2012). *The archaeology of mind: Neuroevolutionary origins of human emotion*. New York: W.W. Norton.

Parker, J. (2010). *Animal minds, animal souls, animal rights*. Lanham, MD: University Press of America.

Parsons, M. (2000). *The dove that returns, the dove that vanishes: Paradox and creativity in psychoanalysis*. Hove: Routledge.

Pennebaker, J. (1993). Putting stress into words. *Behaviour Research and Therapy*, *31* (6), 539–548.

Pereira, K. (2012). The presence of the educator in 'Education to Expression' in the writings of Carl Rogers. *Divyadaan: Journal of Philosophy and Education*, *23* (2), 161–180.

Perls, F., Hefferline, R., & Goodman, P. (1989). *Gestalt therapy: Excitement and growth in the human personality*. London: Souvenir Press.

Phillips, A., & Taylor, B. (2010). *On kindness*. London: Penguin Books.

Piaget, J. (1954). *The construction of reality in the child*. New York: Basic Books.

Plumwood, V. (1998). Intentional recognition and reductive rationality: A response to John Andrews. *Environmental Values*, *7*, 405.

Poland, W. (1975). Tact as a psychoanalytic function. *International Journal of Psychoanalysis*, *56*, 155–161.

Ratnapani et al. (2003). *Metta: The practice of loving kindness*. Birmingham: Windhorse Publications.

Rauch, S., van der Kolk, B., Fisler, R., Alpert, N., Orr, S., Savage, C., et al. (1996). A symptom provocation study using PET and script driven imagery. *Archives of General Psychiatry*, *53*, 380–387.

Rees, M. (2018). *On the future prospects for humanity*. Woodstock: Princeton University Press.

Reeves, H. (1989). *Is nursing caught or taught? An analysis of the way in which nurses learn to do their work* (M.Ed. by research). Norwich: University of East Anglia.

Reich, W. (1927/1961). *The function of the orgasm*. Vienna: Internationaler Psychoanalytischer Verlag. (Re-published by Farrar, Straus and Giroux).

Reich, W. (1949/1963). *Character analysis* (3rd edition). Bellbrook, OH: Orgone Institute Press (Re-published by Farrar, Straus and Giroux).

Revans, R. (1959). *The hospital as an organism: A study in communications and morale*. Preprint No.7 of a paper presented at the 6th Annual International Meeting of the Institute of Management Sciences, September 1959. London: Pergamon Press.

Rizzolati, G., & Sinigaglia, C. (2010). The functional role of the parieto-frontal mirror circuit: Interpretations and misinterpretations. *Nature Reviews Neuroscience*, *11*, 264–274.

Rogers, C. (1959). A theory of therapy, personality and interpersonal relationships, as developed in the client centred framework. In S. Koch (Ed.), *Formulation of the person and the social context. Psychology: A study of a science* (Volume 3, pp. 184–256). New York: McGraw-Hill.

Rogers, C. (1967). *On becoming a person: A therapist's view of psychotherapy*. London: Constable.

Rogers, C. (1980). *A way of being*. Boston: Houghton Mifflin.

Rogers, C. (1986). A client-centred/person-centred approach to therapy. In I. Kutash & A. Wolf (Eds.), *Psychotherapist's casebook: Theory and techniques in the practice of modern therapies*. San Francisco, CA: Jossey-Bass.

Rollin, B. (1992). *Animal rights and human morality*. New York: Prometheus Books.

Rorty, A. (1992). Descartes on thinking with the body. In J. Cottingham (Ed.), *The Cambridge companion to Descartes* (pp. 371–392). Cambridge: Cambridge University Press.

Rutter, M. (2012). Resilience as a dynamic concept. *Development and Psychopathology, 24*, 335–344.

Saayman, N. (2021). The feared therapist: On being part of the psychotic patient's paranoid delusion. *British Journal of Psychotherapy, 37* (1), 36–51.

Salaam Abdel-Malek, H. (2022). Working through apocalyptic times: When the psychoanalytic frame is blown up. *British Journal of Psychotherapy, 38* (3), 457–469.

Saslow, L., Saturn, S., & Willer, R. (2013). My brother's keeper? Compassion predicts generosity more among less religious individuals. *Journal of Social, Psychological and Personality Science, 4* (1), 31–38.

Sandler, J., & Sandler, A. (1983). The 'second censorship', the 'three box model' and some technical implications. *International Journal of Psychoanalysis, 64*, 413–425.

Schafer, R. (1976). *A new language for psychoanalysis*. New Haven, CT: Yale University Press.

Schneewind, J. (2005). Montaigne on moral philosophy and the good life. In U. Langer (Ed.), *The Cambridge companion to Montaigne* (pp. 207–228). Cambridge: Cambridge University Press.

Schon, D. (1991). *The reflective practitioner: How professionals think in action*. Aldershot: Avebury Ashgate.

Schore, A. (2003a). *Affect dysregulation and disorders of the self*. New York: W.W. Norton.

Schore, A. (2003b). *Affect regulation and the repair of the self*. New York: W.W. Norton.

Schwaber, E. (1981). Empathy: A mode of analytic listening. *Psychoanalytic Inquiry, 1*, 357–392.

Schwaber, E. (2007). The unending struggle to listen: Locating oneself within the other. In S. Akhtar (Ed.), *Listening to others: Developmental and clinical aspects of empathy and attunement* (pp. 17–39). Lanham, MD: Jason Aronson.

Searles, H. (1966/1999). The schizophrenic individual's experience. Countertransference and related subjects. *Selected Papers*, 5–27. Madison, CT: International Universities Press.

Sekechi, M., & Chiesa, M. (2022). From hopelessness and despair to hope and recovery: psychoanalytic psychotherapy as effective agent of change in the treatment of a psychiatric patient. *British Journal of Psychotherapy, 38* (3), 483–499.

Shohet, R., & Hawkins, P. (2006). *Supervision in the helping professions* (3rd edition). Maidenhead: Open University Press.

Simpson, D. (2013). A patient who could not allow himself to really get better. *British Journal of Psychotherapy, 29* (1), 25–40.

Simpson, J., & Belsky, J. (2008). Attachment theory within a modern evolutionary frame-work. In J. Cassidy & P. Shaver (Eds.), *Handbook of attachment: Theory, research, and clinical applications*. New York: Guilford Press.

Slater, M. (1991) introduction to Dickens, C. (1850). *David Copperfield*. (New Oxford Illustrated edition). London: Everyman's Library.

Slater, M. (2009). *Charles Dickens*. London: Yale University Press.

Snaith, N. H. (1997). *Distinctive ideas of the Old Testament*. Carlisle: Paternoster Press.

Spitz, R. (1965). *The first year of life*. New York: International Universities Press.

Stiffell, G., & Holtom, R. (2016). Beware the song of the sirens: Reflections on the seduc-tive face of narcissism. *British Journal of Psychotherapy, 32* (1), 37–52.

Strassfeld, M. (2006). *A book of life: Embracing Judaism as a spiritual practice*. Wood-stock, VT: Jewish Lights Publishing.

Suttie, I. (1935). *The origins of love and hate*. London: Kegan Paul, Trench, Trubner & Co.

Talia, A., Muzi, L., Lingiardi, V., & Taubner, S. (2018). How to be a secure base: Thera-pists' attachment representations and their link to attunement in psychotherapy. *Attach-ment and Human Development, 18*, 1–18.

Tansley, A.G. (1935). The use and abuse of vegetational terms and concepts. *Ecology, 16* (3), 284–307.

Tanzer, M., Salaminios, G., Morosan, L., Campbell, C., & Debbane, M. (2021). Self-blame mediates the link between childhood neglect experiences and internalizing symptoms in low-risk adolescents. *Journal of Child and Adolescent Trauma, 14,* 73–83.

Tillich, P. (1962/1952). *The courage to be*. Glasgow: Collins Fontana. First published by Nisbet & Co.

Tomalin, C. (2011). *Charles Dickens: A life*. London: Viking Penguin.

Trevarthen, C. (1999). Musicality and the intrinsic motive pulse: Evidence from human psychobiology and rhythms, musical narrative, and the origins of human communica-tion. *Musicae Scientiae* (Special Issue), 157–213.

Trevarthen, C. (2003). Neuroscience and intrinsic psychodynamics: Current knowledge and potential for therapy. In J. Corigall & H. Wilkinson (Eds.), *Revolutionary connec-tions: Psychotherapy and neuroscience* (pp. 53–78). London: Karnac.

Turner, J. (2000). *On the origins of human emotions*. Palo Alto, CA: Stanford University Press.

Unsworth, T. (2020). My father said I had done something unforgivable. *The Guardian G2*, 4–5.

van der Kolk, B. (2015). *The body keeps the score: Mind, brain and body in the transfor-mation of trauma*. London: Penguin.

Waddicor, M. (1970). *Montesquieu and the philosophy of natural law*. Leiden: Martinus Nijhoff.

Watson, R. (2002). *Cogito, ergo sum*. Jaffrey, NH: David R. Godine.

Watt, D. (2001). Emotion and consciousness: Implications of affective neuroscience for extended reticular thalamic activating system theories of consciousness. In A. Kaszniak (Ed.), *Emotions, qualia and consciousness* (pp. 290–320). Singapore: World Scientific Publishing.

Westland, G. (2015). *Verbal and non-verbal communication in psychotherapy*. New York: W.W. Norton.

White, G. (1789/1993). *The natural history of Selborne*. (Everyman edition). London: J.M. Dent.

Whitehorn, J., & Betz, B.J. (1954). A study of psychotherapeutic relationships between physicians and schizophrenic patients. *American Journal of Psychiatry, 111*, 321–331.

Wilson, A.N. (2020). *The mystery of Charles Dickens*. London: Atlantic Books.

Winnicott, D. (1957). *The child and the outside world*. London: Tavistock.

Winnicott, D. (1960/1965). Ego distortions in terms of true and false self. In *The maturational processes and the facilitating environment: Studies in the theory of emotional development* (pp. 140–152). London: Hogarth.

Winnicott, D. (1960b). Countertransference. *British Journal of Medical Psychology, 33*, 17–21.

Winnicott, D. (1961). *The child, the family, and the outside world*. London: Pelican Books.

Winnicott, D. (1969). The use of the object. *International Journal of Psychoanalysis, 50*, 711–716.

Winnicott, D. (1971). *Playing and reality*. London: Penguin.

Winnicott, D., & The Institute of Psycho-Analysis (Great Britain). (1975). *Through paediatrics to psycho-analysis*. London: Hogarth Press and the Institute of Psychoanalysis.

Wolheim, R. (1971). *Freud*. London: Fontana Press.

Woodhouse, P. (2009). *Etty Hillesum: A life transformed*. London: Continuum Publishing, an imprint of Bloomsbury Publishing Plc.

Workman, L. (2013). *Charles Darwin: The shaping of evolutionary thinking*. London: Bloomsbury.

Yerushalmi, H. (2018). Influences on patients developing mentalization. *International Forum of Psychoanalysis, 27* (3), 157–165.

Young, R. (2017). *The secret life of cows*. London: Faber & Faber.

Index